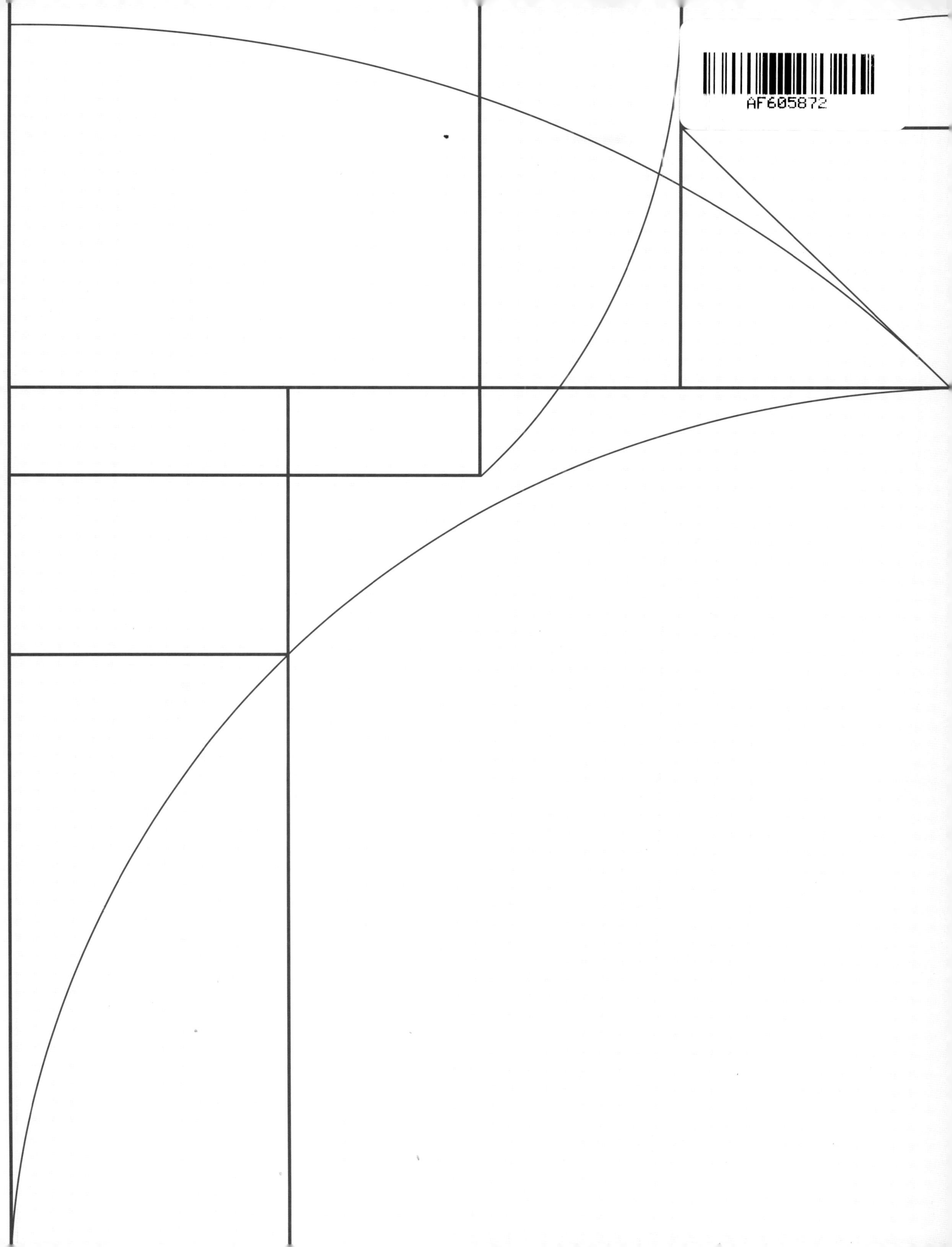

J.W.Power
Abstraction-Création
Paris 1934

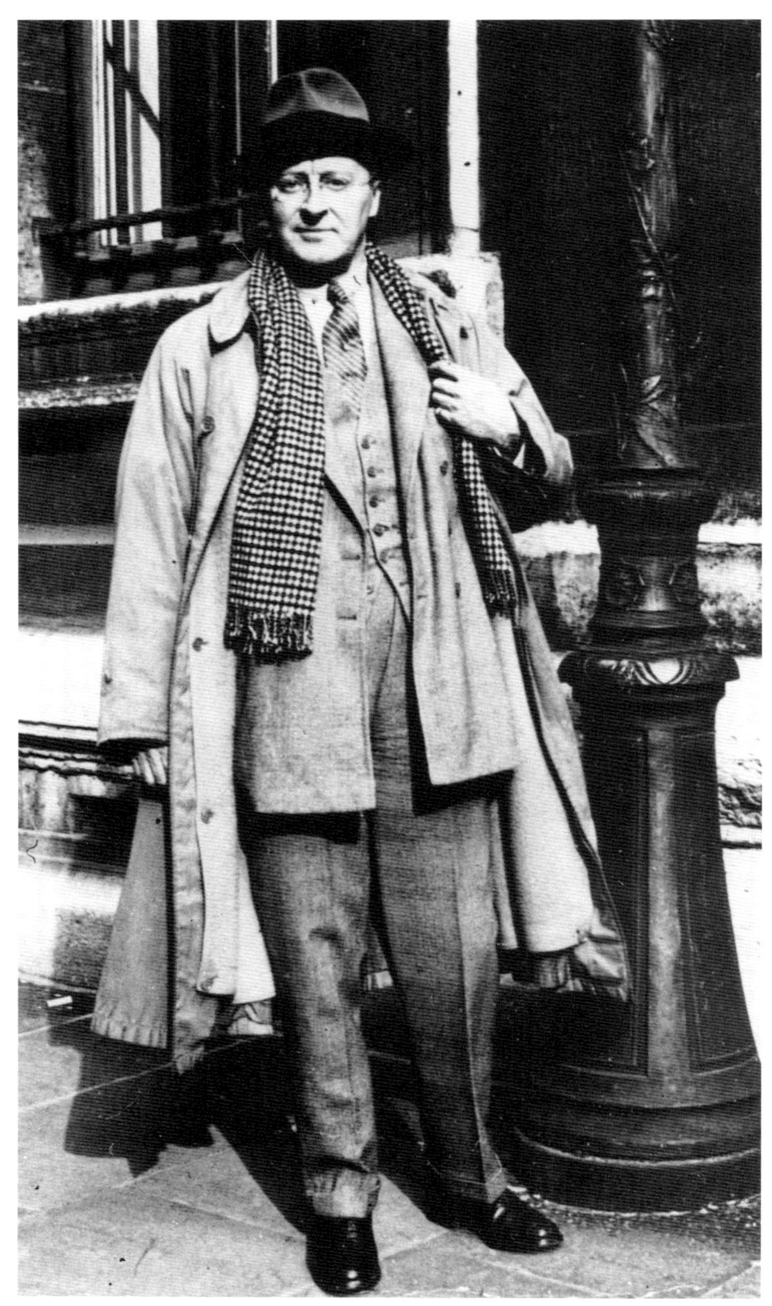

J.W.Power Abstraction-Création Paris 1934

A.D.S Donaldson and Ann Stephen

Contents

Preface

DAVID ELLIS
Director, Museums and Cultural Engagement
The University of Sydney

J.W. Power: Abstraction-Création, Paris 1934, is the companion publication of a groundbreaking exhibition at the University Art Gallery, curated by Ann Stephen and A.D.S. Donaldson, restaging Power's 1934 solo exhibition in Paris.

The book marks the 50th anniversary of the Power bequest, acknowledging the University's visionary benefactor, the artist J.W. Power. Given the continuing significance of building benefaction and support for the University, the exhibition is a timely celebration of one of the University's most generous bequests.

The book provides a permanent record of the most significant chapter in Power's career as an artist. The curators' research places him in the context of the international avant-garde in Paris. In addition, essays by the eminent art historians, Emeritus Professor Virginia Spate and the international scholar Gladys Fabre, reveal the extent of Power's avant-garde network in Paris in the interwar years as well as his artistic process.

It is also the first time that the University Art Gallery has collaborated with Power Publications on a major book and we warmly thank Professor Mark Ledbury, Director of the Power Institute and his staff, particularly Emma White, for their commitment to this remarkable art history project. Their generous support, combined with donations from benefactors and supporters of the University Art Gallery, has allowed us to produce a scholarly and beautifully illustrated publication, as well as a major public program to accompany the exhibition.

I am equally delighted that the University's Chancellor's Committee has supported this project that reveals Power's contribution to our cultural heritage.

I would also like to acknowledge the assistance of the Museum of Contemporary Art who manage the Power Collection on behalf of the University of Sydney. They have provided generous assistance in accessing the collection and archives.

My thanks go to the University Museums team, and finally to the co-curators A.D.S. Donaldson and Dr Ann Stephen, senior curator of the University's art collection. Their initiative, drive and collaborative spirit have seen this important addition to Australian art scholarship come to fruition in this fine publication.

Introduction

PROFESSOR MARK LEDBURY
Director, Power Institute
The University of Sydney

It is always an enormous pleasure to be part of a project that casts an artist in an entirely new and unexpected light, and that pleasure is doubled when the artist happens to also be inextricably and powerfully entwined with the history of the University of Sydney. That is the happy circumstance of this exhibition and publication, both a fundamental re-evaluation of the work of an important Australian artist, and the key marker of the 50th anniversary of the announcement of the Power Bequest to the University of Sydney – a foundational act of generosity which created, ultimately, both the Department of Art History at the University and the Museum of Contemporary Art, one of the premier institutions of contemporary art in Australia.

In part, the generosity of Power the benefactor and creator of a vital and continuing legacy to the visual arts in Sydney and Australia obscured his own importance as an artist and contributor to important European aesthetic and political debates in the turbulent decades between the wars. This book seeks to give Power, the artist, back the place in the spotlight that he enjoyed as a key player in Abstraction-Création and as an artist in constant touch with the restless waves of artistic creation in the interwar years. As Ann Stephen and A.D.S. Donaldson's essay demonstrates, Power was an artist of great earnestness and seriousness of purpose. Constantly engaged with and responsive to the ferment of often competing visions of what mattered aesthetically, he was able to respond to Klee's abstraction, cubo-futurist dynamism, the poetry of Eluard, the engaged, cubist-derived language of Léger, among other tendencies, and sensitive to the stakes of the struggle with plastic form. At the same time, though, as Stephen and Donaldson show, he is an artist of great humour and vitality, whose marvellous heads are playful and sometimes even parodic, whose iconography and formal language is suspicious of a po-faced cubism that could not speak to and of the human.

The work of historical reconstruction that underpins the exhibition is also a work of reconstruction and reframing of a reputation – a coherent and persuasive plea for J.W. Power's place in Australian art. Power is, this exhibition and book proclaim, one of the most important post-cubist Australian artists and among the central figures of early twentieth century Australian art.

In order to make this case, of course, we need to see Power's work first and foremost, and the exhibition takes as its organising principle an unprecedented recreation of the viewing experience that was presented to those who saw his show in 1934. This book extends that recreation by making available for the first time in English the fundamental research of Gladys Fabre, the pre-eminent historian of Abstraction-Création. It also includes an essay of elegant lucidity on *Apollo and Daphne* by Virginia Spate which proves that J.W. Power's work not only can bear such detailed scrutiny but deserves it.

This book is also evidence of our continuing commitment, as inheritors of Power's generous benefaction, to his mission to bring new research and ideas in the visual arts to the people of Australia – a mission to which I remain firmly committed and which is at the heart of everything we do at the Power Institute. The exhibition is a unique moment to both celebrate the man and fulfill the mission.

J.W. Power: Abstraction-Création, Paris 1934

A.D.S. DONALDSON AND ANN STEPHEN

Fernand Léger's Académie Moderne c.1924, from left to right: model, Fernand Léger, Otto Carlsund, Waldemar Lorentzon, J. W. Power, Rudolf Gowenius, unknown seated woman, Elsa Lystad, Franciska Clausen, Siri Meyer, Aurel Bauh, Erik Olson, Balta (?), photograph silver gelatin on paper, 16.5 x 35.5 cm., Edith Power bequest PW1961.1176

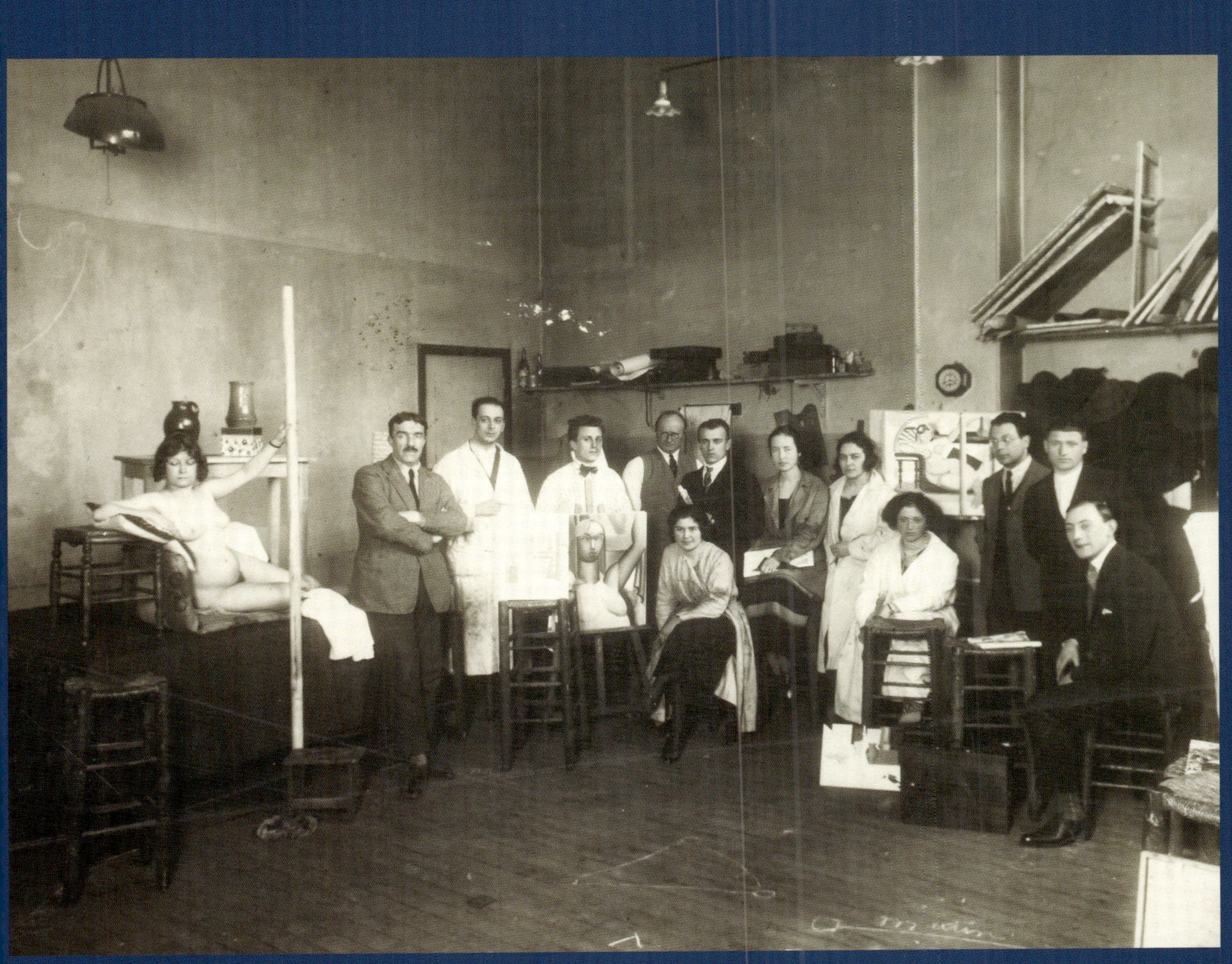

Introduction

We all knew Power, but we knew him as an artist, we did not know him as a rich man or a surgeon.

Daniel-Henry Kahnweiler[1]

THE ART OF J.W. POWER was well known in avant-garde circles in Paris but has been largely unseen in Australia, his career equally invisible. His work is absent from the standard surveys of Australian art and no public collection or state art museum regularly exhibits Power's paintings. His name is well known, however, as the benefactor of a visionary bequest to the University of Sydney.[2] When announced half a century ago, it was accompanied by a gift of more than 1170 art works by him from the collection of his widow Edith Power. While this bequest brought almost all of Power's work to Australia, it did not lead to the recuperation of his work, nor to his rehabilitation into our art history. At the time, the young art critic Robert Hughes commented that 'ironically, had he painted these pictures in Australia between 1927 and 1938 he would possibly be now regarded as the most important figure in our early avant-garde. But he made them in the ambit of Paris, and there they were not in advance of their time.'[3] For Hughes, Power's work could not count because it was not made here, thus effectively estranging his painting from Australian art history. Yet, an artist like Kandinsky, after all, is part of the stories of Russian, German and French art.

Power fared no better at the hands of the paterfamilias of Australian art history, Bernard Smith who consigned him to a kind of art historical purgatory, to a footnote in his canonical *Australian painting* of 1961, for being neither British, French nor really somehow Australian. In the modest Australian literature on Power, he has come to be seen as an isolated, even 'alienated man' who, according to Smith, 'in later years retreated to almost total seclusion from the formal art world'.[4] Power, in our view, however, *is* the most important figure in our early avant-garde and his life and work raise important questions for our art history. In retracing Power's steps we have been able to bring him into focus and to explain many gaps, though at times he still remains an elusive figure. Nonetheless, from the fragmentary record we have been able to recreate Power's 1934 one-person exhibition with Abstraction-Création in Paris. In examining the context of this exhibition our account will show that Power was an artist equally at home in London, Paris and Brussels in the 1920s and '30s. In these interwar years he moved between cities, immersing himself in both contemporary and historical art. This restlessness led to his own unique style of painting, part-abstract surrealism, part-surreal abstraction. Power marked himself as a member of the international avant-garde that converged on Paris in the 1930s by his one-person exhibitions, his participation in small group shows, his contribution to larger shows, his membership of artists groups and societies and by his writings and publication.

Deeply engaged in the art worlds in which he worked, Power's avant-gardism was unprecedented for an Australian. In the 1920s he participated in the modernist art scene in London, but his most significant contribution was made in Paris. It was in the *ville lumiére* that Power studied, and it was there that he showed in step with the avant-garde of his time. From at least the mid 1920s he maintained a studio in Montparnasse, what he later referred to as his 'bolt hole'. He was represented by Léonce Rosenberg's Galerie de l'Effort Moderne, then Galerie Jeanne Bucher, both important champions of interwar modernism. Power was also a member of the artists group known as "1940" and the Salon d'Art Mural but his most important association was with Abstraction-Création, which he helped found, with whom he showed and in whose annual *cahier* he had his work reproduced and his writings published.[5] The art historian Gladys Fabre, whose research on Abstraction-Création is foundational, describes how the group was a fulcrum for the migrating European avant-gardes throughout the 1930s.[6] We will see too how Power, part insider and part outsider, moved in this milieu. For these reasons his work can illuminate the relationships between Sydney and Paris, and between France and Australia, an exchange that goes to the heart of our modernism.[7]

London, Paris and Bournemouth in the 1920s

Mr Power is perhaps the most interesting arrival, showing great individuality and considerable competence ... Even the leaves of his notebook are entertaining: and this certainly is a test.

Osbert Sitwell[8]

LITTLE IS KNOWN OF John Joseph Wardell Power's early art career. Born in 1881, and given the names of both his surgeon father, Joseph Power and his grandfather William Wardell, the pre-eminent colonial architect, he is said to have begun to draw as a boy.[9] There are early sketchbooks, mostly of landscapes painted in Sydney at the turn of the century.[10] Following his father's profession, he studied medicine at the University of Sydney then continued his studies in Vienna and London, where he married Edith James in 1915. During WW1 he served in the Royal Army Medical Corps and following the Armistice, perhaps affected by his experience, he abandoned a two decade long career in medicine for art.[11]

Power's only known war painting from these years, *Ypres* (c. 1918) is an image of a single faceless figure standing sentinel, as if in mourning, amid ruins and acid coloured mists. A memento mori to the devastation of trench warfare, aerial bombing and gassing, it is painted without conventional signs of patriotism. Quiet and reflective, its symbolism strikes a different note to his post-cubist work of the 1920s, and was perhaps painted while he studied in the Paris atelier of Pedro Luiz Correia de Araújo.[12] Power would later attribute his interest in the close analysis of composition to this teacher, writing in 1932 that, 'my own researches extend backwards for about 10 years. I was introduced to the subject by Senhor Pedro Araújo, a Brazilian artist teaching in Paris in 1920 ... though I have confirmed and greatly extended it.'[13] Araújo had briefly taken over the role of Director of the Académie Ranson from Maurice Denis in 1917 but left this position to set up his own school in the following year. Though little, unfortunately, is known about the Cariocan's atelier in Paris, it was 'the first to include a curriculum in the discipline of geometry'.[14]

Typical of the misunderstandings that have arisen in Australia regarding Araújo, was Bernard Smith's misattribution in 1973 of a formal photograph in Edith Power's bequest. In it Power stands at the back and in the middle of a studio amongst a group of eleven students who have apparently interrupted a life painting class to pose for the photographer. Yet the Professor in this photograph with a distinctive moustache standing somewhat apart, arms crossed, beside the model is not Araújo but Fernand Léger. Power had moved, as did others who had studied with Araújo, to the Académie Moderne by 1924, though he was older than most, at forty, the same age as Léger.

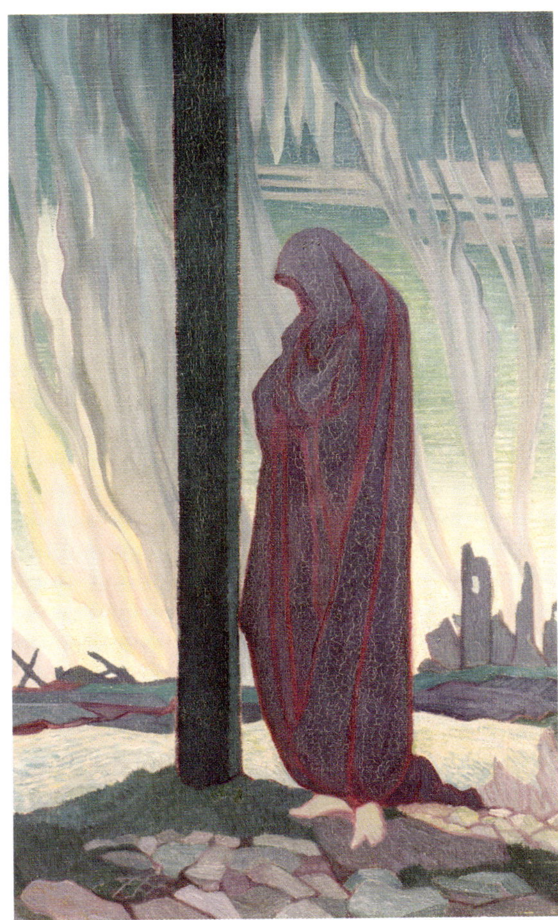

J. W. Power *Ypres* c.1917-18
oil on canvas, 76.4 x 45.8 cm
Australian War Memorial

The photograph was in fact reproduced in Gladys Fabre's 1982 catalogue, *Léger et L'Esprit Moderne*, where Power is listed as an unknown. Our identification places him within the influential Parisian teaching atelier and begins to re-orientate our understanding of him. Léger's first year of teaching in 1924 was a personal turning point, coinciding with his shift towards the Purism advocated by Ozenfant and Jeanneret, and the completion of the 'plotless' film *Ballet méchanique*. In that year, too, he contributed work to Friedrich Kiesler's modern theatre exhibition in Vienna alongside the Bauhausler and future émigré to Australia Ludwig Hirschfeld Mack.[15] Four decades later Mack could still recall Leger's reaction to his question: '"Why don't you have a Modern Art School such as the Bauhaus. You have the best artists in the world, you have won the war, you have the means to develop such an institution." He answered sadly and bitterly that the atmosphere in victorious France was chauvinistic, reactionary and conservative, that no new way of life could be the outcome of this situation. He was jealous of the situation in Germany after a lost war – to be able to build anew.'[16]

Léger attracted mostly foreign students who, as Fabre writes, 'acquired through travel and training, a more open-minded attitude than their French contemporaries at the Beaux-Arts or Arts Decoratif schools in Paris.'[17] Power's colleagues were mainly Scandinavians and included, for instance, the Swedes Otto Carlsund, Erik Olson and Waldemar Lorentzon, the Norwegians Elsa Lystad, Raghnild Haarbo and Ragnild Keyser and the Dane Franciska Clausen, all of whom are foundational modernist figures in the countries of their birth. The Académie Moderne offered classes with Léger in the afternoon, teaching he would begin to share with Amédée Ozenfant the next year until 1928-29. Fabre writes that 'a sense of freedom pervades Léger's classes while Ozenfant's teaching was characterised by close attention to pictorial technique, to precision of detail, to the finish and to the durability of the materials used.'[18] One of Power's drawings *Le Football* (1924) a figure group with 'the volumes treated as cylinders', is an adaption of Léger's machine-like foot soldiers to civilian life.[19] Power's drawing was reproduced that year in *Bulletin de L'Effort Modern*, the influential art journal published by Léonce Rosenberg, Léger's and later Power's dealer.[20]

Fabre's subtitle to her book on Leger's Académie Moderne '*une alternative d'avantgarde à l'art non-objectif*' makes plain that his teaching was an alternative to abstraction, proposing a 'new humanism' in order 'to express the spirit of the age'.[21] Notable for its precision and modernity, Power's painting, like Léger's, uses imagery drawn from the drafting table. The compass was of particular significance to Léger as

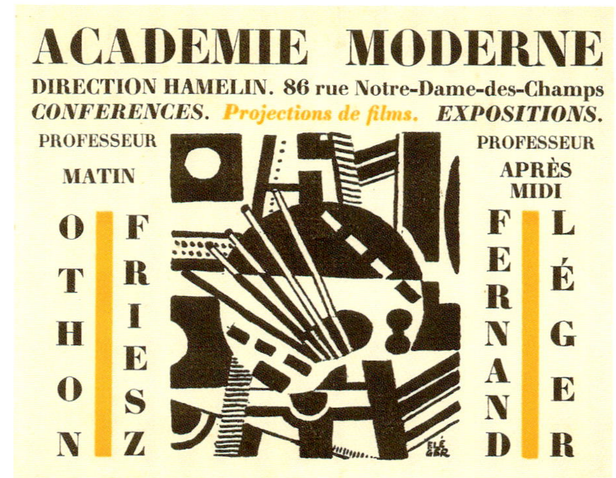

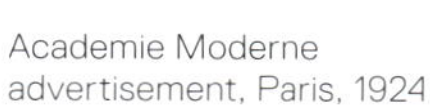
Academie Moderne advertisement, Paris, 1924

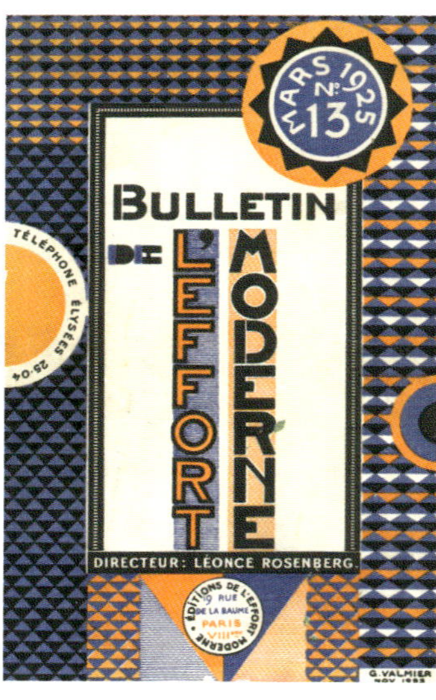

Bulletin de L'Effort Moderne, Paris, 1925, journal, from the library of J.W. Power, National Library of Australia

an image and as a tool for inscribing circles. For him 'every object that has the circle as its basic form is always sought as an attractive force ... it is complete, there is no break in continuity. The ball, the sphere are enormous plastic values.'[22] Like other artists in the interwar years Power, an amateur mathematician and a scientist before he was an artist, was fascinated by geometry and the way laws of proportion inform visual perception.[23] In his correspondence Power wrote that when he was 'too worried to draw or paint' he 'got hold of an algebra book and a penny notebook & work[ed] at the Binomial theorem and exponentials.'[24]

When designing arched panels for his apartment, Power made a pair of triangular compositions or 'ogee' panels: one based on drafting tools for the studio, contrasting the circular lines of French curves and protractor with compass, t-square and grid.[25] For the bathroom, he painted hard and soft forms like sponges and towel with shaving gear, brushes, combs and a mirror. The geometric order of this masculine tableau belies a nervy, almost chaotic energy. The art historian Virginia Spate, writing about another of his paintings based on bathroom accessories, suggests the subject matter is ironic, as 'no Cubist so far as I know, included objects as banal as a toothbrush and a red-and-white fringed muffler in ways that undercut the seriousness of the style.'[26] *Untitled (Still life with toothbrush)* (c.1930) has a particular Parisian twist, drawing upon the window displays and the retail packaging of a well known brand of French toothpaste, Eotot. Worked into this cubist still life is its packaging, a tooth brush advert, a circular *savon*, with a grey roll of cotton wool all diagonally layered onto a brilliant orange rubber mat and checked towel, framed by pointillist dots, faux marbling and wood grain. In much of Power's painting the relationship between the space inside his canvas and the work's frame is a highly considered element of his work. Power painted outside and off the canvas, in this work introducing rust coloured paint onto its gilded frame, blurring the line between framing device and painting.

Throughout the 1920s, when not in Paris, the Power's home was Therapia, a house on the south coast of England at Bournemouth, which he considered initially as a retreat but then a millstone, until its eventual sale in the early 1930s. His paintings from these years are based on what his friend, the art critic Anthony Bertram describes as a 'watering place for the well-to-do particularly favoured by the elderly and old' transforming its beach, bandstand and harbour into unlikely cubist landscapes.[27] Many of Power's sketches are drawn on concert programs from Bournemouth's renowned music festivals of the 1920s featuring such musicians as Sibelius, Elgar, Holst and Bartok. In *Seaside still-life* (1926) three horizontal bands,

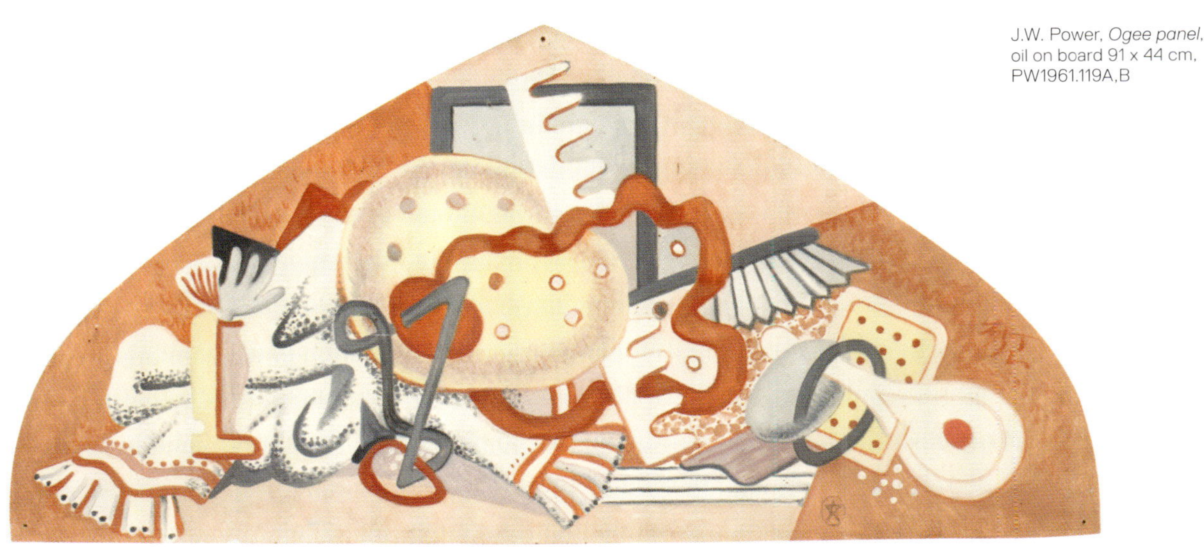

J.W. Power, *Ogee panel*, c.1930
oil on board 91 x 44 cm,
PW1961.119A,B

of pebbles, sea and sky, provide a shallow stage for a slippery game of appearances that alternate between geometric and quotidian forms. Power rotates the sides of parallelograms across the canvas, their diagonal edges reading sometimes as geometrical line and sometimes as object from red sail to green sea-filled cone, from bucket to spiral in complimentary colours. The radial symmetry of a star fish mimics in a biomorphic form Power's adopted signature of the pentagram, marking or masking his surreptitious presence on the pebbly English beach. His tightly ordered cubism of the late 1920s looks to the geometric order of Juan Gris, an artist Power admired and whose Sorbonne lectures he refers to and may well have attended.[28] It was there that Gris explained the abstract order underpinning his cubism: 'I make a bottle – a particular bottle – out of a cylinder … I compose with abstractions (colours) and make my adjustments when these colours have assumed the form of objects.'[29]

From his retreat on the south coast, it was to London that Power turned in embarking on a career in post-war Europe. In 1922 he was briefly a member of the 7 & 5 Society, a group that initially brought together seven painters and five sculptors from across the modern/conservative divide. By the end of the decade it had become, according to the art historian Denys Wilcox the 'cradle of English abstraction'.[30] Power was elected a member of the more progressive London Group in 1923 and exhibited annually, except 1926, with that broad church of mostly British modernists, till 1930.[31] When Power held his first one-person exhibition at the Independent Gallery in London in 1926, *The Sunday Times*' art critic Frank Rutter observed that rather than British, his work was aligned to 'the most advanced painters of Paris. He usually pitches his colour fairly high, and ranges from geometrical abstraction to the outlined primitiveness of Severini's later work.'[32] *The Observer* noted 'he stands alone among Australians in his intelligent appreciation of modern ideals.'[33] Bertram, the art critic on *The Saturday Review*, was the most positive: in his view 'Power is to be very seriously reckoned with. He combines a masterly sense of construction with a forceful content. In certain abstract painting … the best of its kind that I have yet seen by an Englishman [sic] – his formal powers are clearly perceived.'[34] That review initiated an enduring friendship over the following decade as Power turned away from London and towards Paris.[35] During this time, Bertram maintained an extended correspondence with Power, and forty years later annotated his letters. These letters are key documents for understanding Power's life and work over this period.[36] In them, Power confided to Bertram about his art and his exile, writing that he had found 'life unendurable in my native land' whilst loving 'travelling to new places above all things & would do so more if it were only compatible with painting.'[37]

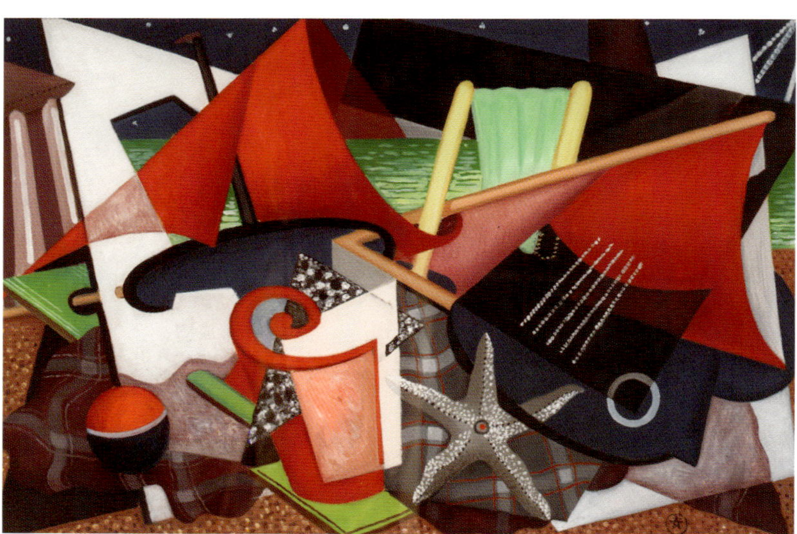

J.W. Power, *Seaside still-life* 1926
oil on canvas, 50.6 x 76.5 cm, PW1961.55

From 1926, if not earlier, Power maintained an apartment studio in Paris overlooking the Cimetière Montparnasse, just off the Boulevard Raspail. The landmark modernist block at 11 bis Rue Schoelcher was an *atelier d'artistes,* then newly designed by the architects Gauthier & Gauthier, on a quiet edge of Montparnasse, a short walk down to the quarter's bohemian studios and cafes. There, in the so called *quartier anglais*, he could frequent La Rotonde, La Select, La Coupole, or indeed Le Dingo.

One of the most significant relationships that marked Power's first decade in Paris was that with his gallerist Léonce Rosenberg, with whom he showed until 1933 – he was even identified by the art critic and art historian Maurice Raynal as a member of the 'l'école Léonce Rosenberg'.[38] Opened in 1918, Rosenberg's avant-garde Galerie de L'Effort Moderne was the site of De Stijl's landmark 1923 exhibition and the only French outlet for the work of Piet Mondrian. Rosenberg was best known, however, as a supporter of the Cubists; beside Gris, he represented Braque, Léger and Picasso, before they moved on to his brother Paul's gallery, just down the rue de la Boétie – the brothers were a powerful pair in the Parisian art world. Léonce published 40 issues of the *Bulletin de l'Effort Moderne* (1924–27), an important forum for avant-garde ideas in Europe, and Power's work was first reproduced in this journal.[39] From Power's letters, it is clear that he was commercially successful and in fact became frustrated with the pressure his gallerist exerted. 'Rosenberg is squeaking for more. I cannot produce rapidly & at the same time say all I want to say', he wrote, 'so we are constantly at loggerheads on this point'.[40]

Power had by then begun to collect contemporary Parisian art, and amassed a substantial library of art books and journals. Recalling his visit to their house in 1929, Bertram remembered the interior being 'hung with paintings by the leading modernists of the day. This was unusual and a further demonstration of his interest in other people. Most artists that I have known have decorated their rooms with their own paintings.'[41] The inventory of Power's collection reveals that about a third of the works are from before 1920, including those by Léger, Ozenfant, Gris, Jean Metzinger, Albert Gleizes, Diego Rivera and Louis Marcoussis. All these artists he could have come to know while he was at the Atelier Araújo, the Atelier Moderne, or more likely, through the Rosenberg brothers. He also owned several drawings and a set of ten *pochoir* prints by Pablo Picasso from his 1920 designs for the Ballet Russe production of *Pucinella*, as well as El Lissitzky's lithograph *Totengräber* (The gravediggers) (1923), characters from his 1921 production of *Victory over the Sun*.[42]

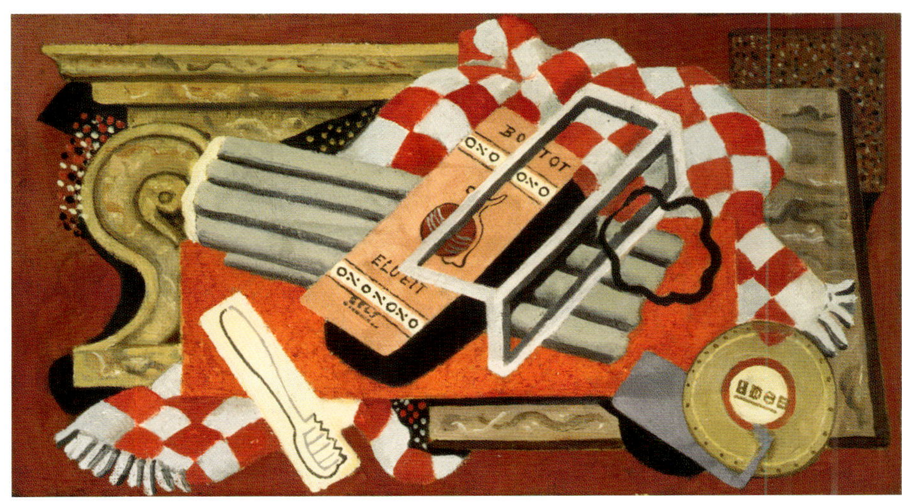

J.W. Power, (still life with toothbrush) c. 1930
oil on canvas 25 x 46 cm PW1961.67

Like many artists at this time, Power was interested in the idea of the relationship between colour and music and drew inspiration from the stage, screen and other popular entertainment. *Danseurs à l'accordéon* (c.1928) is based on a pair of dancing cowboy puppets in ten gallon hats and tiny boots, their rhyming outlines backed by paper-thin cubist panels of accordion keys against a Spanish mission set. The reduced palette and smooth, unmodulated surface are characteristic of Léger's atelier. At the time, Léger was focused on 'the architecture of the mechanical', which lent his own *Accordéon* (1926) a monumental presence. Spate makes an 'Australian' reading of Power's 'cowboy' painting, proposing that as 'he came from a country that did not have a deeply rooted tradition of large scale figure painting ... Power took an ironical approach to Parisian avant-garde art ... laughing not only at the cowboy myth, but also at the high-toned nature of the avant-garde's flirtation with popular culture.'[43]

In a parallel study, French art historian Jocelyne Rotily observes of the American expatriate artist Gerald Murphy, a close friend of Léger's in the 1920s, that he was 'neither completely cubist nor totally Purist.'[44] Drawn to the *ville lumiére*, as expatriates from 'the new world' with 'new money', both Murphy and Power use imagery from popular culture and modern life. Though painted in France, Murphy's *Razor* (1924), was based on distinctly American mass-produced commodities, thus in a sense he 'nationalised' his art. Power, a confirmed cosmopolitan was thoroughly versed in the history of art, both Western and Eastern, and drew on this knowledge as well as from everyday life. His many painted blooms are *fleurs de mal*, never Australian native flowers and his 'cowboys' are steeped in the Parisian avant-garde and its taste for American culture. Paris had its own Jazz age with Josephine Baker its star. For its part the avant-garde had its own take on American popular culture, amongst them: the so-called American Manager in cowboy boots,

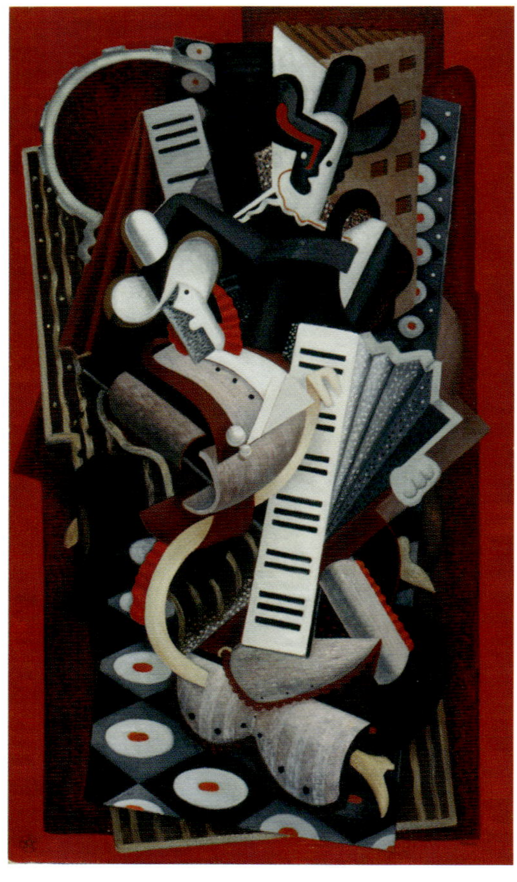

J.W. Power, *Danseurs à l'accordéon* c.1928
oil on canvas, 132.5 x 76.5cm, PW1961.82

megaphone in hand against a papier maché skyscraper that Picasso designed for Satie and Diaghilev's production of *Parade* (1917), which launched cubism onto the Parisian stage; Léger's Charlot (Charlie Chaplin) marionette in the opening and closing sequences of the film *Ballet mécanique* (1924); and the American sheriff that Murphy designed for the Ballets Suédois production backed by a Cole Porter jazz score, *Within the quota* (1923).

Power's art always gives great emphasis to rhythm and movement. Late in life he reflected on its centrality to his work, writing that 'art is the rhythmical expression (or statement) of feeling. Plastic art is the rhythmical expression of a plastic experience ... No rhythm no art. No feeling no art'.[45] Linear rhythm (and music) was also crucial to Paul Klee, an artist Power admired so much that he translated a German monograph on him at a time when there was very little available in English.[46] Indeed Power may have visited Klee, as his Berne sketch book is dated 1934, the year Klee resettled in Switzerland after being forced to abandon his teaching in Germany.[47] Power kept abreast of developments in contemporary German art and architecture. He explained to Bertram that while he had not been in Germany since 1910, he was informed 'by means of books, magazines and photographs. I know Eric Mendelsohn's work by pictures fairly well & Walter Gropius who built the marvellous new art school, or "Bauhaus", at Dessau and I have [Carl] Einstein's book on their modern painting and one or two others ... I see that both of them [Klee and Kandinsky] have been appointed art masters ... and if the resumé of their course of teaching in the last number of *Cahiers d'Art* is true it must be a l very wonderful. I should very much like to exhibit in Berlin.'[48] He never did.

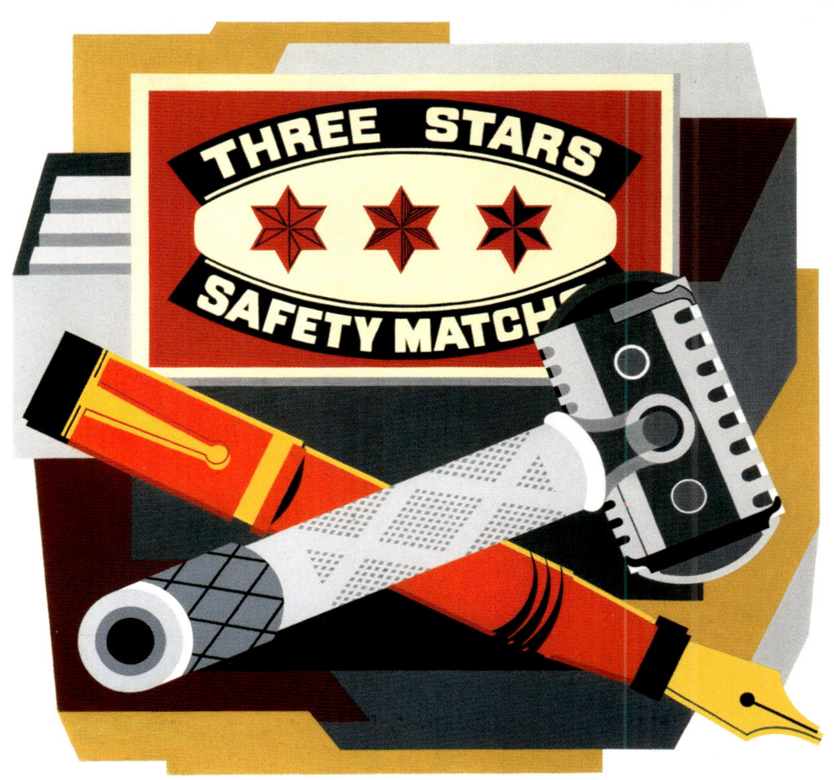

Gerald Murphy, *Razor* 1924
oil on canvas, 81.44 x 92.71 cm
Dallas Museum of Art, Foundation for the Arts Collection, gift of the artist

Paris and Brussels in the 1930s

Paris is the fountain of fresh ideas.

Anne Dangar[49]

IN 1929 POWER ANNOUNCED to Bertram that his painting had come to 'the end of a period' and that he must now put his 'energies into a richer and more complete development.'[50] What triggered Power's decision to sever ties with the London art scene and the domestic comforts of Bournemouth? Writing from Paris he advised his friend that there was a 'distinct development here in the last 6 months, the first step forward for some time. We have seen some lovely things – though none were quite in the central line of tradition with proper plastic composition that one sees in Rubens, el Greco & Cézanne – but they are so beautiful that one forgives them everything.'[51] What could he have seen in 1929? In January Kandinsky held his first one-person show in Paris at Galerie Zak, Etienne Beöthy also showed at the same gallery in April and later Friedrich Vordemberge-Gilderwart held his first exhibition in Paris at J. Povolosky & Cie; it was the year Picasso's Dinard series of *Bathers* was featured in the new journal *Cahiers d'art*.[52] Perhaps he had seen some group exhibitions: the *Exposition d'Art Abstrait* at Éditions Bonaparte in summer, included paintings by John Graham, Léon Tutundjian, Andreas Walser, Otto Freundlich and Georges Vantongerloo. At the inaugural Salon des Surindépendants he could have seen work by Auguste Herbin, Theo Van Doesburg, Serge Charchoune, Tutundijian and Carlsund, artists with whom he would soon show. It was also the year that Salvador Dali held his first solo exhibition in Paris and Georges Bataille broke with Breton to launch *Documents*. All these avant-garde experiments would feed into Power's painting.

Moving to Paris, and into the milieu of the avant-garde, Power confessed to Bertram that 'having been drawn into the quarrel in the Surindépendants & now being one of a new lot, I have to walk more carefully than of yore, lest I be assassinated by some young romantic paint slinger who wastes his passion rather than builds with it.'[53] Herbin had co-founded Les Surindépendants as an alternative to the conservative Salons; its membership had a broad base, with open, unjuried, non-commercial exhibitions and included surrealist and abstract artists. International in nature, it also included many women such as the English artists Paule Vézelay and Marlow Moss, the Dutch-Indonesian Christine Boumeester, the Portuguese Maria-Helena Vieira da Silva and the Swiss Sophie Täuber-Arp. However by 1931, as Power's letter attests, that very inclusiveness had become unworkable. That same year Power also exhibited in another initiative of Herbin, the short-lived association known as "1940" that included numerous artists who would soon become members of Abstraction-Création.

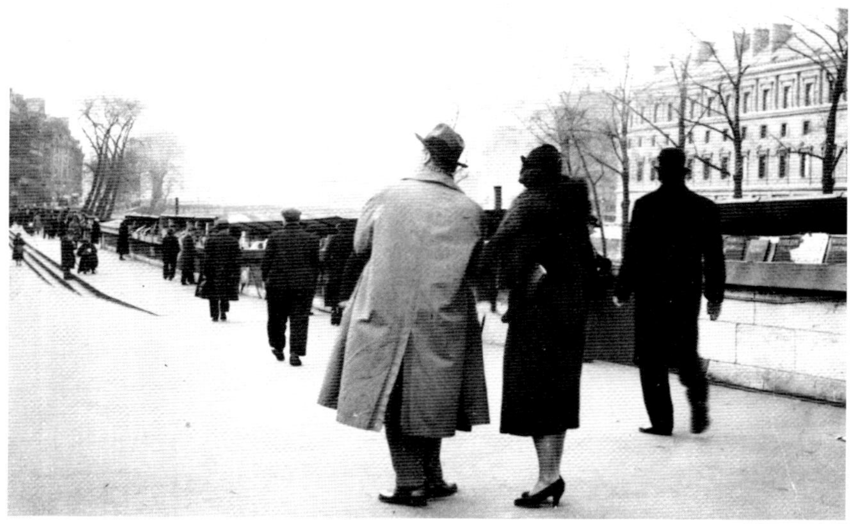

J.W. Power and Edith Power, Paris, c.1930, photograph, Power Institute archives.

By 1930, for the first time, Paris had become the centre of abstraction in Europe, what Fabre has called 'la capitale de l'avant-garde artistique internationale'.[54] Long term residents Robert and Sonia Delaunay, František Kupka, Piet Mondrian, Jean Hélion, Jean Gorin, Herbin and Freundlich had been joined by Joaquín Torres-García from Uruguay, Vantongerloo from Belgium, van Doesburg from Holland, Ivan Puni from Russia, Beöthy and Henri Nouveau from Hungary and the Arps, Jean and Sophie Täuber, fresh from their work on the Café Aubette in Strasbourg. By 1933 their ranks were swelled with the arrival of the Russians Naum Gabo, Nikolaus Pevsner and Kandinsky and by an increasing number of artists from Denmark, Sweden, Switzerland, Japan, Germany, Poland, and Australia. Together they stood up for abstract art, and at the same time stood against representational art and official surrealism.

Abstraction-Création would gather all these artists together. In December 1930, Power, then in Britain, received word of developments from Paris. He explained to Bertram: 'I've just had a letter from Herbin telling me that all the "disciplinés" are leaving the Surindépendants following the fracas with the Secretary and asking me to be on the Committee of a new Society which I shall probably agree to if further details are favourable.'[55] Herbin was the group's first president with Vantongerloo as its vice-president and they worked with a formally organized committee and a secretary-treasurer. Power wrote again to Bertram on the 10th February 1931, just five days before the official founding of Abstraction-Création. 'You will be sorry to hear that we are selling up & cleaning out ... we go to France on the 23rd for good (or evil). The crash in Australia is, I think, going to ruin me ... I had better go to Paris where I already have a studio & where I

Key to map

1. J.W. Power's first studio. 11, bis rue Schœlcher. 14th Arr.
2. J.W. Powers's second studio. 31, rue Campagne Première. 14th Arr.
3. Abstraction-Création's exhibition space. 44, avenue de Wagram. 8th Arr.
4. Academie Moderne. 86, rue de Notre-Dame des Champs. 6th Arr.
5. Galerie l'Effort Moderne/ Galerie Léonce Rosenberg. 19, rue de la Baume. 8th Arr.
6. Galerie Jeanne Bucher. 5, rue de Cherche Midi. 6th Arr.
7. Otto Freundlich's studio. 10, avenue Denfert-Rocherau. 14th Arr.

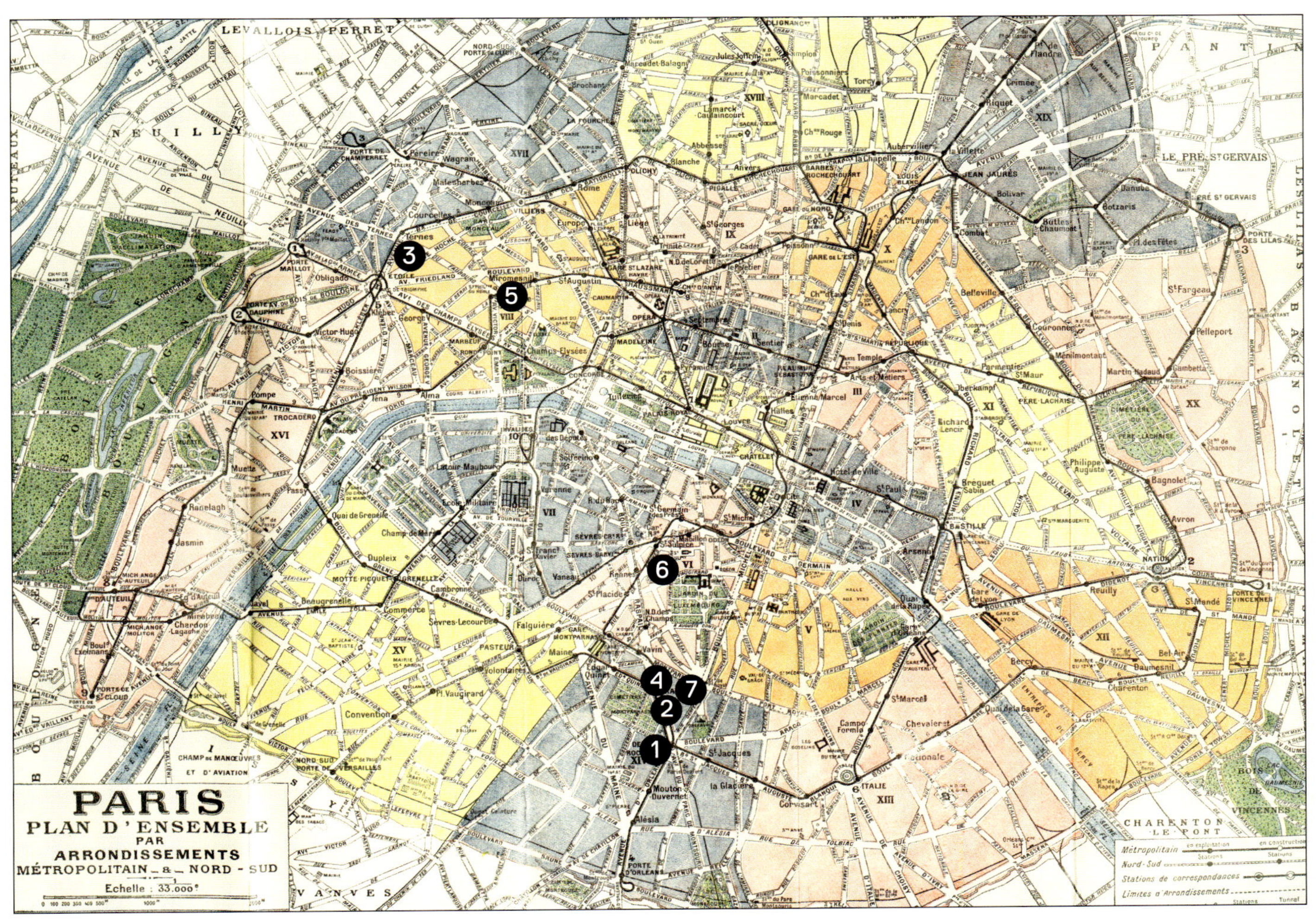

hear I have been elected to the committee of a new art gallery'.[56] At the time the Depression shadowed everything. The art market crash in London 'resulted in the virtual death of modern forms of easel painting' and in Paris the collapsing exchange rate would exert pressure on even Power's substantial resources.[57] While his name never subsequently appeared on any committee lists, nonetheless, he proved to be an important contributor to its presence in Paris, covering costs and funding some of the group's publications, besides collecting the works of his friends.[58]

Abstraction-Création brought together geometric abstract artists alongside their colleagues who were more concerned with an organic or biomorphic version of abstraction, and it was with this latter tendency that Power can be identified. 'Our new revue *Abstraction-Création* has now appeared', he wrote to Bertram, '& is full of interesting & intelligent articles by the painters represented, but it is still a paradox to me that such intense intelligence should end in a picture of two black bars on a white ground as it does with Hélion, Mondrian, Moss and Gorin.'[59] In fact the work of many Abstraction-Création artists, including Hélion, Gorin, and Vantongerloo were part of Power's collection, but it was Herbin, with seven works, who was the most represented artist in his collection. Though Power was not uncritical of him, he wrote to Bertram of Paris at this time that: 'Surrealism holds the floor, that is amongst the young & thoughtful ones ... Herbin, that mirror of the mode, is also more suave in design ... The cubist rigidity markedly softened.'[60]

Abstraction-Création was able to bring together artists from both the geometric and surrealistic streams within non-figurative art. It functioned as an exhibition platform for its members and through the publication of its *cahier* it sought to promote its artists and compete with surrealism's distribution of diverse ephemera. In February 1934 Power was part of the exhibition *Hepworth, Béothy, Closon, Fernandez, Hélion, Power, Prampolini, Seligmann, Täuber-Arp, Valmier*, Abstraction-Création's group show that brought together its artists who shared a concern for organic forms and biomorphioc imagery in their abstraction. This show and these artists best frame our understanding of Power's place in Paris in the 1930s. Of the ninety-four artists who contributed to *Abstraction-Création* over the six year period in which the *cahier* was published, Power was one of only eleven artists to contribute to every issue. The others were Béothy, Gleizes, Gorin, Herbin, Vantongerloo, Moss, the Hungarian László Moholy-Nagy, the Swiss Kurt Seligmann and the Irish Evie Hone and Mainie Jellett.[61] Both Hone and Jellett, like the Sydney artist Grace Crowley, had been students of Gleizes and were friends of Anne Dangar. Indeed, in a letter to Gleizes, Jellett reported her admiration

BARBARA-HEPWORTH	POWER
BEOTHY	PRAMPOLINI
CLOSON	SELIGMANN
FERNANDEZ	TAEUBER-ARP
HELION	VALMIER

ABSTRACTION - CRÉATION
44, AVENUE DE WAGRAM, PARIS-8e
DE 10 h. A MIDI ET DE 15 h. A 19 h.
DEUXIÈME SÉRIE DU 2 AU 14 FÉVRIER
VERNISSAGE LE 2 FÉVRIER DE 16 h. A 19 h.

Abstraction-Création invitation, Paris, 1934

for Power's work, along with that of Georges Valmier, Alfred Reth and Laure Garcin.[62]

Interestingly, Power was not the only Australian member of Abstraction-Création. Crowley was invited to join by Dangar, the Sydney potter then living at Gleizes' art colony Moly-Sabata south of Lyon. Dangar wrote that 'Monsieur Gleizes is insisting on me joining Abstraction et Création Société & told me to tell you'. She confided, 'I didn't tell him but I am not sure if you ever paint non-representative work? One has to send three works to be judged & it costs 150 fr. to be a member'.[63] Crowley was not yet an abstract painter, it would be another eight years before she became a non-figurative artist, so it is understandable that she declined this offer.

In the midst of the Parisian avant-garde in 1932, Power released *Éléments de la Construction Picturale*, his analysis of painting and the history of its relation to geometry, the first artist-book by an Australian. Published by Antoine Roche, well known not only for producing lavish limited editions books but also for being 'a wealthy dilettante, very cultured, an opium addict and a homosexual.'[64] Power's book may also have been produced in conjunction with his friend Rose Adler, the renowned bookbinder. It was she who designed the striking snakeskin binding for Matila Ghyka's *Esthétique des proportions dans la nature et dans les arts* (1927), a book Power owned and admired, calling it 'by far the most profound and exhaustive work on proportion'. Both Power's and Ghyka's book-covers make use of a mirror design, Power's more austere cover reproduced his mathematical diagram for squaring out a canvas on its front and back.[66] His book is foremost an attempt to connect then contemporary painting to the past – through the work of Duccio, Raphael, Rubens, and Gris – it aims to show how artists have borrowed from and extended past compositional methods and systems of proportion. It includes a back pocket section containing a photographic reproduction of a work by each of the artists with various diagrams and celluloid overlays for analysing each work. Power intended that 'these should be placed upon the photograph one at a time in numerical order while reading the description.'[67] Ten years in the making, it can be seen as Power's farewell to Cubism, a movement he described as both 'the very symbol of liberation and the means towards one of the purest aesthetic periods in history.'[68] The precision of his analysis testifies to how he harnessed his own deep knowledge of art and mathematics to move towards abstraction. In 1939 his psychedelic *L'homme calculateur*, surely in part a self-portrait, was published in Christian Zervos's *XXe siècle*.

Celebrated in Paris, Power's book was launched at an exhibition he shared with Jean Lurçat and André Masson at the Galerie

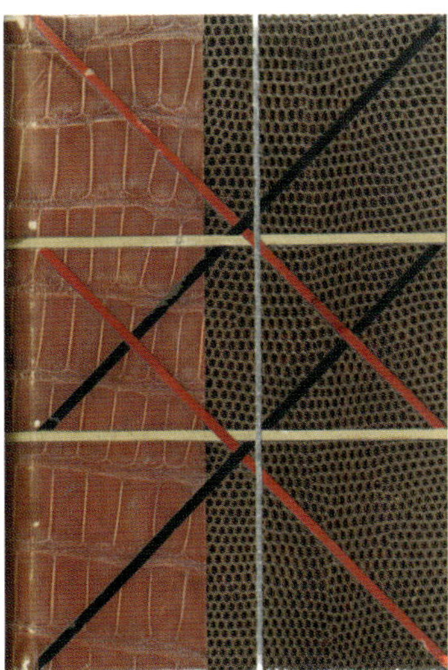

Matil Ghyka, *Esthétique des proportions dans la nature et dans les arts*, Paris, 1927, book, binding by Rose Adler, from the library of J.W. Power, National Library of Australia.

Jeanne Bucher in June 1933, a show that marked his move from Rosenberg to Bucher.[70] Léopold Survage was among the artists who responded to this work, sending Power his monograph inscribed with the words, 'in thanks for your beautiful book and your work ... which has added to the valuable knowledge of painters... .'[71] Called by the art critic Marcel Zahar 'a monument of science', significantly Power's book was recognised by the communist art historian Konrad Farner in the catalogue for the landmark 1936 exhibition *Theses, Anti-theses, Syntheses* in Luzern.[72] In his 'Bibliografie' Farner lays out an intellectual tradition for abstraction, and under the category 'mathematik', lists *Éléments de la Construction Picturale*, describing a lineage that runs: 'Fiedler – Marés – Hildebrand – Dehio – Hölzel – Fischer – Power – Kandinsky – Moholy'.[73] That same year the Italian art historian Lionello Venturi, in his comprehensive study *History of Art Criticism* (1936) placed Power's book alongside those by other cubist painters such as André Lhote, Gleizes and Ozenfant. Venturi wrote that it provided a post-cubist synthesis capable of reconciling the sensorial with the ideal through 'the ascendency of sensation ... expressed in purely geometric terms.'[74] Indeed Lhote would also cite Power's book in his own influential *Treatise on Landscape Painting* (1939), a book that was known to Australian artists from this time on, and in it he acknowledged Power's 'ingenious system of mechanics'.[75] Perhaps its most enduring legacy, however, was on the art of a generation of post-war English constructivists such as Victor Pasmore, Adrian Heath and Kenneth and Mary Martin who seized upon Power's exposition of the 'moving format', an analytical procedure for creating movement by rotating a geometric unit across the picture plane, as the basis of their constructions.[76]

Power also wrote for *Abstraction-Création*, the group's annual *cahier*. In the first issue Power, in common with other members, identified abstraction with freedom, acknowledging 'the accomplishments of Cubism, Expressionism, Constructivism, Surrealism and pure abstraction. While the material world struggles and groans under the burden of financial and political crisis, we, the creators of the spiritual world, painters, sculptors, writers, poets, musicians, are richer than ever in our means of expression.'[77]

For the next issue the committee sent members a questionnaire that sought a response to a series of provocative, even nonsensical questions. Power replied logically:

> 'Is a locomotive a work of art? Not at all! A locomotive is not a work of art. A work of art is a harmony created as an end in itself, and an artist is someone who "only" concerns himself with the harmony of forms and colours as ends in themselves. If the harmony of forms is the result of a practical function, such as, for example, speed, lightness, solidity, it is not an end

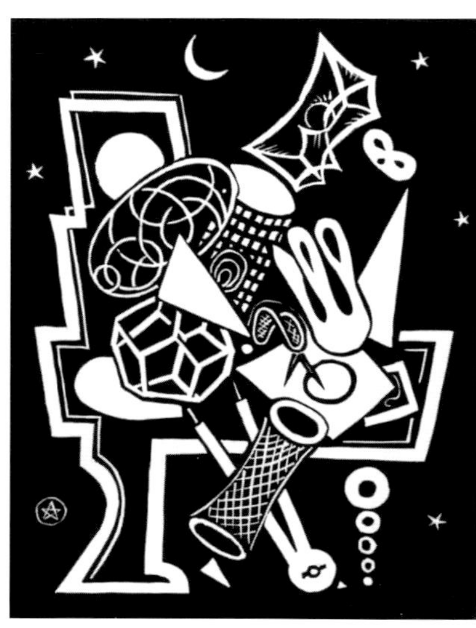

J.W. Power, *L'homme calculateur*, linocut, 31 x 23.4, UA2000.60, inserted in *XXe siecle*, Paris, No. 5/6, 1939, University Art Gallery

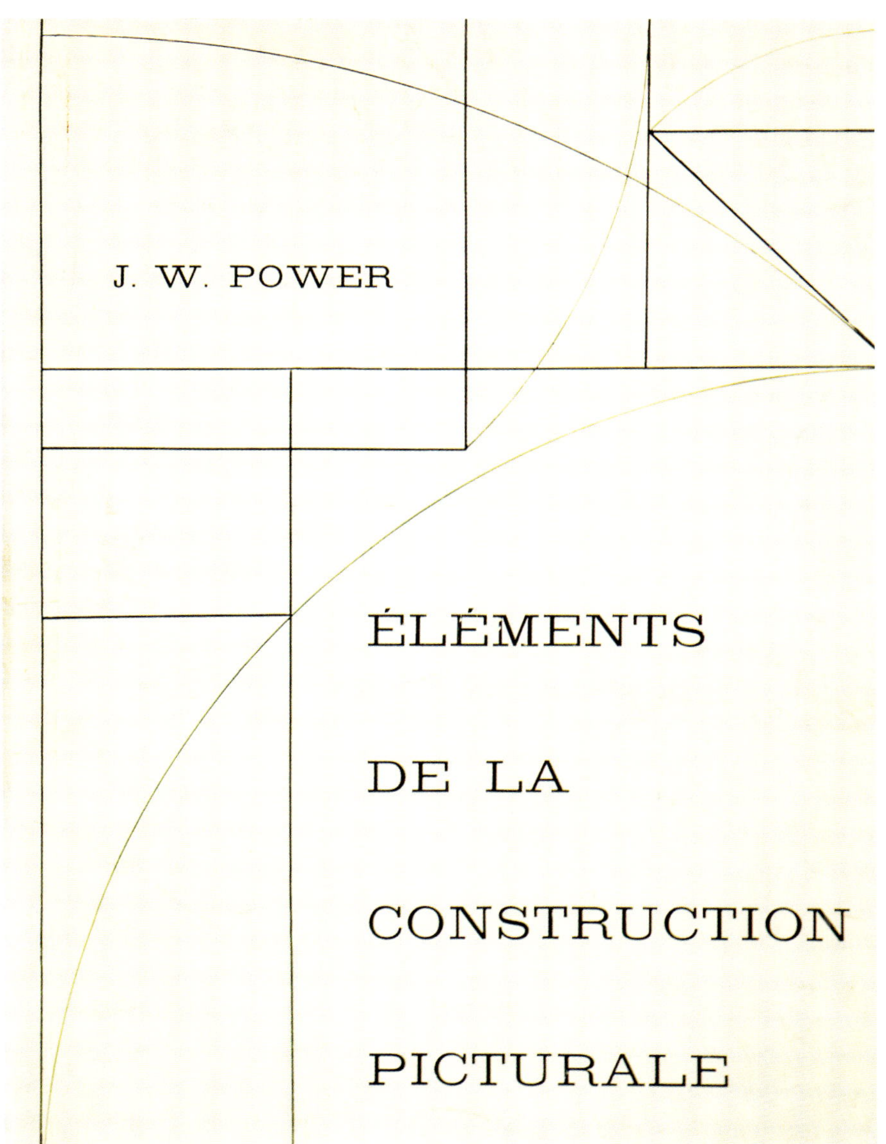

J.W. Power, *Éléments de la Construction Picturale*, Paris, 1932, book, Rare Books & Special Editions Library, Fisher Library, The University of Sydney.

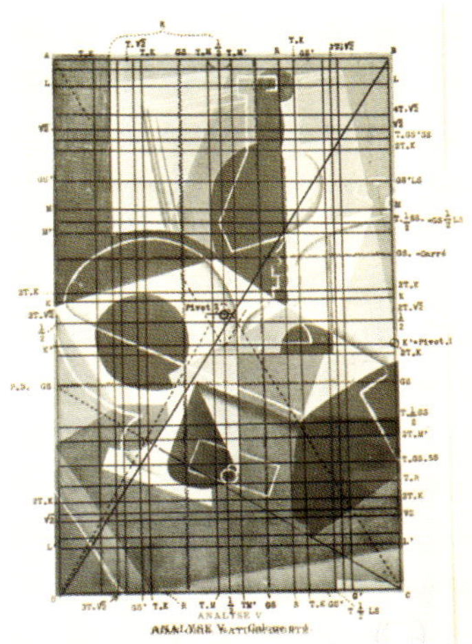

J.W. Power, *Éléments de la Construction Picturale*, Paris, 1932,photographic reproduction of Gris' *Nature Morte*, with celluloid overlay.

in itself, it is, rather, the means towards an end. It is therefore not a work of art. There might well be one part of a machine where its maker is free to choose the most beautiful curve, the finest proportion, and that element alone might have an aesthetic value, but if he allowed the aesthetic value to prevail over the practical function, he would be a bad engineer; and if he is a bad engineer, he would be better off dead. An artist, in looking at a perfect machine, might be inspired and create a work of art, but that is quite another thing.'[78]

For Power painting was 'an end in itself', nonetheless, as we will see, he would show his work in highly charged contexts.

The intensity of art world politics created great pressures within the group. Power wrote to Bertram that there was 'too much stimulus in Paris, one feels in a continual flutter ... Everyone is on tenterhooks about Something.'[79] In 1932 he let a house in Brussels by the forest at 41 Avenue des Courses, 'a new ferro-concrete structure, 1927, with a flat roof'; he also rented a studio at 205 Avenue Louise, the distinguished Brussels boulevard, that city's equivalent of the Avenue des Champs-Élysées.[80] Throughout these years, shifting between Belgium and France, Power studied the art of the past while travelling extensively throughout Europe. The history of painting is as present in his work as the modern and the contemporary. 'The subject', he wrote, defining his position, 'must be studied for a long time to sort out the felt from the unfelt & the newest means of "expression of the thing" felt.'[81]

Installation view of *Abstraction-Création* exhibition, December 1933.

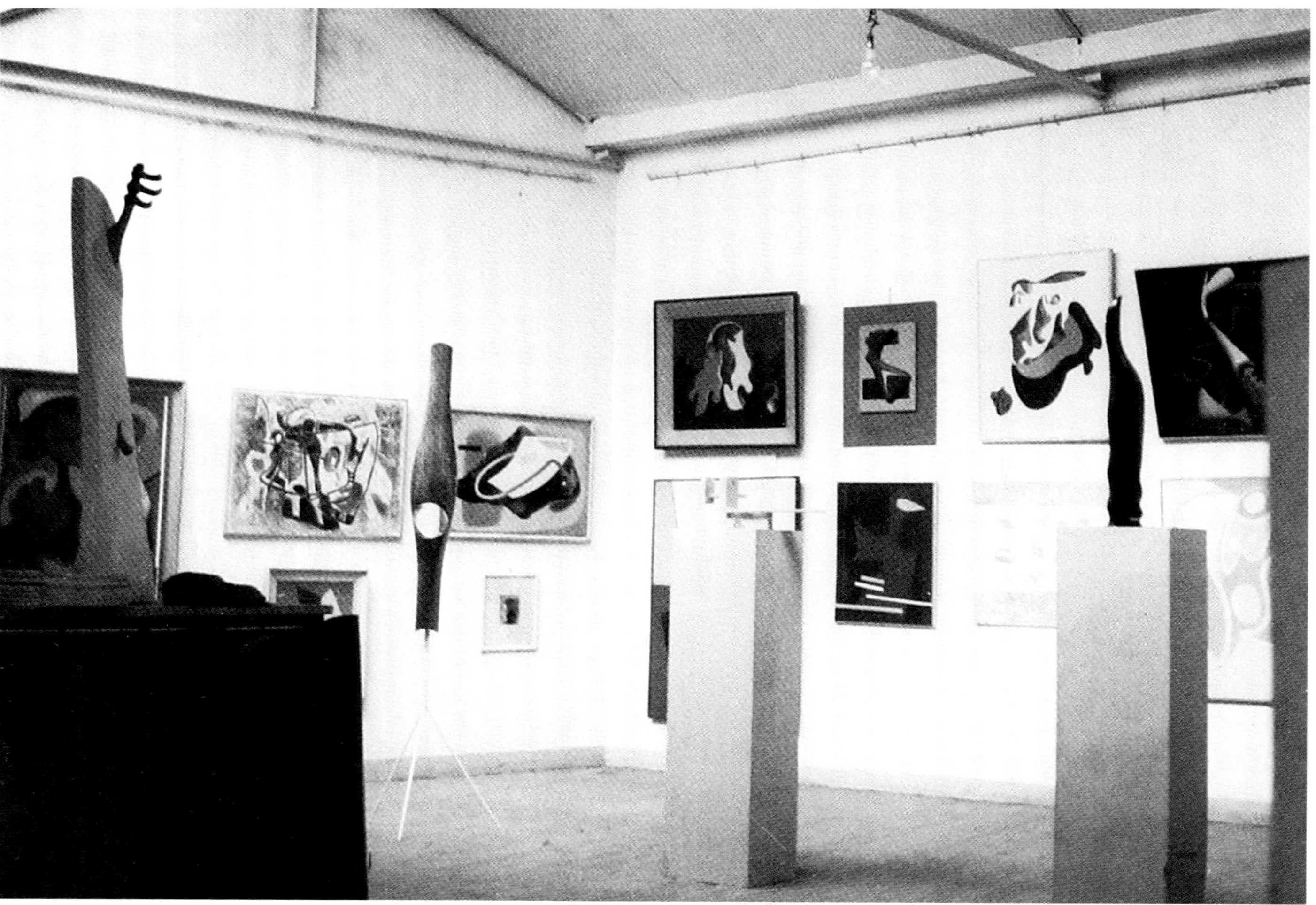

J.W. Power at Abstraction-Création 1934

Every year that passes convinces me that I was wise to take up the more abstract forms of painting in all their various manifestations.

J.W. Power[82]

IN 1934 POWER HAD the first one-person exhibition at Abstraction-Création's gallery at 44 Avenue de Wagram. Their 'salle d'exposition' was located in a rear courtyard behind a building off the Étoile. Not large by today's standards, it was generous by comparison to the compact spaces of the then evolving Parisian gallery scene. Paintings could be hung from a hanging rail that ran around the top of the nearly three metre high white walls, and a high window that ran the length of the long wall allowed natural light into the space. Visitors entered through the courtyard and stepped into a small anteroom that opened out onto the main gallery.[83]

Opened in winter before the New Year, the space was a platform for an intense series of exhibitions and events that lasted only as long as the following summer. International in character, the group formed a block against the dominant tendencies then holding sway in Paris. By July 1934 Abstraction-Création had held one large group exhibition, four small group exhibitions, two two-person exhibitions, a conference around Gleizes, and two solo exhibitions, the first by Power, the other by Moholy-Nagy. Power's exhibition was thus at the heart of the group's most public life. Most of the visitors to the gallery came from the group's immediate circle of artists, friends and supporters and their exhibitions had little impact on the wider Parisian art world, with none being reviewed.[84]

Two months after the group show in which he had participated, Power's own exhibition opened in the spring, running from 14–28 April, 1934. For the installation he prepared a detailed '*Plan de l'exposition*', [see pages 44–45] on which he measured and positioned miniature gouache versions of the twenty eight paintings, such care consistent with his highly ordered practice. While no roomsheet or catalogue survives, this plan has enabled the precise recreation of Power's exhibition including 26 of the 28 works.[85] It reveals that the show was a survey of his work over seven years, and traces his move away from cubism towards his own combine of abstraction and surrealism. His layout and hanging schema, with five symmetrical pyramid groupings in which one, two or three mostly vertical panels frame a larger central work, are laid out like a secular version of a multi-panelled altar piece.

Power was always particular about the framing of his painting. Even in the coloured plan of the exhibition, around the small sketch of each work he painted an image of the frame. All his frames are bespoke, those on the earlier works are elaborate hand-carved wood with gesso; some of them are over-painted to match or contrast with the painting's palette. Most of the frames are burnished with silver or gold, generally with mirror finishes made by water gilding. By sometimes painting on the inside edge of the frame – the lime green beading around *Marine* (c. 1934) [Plate 20] and the bright orange line around *Danseurs* (1934) [Plate 19] for example – Power deliberately blurred the line between it and the canvas. His frames, though they make clear the distinction between the wall and the painting would, nonetheless, have helped anchor the work in the interiors of the day, replete as they were, with frames on everything from the mirrors to the doors and windows. Even in his extensive collection of informal oil sketches never intended for exhibition, Power painted in the frame as if he was unable somehow to see the work without it.[86] Such decisions about framing raise questions about the line between art and not-art. When Bertram asked his advice about removing frames from several works that Power had given him, it prompted an expression of mock horror. 'Having taken off the frames from your pictures you must now take off the paint & leave only bare canvas to express perfect purity! I hope Ben Nicholson has not been once again misled by seeing pictures without frames at the Abstraction-Création shows!'[87]

Power's decisions about framing shift over time. The earliest work in the exhibition, for instance, has an ornate two-tone frame which is partially overpainted, while the later paintings have plainer gilded frames. Beginning in the ante-room on the left with his cubist *Paysage Cannes* (1927) [plate 2], the clockwise order of works around the room is loosely chronological.[88] Further around the wall is *Paysage* (1934) [plate 6] the only other 'landscape' on display. In it Power replaces the dark palette of the earlier view of Cannes with pastel pink, white and yellow, articulating an artificial space of curved, interlocking panels fixed by plugs and pins. Pairs of translucent grey globules and clouds inhabit a dream architecture built on an underlying harmonic symmetry.[89]

As we have seen, in the 1920s Power was fascinated by popular dance, and several of his earlier paintings were directly inspired by crazes sweeping across Paris such as the tango and the foxtrot. In the 1934 exhibition he included at least five variations on the theme of bodies in motion using figures to explore formal colour relations. In this way he contributed to the line of painting that sought correspondences between colour and sound. The earliest *Danseuses à la harpe* (1929) [plate 9], is a fantasy embrace between a naked female and a cartoon male in a brown check suit, complete with reverberating lines suggesting motion. Their elastic bodies enact an erotic moment, with the female nude's phallic, Picasso-like head penetrating the golden aura of the embrace, the whole scene framed by musical instruments. Power's dance compositions imagine an ecstatic Dionysian state, like Aby Warburg's foundational studies of the Renaissance revival of antiquity that emphasise accessories in movement. Take Warburg's description of Botticelli's goddess of Spring: 'Her gown ... clings to her body ... a fold curves gently downward to the right from the back of her left knee, fanning out in small folds below... Most of her fair hair wafts back from her temples in long waves, but some has been made into a stiff braid that ends in a bunch of loose hair.'[90] Power's circular *Danseurs* (1933-34) [plate 27], celebrate a Brazilian samba (perhaps a backward glance to his old teacher), their rubbery forms coil and stretch in animated motion across a pointilist field. The red petals of her skirt fans out behind a swirling white bandana, matching another smaller one braided with loops – Carmen Miranda-style – above her head.

Though documented in Power's photo-album, two paintings are missing from this recreation. In these works, both studies of frozen movement, whip-like lines penetrate or encircle cones and rings, trailing ejaculations of spilt pearls and strings of fluid [plate 24 and 25]. At this time, the avant-garde's interest in the body in motion coincided with the rise of popular physical culture ideologies aimed

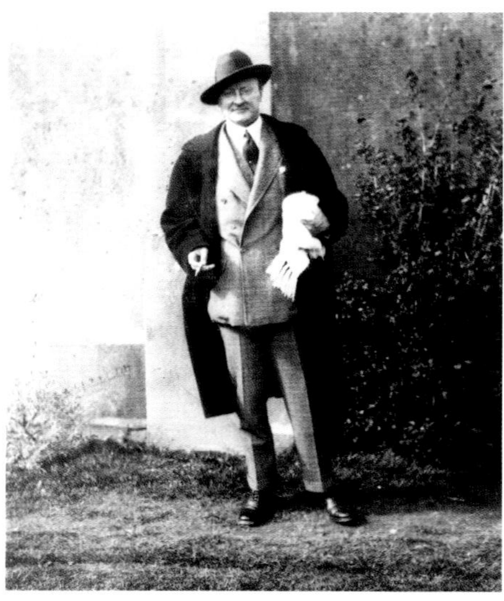

J.W. Power at the Bertram's house, c.1930, photograph by Barbara Bertram.

at reawakening and revitalising the body. The influential teacher and theorist Bess Mensendieck, for instance, 'focused on the "elastic" capacity of joints and muscles to flow in what she called "physiologic rhythm"'.[91]

Another favoured genre in Power's oeuvre that features in his 1934 exhibition is portraiture. His *Tête* (Head) (1931) [plate 10] (reproduced in Abstraction-Création's first *cahier*) retains a cubist layering with its single eye, securing the features by overlapping flat and volumetric forms such as waves of hair and striped and polka dotted fabrics. In a later portrait *Tête* (1932) [plate 13], gravity has intervened, the tubular profile rests on a thin plinth, wedged between a liquefying easel, a spiralling hair-bun and a skyscraper. These recurring *Tête* paintings are as much images of the micro-cosmic, drawn equally from the unconscious as from the everyday, as they are portraits of individuals. Each smooth surface – and the surface of his work is always important to Power – appears to fold, wave, peel or loop, transmogrified by his imagination. Though Power was never officially a Surrealist, just months after the 1934 exhibition he wrote:

> 'I have just finished a book *La petite anthologie poétique du Surréalism* with an introduction by Hugnet who is of the party. It is excellent, so clear and unequivocal & is I think the best thing extant on their aims and ideals which seems mainly psychoanalytical. It speaks much of Dali & shows his recent pictures and his photograph. He is very proud of his "paranoia". Apparently they cultivate wilfully the most ridiculous & impossible juxtaposition of object & thoughts in the hope of liberating their subconscious & then (awful thought!) sitting down to study it! They are definitely more interested in psycho-analysis than anything else and admit it frankly & are "anti-art". But some of their writing is quite beautiful at times especially Paul Eluard. Some of them cannot help being artists in spite of their theory.'[92]

Clearly engaged by Surrealism's intellectual project, Power's words often belie his painting. Later he recognised that Surrealism, 'opened up a channel of revolt against the Cubists & therefore they are worthy. Perhaps the most perfect art has more content and contact with life than Cubism pure and simple.'[93]

In Abstraction-Création's exhibition space the two long walls offered the most prominent and uninterrupted sight lines. On the first, Power placed two vertical works either side of *Conversation* (1930) [plate 12]. One of the larger works in the exhibition, it recalls Vermeer's *Music lesson* (c.1663) in which a woman plays a keyboard beneath a mirror as a man listens. Like other of Power's figure groups, *Commérages* (Gossipers) (c.1930) [plate 4] or *Moonlight flirtation* (c.1930) [plate 8], the intense exchange dissolves individual forms into loops and spirals bound by streaky slashes of ribbon. Behind them a long mirror or window, set in a lime green field, frames a sea of protoplasmic forms as seen through a microscope, not unlike a Kandinsky painting.

Kandinsky's own arrival in Paris co-incided almost exactly with the opening of Abstraction-Création's gallery. His exhibition at Christian Zervos's Galerie des Cahiers d'Art in late May 1934, the year he became a member of the group, opened as Abstraction-Création's program of exhibitions was coming to an end. Power shares an affinity with Kandinsky's 'scientific' concerns and with his imagery, and both owned copies of Karl Blossfeldt's influential *Urformen der Kunst* (Original Forms of Art) (1929). Power's well-thumbed copy of this photographic study of magnified and abstracted flowers and leaves was an important source for his spirals and vegetable forms. Kandinsky's presence in Paris lent support to those artists who were already developing so-called biomorphic modernism, the term coined at this time in order to distinguish between the various emerging forms of abstraction. The British poet and art critic Gregory Grigson, having been introduced to Abstraction-Création while in Paris in 1934, applied the term to differentiate between geometric abstraction and the work he favored. In his view 'biomorphic abstractionists' were 'the beginning of the next central phase in the process of art. They exist between Mondrian and Dali, between idea and emotion, between matter and mind, matter and life.'[94] For artists biomorphism meant more than just a style, rather, as the art historian Jennifer Mundy argues, it was a means 'to figure the conceptions of "life", "origins", and "nature." While these are all themes and motifs that refer to the life sciences or to concepts current within the Biocentric discourses, there is no necessary connection between ideological background and style.'[95] Like Kandinsky, Power did not fit the Surrealist mould, neither, for instance, were Communists. Both, however, came to modify their initial irritation with Surrealism driven in part by their fascination with biomorphic and cosmological imagery. It is difficult not to think that Power's biomorphism was also informed by his previous work as a doctor and research scientist, particularly as he is said to have 'maintained an interest in bacteriology throughout his life.'[96]

In the centre of the other main wall in the gallery, Power placed his three elongated 'ribbon' paintings, each one titled *Abstraction* [plates 17, 18 and 21]. Completing the wall, he bookended this triumvirate with *Groupe* (1931) [plate 15] and *Danseurs* (1934) [plate 19]. These works forming the base of a triangle, its uppermost point was made by hanging the horizontal format *Marine* (c.1932) [plate 20]. Traces of a recumbent nude haunt Marine's curvy armature, modeled in feathery strokes of white and pink. Like *Paysage*, translucent globes and amoeba-like forms – here covered with dots and sprigs – float or hover in a weightless aquatic environment. Power's sketchbooks are filled with classical nude studies both from the model and drawn after works by Picasso as well as Rubens, Ingres, Titian and Poussin. In *Groupe* (1931) the figures rise like those in Botticelli's *The Birth of Venus* (1486) bound together by decorative linear loops and curves, suggesting draperies of figures in motion. Power transformed Botticelli's diaphanous fabrics into contemporary spotted bathing costumes, with spirals for breasts, and pegs and holes for heads. While more gentle than the sexual energy of Picasso's Dinard *Bathers* series (1928), Power's metropolitan figure dressed in hat and suit is camouflaged between the female figures, his erection pressing in on the group.

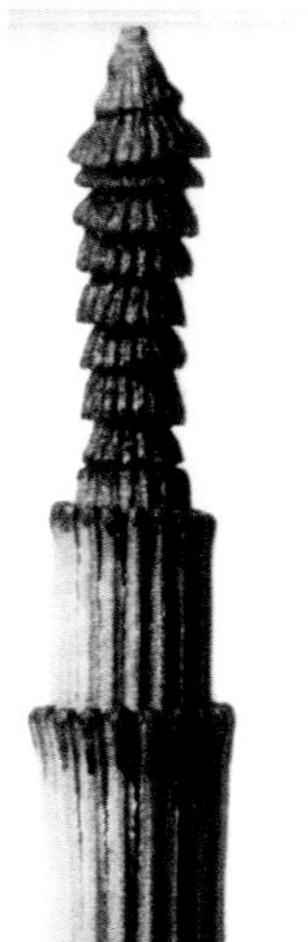
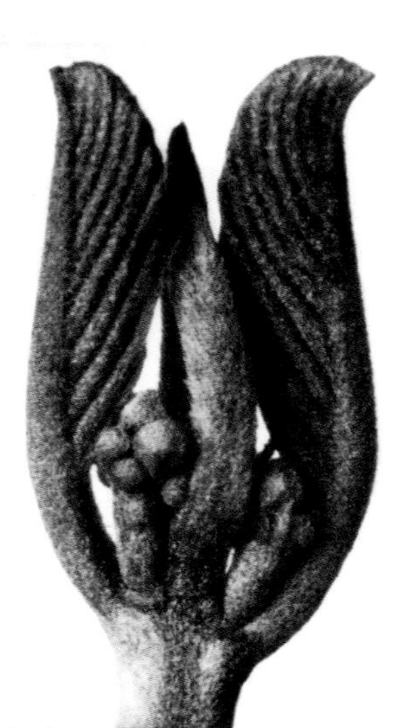
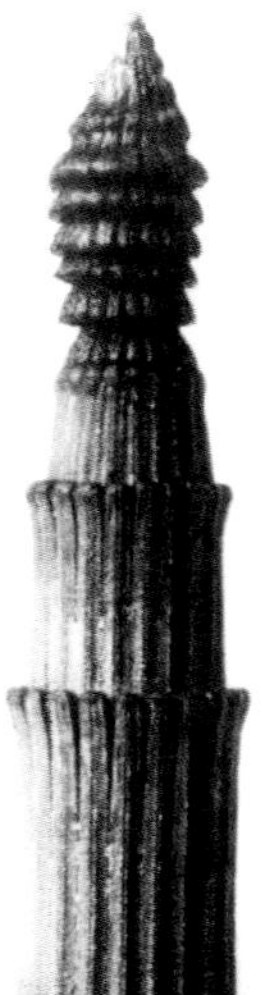

Photograph from Karl Blossfeldt, *Urformen der Kunst*, Berlin, 1929, book, from the library of J.W. Power, National Library of Australia

On the 'third' wall in the gallery hung one of Power's most playful raids on the iconography of western art. His *Susannah and the Elders* (1931–32) [plate 23] re-presents a scene of lechery taken from the book of Daniel in the Old Testament. Power uses a palette of rose and orange against grey and dark green, his grafted figure of the cross-eyed 'elders', painted around the surface of twin dark pink cylinders, leers out over a ribbon of flesh, shielded by rose dapery. While an unusual source for avant-garde artists, this parable of sexual violation appears, as the art historian Mark Antliff has recently suggested, to have also been the source for Raymond Duchamp-Villon's *Femme assisse* (Seated Woman) (1914), with its 'side-long glance and a gesture of modesty'.[98] Another version much closer to Power, was carved by Étienne Beöthy, who also showed with Léonce Rosenberg and was a founding member of Abstraction-Création. Beöthy's organic sculpture, *Susanne* (1929) formed from a series of arcs balanced atop a pedestal, looks uncannily like a model for Power's figure. His painting recalls both the history of the representation of *Susannah* but also looks forward to a lighter, even slapstick, approach to painting.

In his exhibition Power hung *Susannah and the elders* beside the larger *Flower in parenthesis* (1932–33) [plate 22] Set against a green-gold field, the flower's shimmering flesh is painted in pink, orange and vibrating yellow on a base of olive green. Power's exhibition ended, around the corner, with a smaller version of *Flower in parenthesis* (1932–33) in which he used a palette of red, green, brilliant purple and pale violet painted on a wood panel, the only work in the show not painted on a canvas [plate 28] These blooms, like Blossfeldt's magnified studies, seem more 'central core' jewels than botanical specimens. In the 1920s Power painted and drew many landscapes with distinctive sinuous and bulbous trees. As a modernist and a scientist, biomorphic imagery offered him a way of reconciling nature and artifice. Power may well have known Alois Riegl's *Stilfragen: Grundlegungen zu einer Geschichte der Ornamentik* (Problems of Style: Foundations for a History of Ornament) (1893) that sought to understand the ancient roots of ornament. Recently the art historian Spyros Papapetros has shown how the complex form of the spiral (that Riegel traced through many cultures) in fact also 'simulates Charles Darwin's diagrams ... the perpetual spiralling of the tendril was abstracted into an angular network of points, arrows and dotted zig-zag lines.'[99] Such a synthesis between science and art lies behind much of Power's painting.

In the 1934 exhibition Power's most recent works mark a decisive shift towards abstraction. Though he often maintains figure/ground relations, his paintings dislocate objects and delight in spatial ambiguities. The impossible forms floating in the foreground – whether seen, for instance, as interlocked ribbons, or pipes pierced by tumescent horns, or rings set amongst a spray of transparent liquid pearls or semen – all effect uncertainty. They are remarkable for embracing an intimate yet disembodied erotic imagery. Often set in deep space, Power, like Klee, imagined his paintings as a universe, replete with planetary spheres, moons and asteroid belts, through which 'the artist floats in cosmic serenity over real things.'[100] These artists, inspired by science, painted personal cosmologies subsuming their subjectivity into images of the universe.

Although Power was assiduous in working up his painting, bringing all his geometry, mathematics and scientific knowledge to bear on any work, he was not rigid in making the sketch the rule. As with all his work, Power rehearsed various permutations of each painting in his small oil sketches. He insisted that, 'the colder passages must have warmer touches, the warmer must have colder in painting flat planes of colour in an "abstract" ... Contrast all the time, not only in colour but in texture quality, line, surface, etc'.[101] It is interesting to note that in the early 1930s Power developed his *Colour Transposition Chart*, a system to be used by artists. He approached Windsor & Newton with the system but the matter went no further and Power's work in relation to this proposal has been lost.[102]

As Power's painting moved away from explicit representation, the act of painting itself became more important to him. In his notebook he explains how his painting evolved 'in the working out. This is a part which is often misunderstood. Hence abstract art.'[103] The final painting, then, may go beyond its initial conception. The artist is 'obliged to create a unity from our experience' and thus we are 'deliver[ed] from the tyranny of classical cubist construction.'[104] His comments here are revealing because it is tempting to see all his work as cubist, as for instance Bertram does, when he refers to 'Power's classical cubism'.[105] Power went beyond this crucial initial influence, though he was never an entirely abstract nor surrealist artist either. For Power, paint, his medium, is distinct from colour. In a very contemporary way, he understands the painter 'must be true to the mediums used and conditions of use.'[106] In his view the 'quality of surface is a very important modifier of colour. To a man who knows his metier the number of ways of painting any single colour is infinite.'[107]

Paris and Jersey 1935–43

If there is a person who hates uniforms, flags and parades more than I do I should love to meet him. If men would only choose a middle course and leave me to my painting how happy I could be.

J.W. Power[108]

FOLLOWING HIS EXHIBITION, Power continued to be a member of Abstraction-Création and participated in a number of group exhibitions in Amsterdam, New York and Paris. By this time the Powers had moved back from Brussels into 31 bis rue Campagne-Première not far from his first residence, another purpose built studio structure perhaps best known then as the address of Man Ray. In these years his social relations and political sympathies can be discerned from his friendships as much as from his participation with artist groups. He showed with the Groupe d'artistes Anglo-Americains in 1935 and 1936, and in the survey exhibition *Origines et développement de l'art international indépendant* at the Jeu de Paume in 1937, but most significantly he showed with the Salon Art Mural in 1935 and 1938.[109] Founded in 1935 by the artist Saint-Maur to raise the profile of the mural, the group sought to integrate art into architecture and to bring modern artists together with artisans.[110] Abstraction-Création formed an internal grouping within Salon Art Mural and in their first exhibition Power's work was hung beside Robert Delaunay, Gorin, Hone, Jellett, Henri-Jean Closon, Paul Roubillotte and Alexandra Povorina. Vantongerloo had recognised the compatibility of the two organisations and in the Salon's 1938 publication he wrote of the social dimension inherent in the relationship between painting and the wall for abstract artists.[111]

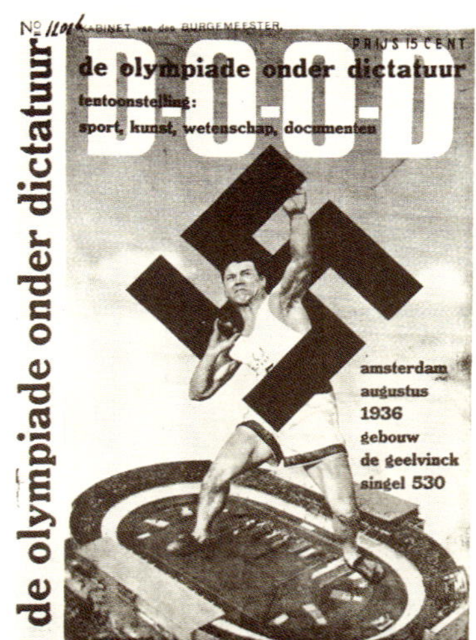

De Olympiade Onder Dictatuur [D.O.O.D], Amsterdam, 1936, catalogue

In 1936, again through the agency of Vantongerloo but also through his association with Art Mural, Power contributed to *De Olympiade Onder Dictatuur* (The Olympic under dictatorship) held in Amsterdam from August 1 to September 17. It was the signal exhibition of the Netherlands resistance to Nazism, its acronym D.O.O.D in Dutch spells 'death' and was timed to coincide with the Olympics in Berlin. It was organised in response to the German invitation for Dutch artists to compete in a parallel art exhibition with the Games.[112] Held in two parts in two separate spaces, the first was a documentary show reflecting on the social and cultural situation in Germany, the second an art exhibition of Dutch and international artists including Power alongside, for instance, Max Ernst, Lurçat, Vantongerloo and Freundlich.[113] While anti-fascist in sentiment, for the most part the works were not avowedly political incorporating the avant-garde alongside more traditional painters. Power sent two works, *Flowers* (1934) from his 1934 Abstraction-Creation show and a new wilder *Tête* (1935).[114] Not in any sense an overt ideological statement, this work would nonetheless have been condemned in National Socialist terms as 'degenerate'. Following the appearance of the show's poster in the streets, German pressure was applied in the Town Hall, leading to works being removed from display and when it moved to Rotterdam (in a much reduced version) it was closed down after just a few days.[115] In the Netherlands, according to the journalist and co-organiser Leo Klaster, 'the *D.O.O.D* exhibition achieved more prominence than the actual artistic competition in Berlin itself – which suffered from lack of foreign participation. The exhibition ... was for some time closer to the centre of public interest than even the Olympic Games.'[116]

By the time of Abstraction-Création's demise in 1937, its battle with surrealism had been fought, and in the art historian Willy Rotzler's

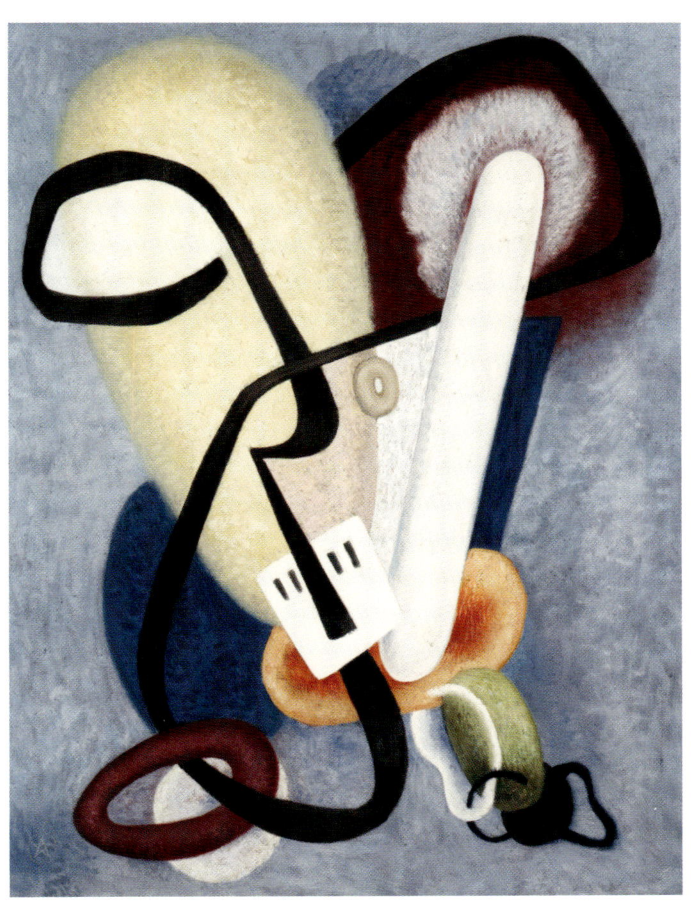

J.W.Power, *Tête*, c. 1935
oil on canvas, 66 x 50.7 cm, PW1961.59

view, abstraction had established itself as 'a legitimate form of artistic expression [that] had been publicized all over the globe'.[117] Many of its artists continued their migration westward at this time, but for the Powers' part, they sailed eastward for three months. Leaving Marseille for the Suez Canal and beyond, Power kept a sketchbook and in them he recorded the 'colour' of Aden, Bombay, Singapore, Malacca, Canton, Hong Kong, Penang, Kowloon, Shanghai, Japan and Hawaii before arriving in Vancouver in April 1937.[118] From there they headed east across Canada to New York, their arrival coinciding with Alfred Barr's landmark exhibition *Cubism and Abstract Art* at the Museum of Modern Art. Power, in his copy of the catalogue, underlined the names of the artists who mattered most to him such as Léger, Kandinsky, Picasso, Kupka, and Vantongerloo, and highlighted details of their biographies. Power also contested certain of Barr's claims, questioning in his copy of the catalogue the significance Barr gave to Nicholson and the role he ascribed to Pevsner and Gabo as the 'leaders of Constructivist element in Abstraction-Création '.[119] As a Parisian insider he was alert to the inherent bias in Barr's account.

Though always restless, Power nonetheless maintained friendships with artists in the cities where he lived and in those he had left behind. After he left England, Power kept up contact with old friends; from his letters it is his relationship with Anthony Bertram we know best. In this correspondence, Power expresses his regard for various artists and writers including the poet Martin Armstrong and others, such as Paul and John Nash. The Bertram's photo album and visitors' book for their house in Bignor, Sussex record a worldly circle of European guests, including French, Poles, Austrians and Germans, many from the art world, the BBC and the stage. Power appears to have known them all. The painter John Armstrong was part of this circle, the two sharing an interest in littoral imagery so characteristic of British surrealism in the 1930s, and Armstrong worked in the theatre as a designer, another of Power's pleasures in the 1920s. Edward Wadsworth, the first English artist to participate in Abstraction-Création and like Power previously a member of the Surindépendants and the association "1940", was another friend. Also financially independent, Power and Wadsworth corresponded though, unlike Power, Wadsworth lived and worked throughout the 1930s in England.[120]

Though resident in Paris, Power continued to show in London. In 1931 he was part of *Recent Developments in British Painting* at the Tooth Gallery where he was hung beside John Armstrong, John Aldridge, John Bigge, Edward Burra, Henry Moore, Paul Nash, Nicholson and Wadsworth. Favourably received, with the nucleus of this exhibition Moore and Nash went on to found Unit 1, the vehicle for English abstraction. Curiously, in 1934 Power showed alongside the Sydney painter Roy de Maistre at the galleries of Arundell Clark in New York with others including Wadsworth, Paul Nash, Ben Nicholson, John Bigge, Tristan Hillier, Edward Burra and Ivon Hitchens. He showed again with de Maistre in 1937 in his final outing with the London Group.[121] However, by 1934 Power was better recognised as a Parisian artist, when in that year four of his paintings were reproduced beside his biographical entry in Édouard-Joseph's *Dictionaire Biographique des Artistes Contemporaines 1910–1930*.[122]

Perhaps like Man Ray, of whom the art historian Sophie Lévy has written that 'like others [he] understood that he had to play the foreigner in order to be included in Parisian groups', Power was both an insider and an outsider in Paris.[123] A French speaking anglophone, Power numbered amongst his close friends Herbin, a relationship established in the 1920s, when both were represented by Léonce Rosenberg. Herbin felt able to call Power to Paris, precipitating his final move from England. Power was close to Vantongerloo too, an important protagonist beside Herbin in the formation of Abstraction-Création, and its erstwhile treasurer. It is likely that Power was a friend of Gris, who died aged 40 in 1927 and whose painting *Nature morte* (1917), now known as *Moulin à café et bouteille*, was analysed by Power in his book. Perhaps the Czech artist František Foltyn who owned Power's work and was a member of Abstraction-Création while based in Paris, was also a friend.[124] Certainly Pierre Chareau, renowned for his Maison Verre completed in 1932, and his English wife, were friends of the Powers. In his 1938 exhibition at Galerie Jeanne Bucher Power included a surreal pen portrait of Madame Chareau.

The majority of Power's own art collection, drawn if not from friends then from those he knew, was dated from the 1930s including work by, Enrico Prampolini, Roger Bissière, Gleizes, Freundlich, Herbin, Marcoussis, Masson, Ozenfant, Picasso, Survage, Vantongerloo, Valmier and Gorin.[125] It is one of the great losses to Australian art that Power's collection was auctioned shortly after the Power bequest was announced in 1962. At the time the Parisian writer and art historian Robert Lebel spoke of Power's spirit of commitment to the art and artists of his time. Lebel recalled that he had 'bought many of the paintings for far more than they were worth to help the artists ... by so doing [he] also helped to make many of them famous.'[126]

Yet all these relationships remain elusive, pieced together from scattered evidence. Power's social life in particular has remained hidden, the only surviving letter that directly records his friendship with another artist is from the expatriate German sculptor and painter Otto Freundlich who was a long time resident in Paris. Freundlich, who was Jewish, became a prominent target of Nazi propaganda when his early sculpture *Der neue*

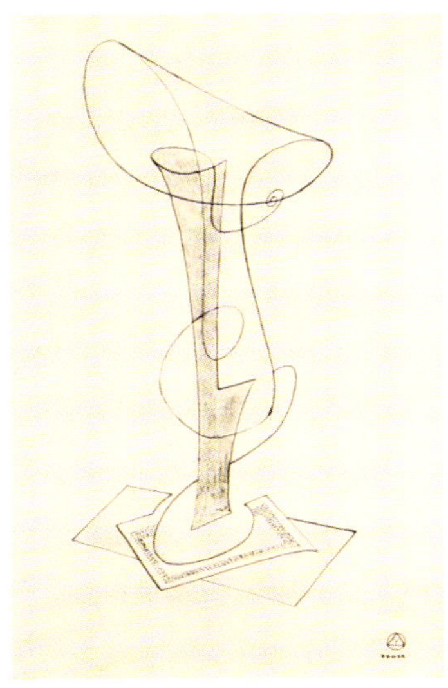

J.W. Power, *Madame Chareau*, 1938, pen and ink drawing, J.W. Power photo album, Rare Books & Special Collections Library, Fisher Library, The University of Sydney, RB571.4/2

Mensch (New Man) (1912) was featured on the cover of the catalogue of *Entartete Kunst* (Degenerate Art) in 1937. Their relationship developed within such a climate of anti-Semitism, in France as well as Germany.

They had been in many of the same exhibitions from the Surindépendants, through Abstraction-Création and up to *D.O.O.D.* They shared the same gallerist and both held exhibitions at Galerie Jeanne Bucher in 1938. Power's exhibition, *Peintures sur verre et toiles de John W. Power*, besides his paintings on canvas, also included experiments with collage, chalk drawings, ink drawings on gold paper, a brush drawing on marble dust, watercolours and pastels. Most remarkable in this exhibition, however, were his paintings on glass. Double sided, like his cigar-box oil sketches, these small mostly abstract paintings with their apparent incompleteness seem at odds with Power's earlier work. Transparent and unframed, they challenge our ability to see them even as paintings and extend our understanding of his art.

Three years earlier and on the occasion of Freundlich's sixtieth birthday, Bucher sought to raise both funds for and the profile of the impoverished artist. Samuel Beckett remembered, 'I went to Otto Freundlich's exhibition at Jeanne Bucher's. A subscription list has been opened to buy a picture and to present it to the Jeu de Paume ... a very fine one, far and away the best in the show ... I met him once a couple of months ago and found him very sympathetic'.[127] In the end the effort came to nothing.

In 1938 Freundlich wrote to Power having recently received a *pneu* from him, a letter sent by the then modern pneumatic dispatch network that connected Paris by tube.

> *Paris, 5th arrondissement 12.II.1938*
> *38, rue Denfert-Rochereau*
>
> *My dear Power,*
>
> *I thank you with all my heart for your kindness. The pneu arrived safely with your generous gift; you have done me a very great service. Again, all my thanks.*
>
> *I was glad to see your recent paintings, which are full of originality and wholly new artistic possibilities. In these wretched times, it is comforting to see a few artists diligently following the paths that are opening up new perspectives for art, perspectives which, sooner or later, will benefit human culture. I hope that you will give us the pleasure of coming to visit; you will be able to see the beginning of the mosaic. And once I have finished it, I will make a little mosaic for you.*
>
> *With my sincere gratitude and warm friendship,*
>
> *Otto Freundlich*[128]

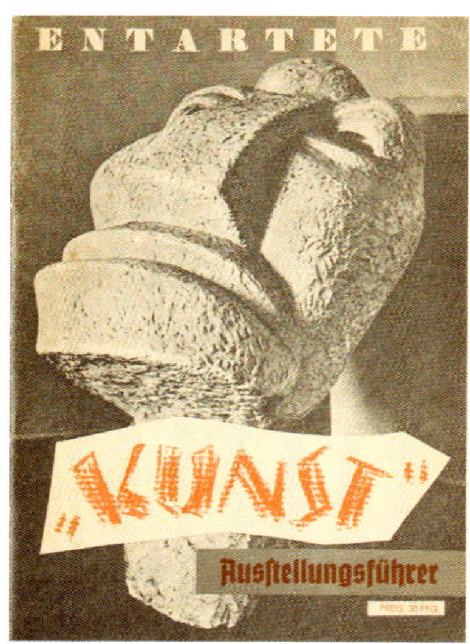

Entartete Kunst, Munich, 1937, catalogue, featuring Otto Freundlich's *New Man*.

The exact nature of Power's 'kindness' is not known but as the *pneu* was a system for delivering paper it is not hard to imagine that Power was helping Freundlich out financially, as he had years earlier when Bertram had begun his family.[129] What is clear from this letter, however, is that Freundlich had recently visited his studio in the months leading up to what would be Power's last one-person exhibition. The two artists were friends, their studios never very far apart, and it is notable that at the sale of Power's collection in 1962, lot number 16 was the small mosaic *Bild in ceracolor* by Otto Freundlich.

Unfortunately, the years after their exhibitions in 1938 were neither full of 'opening up new perspectives for art' nor of explorations in 'new artistic possibilities'. Instead, war drew nearer. Freundlich stayed on in Paris after the Occupation, was arrested by the Germans and released under pressure from Picasso and others, but was eventually betrayed in Vichy France trying to cross into Spain in 1943. Returned by the authorities to Paris, he was interned at Drancy before being transported to occupied Poland where he was killed on arrival at the concentration camp at Lublin-Majdenak. Power, likewise, died in 1943, in occupied Jersey, just 30 kilometres off the French coast. It was there that he had made his last home in 1939. A matter of days after war was declared he wrote his will which included the bequest that conceived of bringing 'the people of Australia in more direct touch with the latest art developments in other countries'. In the midst of war and in the face of Fascism, Power had the vision to imagine a future in which contemporary art could play a crucial role in making Australia a more cosmopolitan culture. With a similarly expansive world view, Paul Rosenberg, likewise in exile, wrote for *Art in Australia* from New York in 1941 that 'artists, creating what the Nazi caste in their lack of culture call "degenerate art", may no longer exhibit or manifest themselves in Paris ... Unknowingly, Europe is permitting the torch to escape ... The new world is inheriting the civilisation of the old. A new field of culture will form here, which in turn will spread throughout the entire universe.'[130]

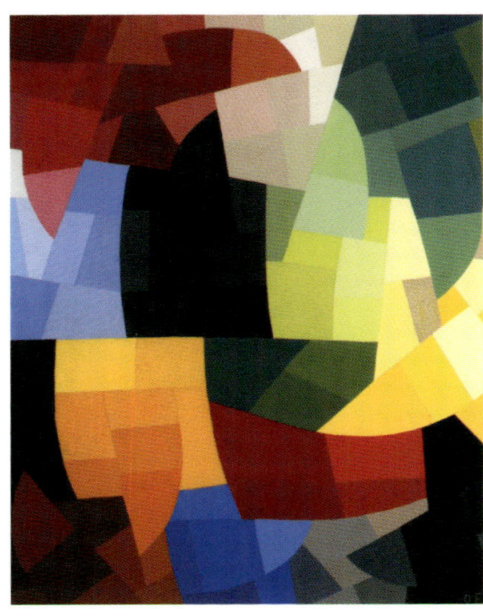

Otto Freundlich (1878-1943)
Composition 1939
Gouache on paper 54 x 43 cm, Collection Musée de Pontoise Donation Otto Freundlich - Wvz.196

Conclusion

Had [Power] painted these pictures in Australia between 1927 and 1938 he would possibly be now regarded as the most important figure in our early avant-garde.

Robert Hughes[131]

WHAT, THEN, can J.W. Power's 1934 exhibition tell us about art in Paris and how should it be understood in Australasian art history? Retrospectively, the exhibition can be seen as remarkable for an Australian in Paris and the highpoint of his career, yet it has remained out of sight for eight decades. Its restaging brings into focus the relations between the paintings and the wider company they kept. Seeing them together also allows us to acknowledge Power's contribution to Abstraction-Création's project of building an outward looking international community of artists through publications, events and exhibitions. As Power's exhibition took place at the epicentre of the avant-garde of the 1930s, when questions about painting were a matter of dispute, his work, neither completely abstract nor surreal, stood at the crossroads of this debate. Power's cosmopolitan art, even then, exposed the differences and the similitude between these dominant tendencies. His work thus demands a rethinking of our art history. Contra Hughes, Power is 'the most important figure in our early avant-garde', precisely because his work was made within the ambit of Abstraction-Création.

Australian artists have always looked to Paris and many have lived and worked there. Drawing from the archives, museums and libraries of continental Europe, resources largely ignored by Australian art historians, we can see that Power contributed significantly to cultural life in the twilight years of the Third Republic. We can see now that Power's experience was not unique but can be compared to the earlier generation of Australasian expatriate artists such as John Peter Russell, Rupert Bunny, Charles Conder, Ambrose Patterson, Max Meldrum, Frances Hodgkins, Kathleen O'Connor, Bessie Davidson and Agnes Goodsir. Power's career, too, overlaps with his contemporaries in France such as Anne Dangar and Sam Atyeo. After the war, Mary Webb, Helen Lempriere and Stacha Halpern continued this line. In her essay on the School of Paris, Gladys Fabre points out that exile, even when temporary, imposes a sense of otherness which she compares to an amorous relationship in terms of the energy and creativity that it engenders.[132] Power's self-imposed exiles – from Sydney in London, in France from England, in Belgium from France, and then back in Paris from Brussels – were fuelled by his insatiable cosmopolitanism.

Expatriates, particularly those who lived and worked in non-anglophone countries, have largely been overlooked in Australian art history, shunned in our nationalist narratives for their apparent disloyalty. Power's exhibition and career reorients our cultural map and reveals the depth of such engagements with Europe. These exchanges underpin many of the cosmopolitan values of contemporary Australian society – the multi-cultural, the urbane, the heterogeneous. By reinscribing such an important expatriate artist into the story of Australian and French art, we have shown that the present can have a new past.[133]

Notes

1. Daniel-Henry Kahnweiler in conversation with Bernard Smith, in Bernard Smith, 'The Role of an Institute of Fine Arts in the University of Sydney', *Arts: The Journal of the Sydney University Arts Association*, Vol. 6, 1969, p. 5.
2. J.W. Power Will, 1939, announced by the University of Sydney in 1962. University of Sydney Archives, General Subject Files, G3/185/26/0023. The bequest to the University of Sydney established the Power Institute of Fine Art, the Power Collection, the Power Studio at the Cité International des Arts, Paris and the Museum of Contemporary Art in Sydney. See Julia Horne and Geoffrey Sherington, *Sydney: The making of a Public University*, The Miegunyah Press, Melbourne University Publishing, Carlton, Victoria, 2012, pp. 220-221.
3. Robert Hughes, 'Bequest and behest', *Nation*, Sydney, 28.7.1962, p. 16. Hughes' commentary was made in his review of Power's exhibition at the University of Sydney in 1962. Under the direction of Leon Paroissien and Bernice Murphy, the Museum of Contemporary Art, a major recipient of the bequest, exhibited Power's work several times, most notably in 1991, publishing a modest catalogue *John Power*, with texts by Donna Lee Brien and Virginia Spate. In 1993 Murphy dedicated *Museum of Contemporary Art: Vision & Context* to 'John Power – artist' and in it she chronicled the establishment of the museum and acknowledged that Power's 'own work as an artist still awaits a full and exhaustive treatment, and a major publication.' Bernice Murphy, *Museum of Contemporary Art: Vision & Context*, Museum of Contemporary Art, Sydney, 1993, pp. 44-45.
4. Bernard Smith,'The role of an Institute of Fine Art in the University of Sydney', *Arts: The Journal of the Sydney University Arts Association, Sydney*, Vol. 6, 1969, p. 5.
5. Power's biographical entry indicates he was on the committee of Abstraction-Création and showed with Léonce Rosenberg, 1931-1933, in Édouard-Joseph, *Dictionnaire Biograpique des Artistes Contemporains 1910-1930*, Librairie Grund, Paris, 1934, pp. 158-59.
6. Gladys Fabre, 'Abstraction-Création 1931–1936', *Abstraction-Création 1931–1936*, Musée d'Art Moderne de la Ville de Paris, Paris, and Westfälisches Landesmuseum, Münster, 1978, pp. 304-306.
7. Sydney's art developed in the studios of two atelier-school teachers, the Italian Antonio Dattilo-Rubbo and the Englishman Julian Ashton, both influenced by the various 19th century Schools of Paris. Dattilo-Rubbo made colour a key concern for his students, such as Grace Cossington Smith, Roy de Maistre, Roland Wakelin, James Cant, Mary Webb and Margo Lewers. Ashton, who had worked at the Académie Julian in Paris, was concerned to work *en plein air*.
8. Osbert Sitwell 'The London Group Exhibition', *New Statesman*, London, 1.11.1924, p. 110.
9. Édouard Joseph, *Dictionaire Biographique des Artistes Contemporaines 1910-1930*, Librarire Grund, Paris 1934, pp. 158-159. The entry in this dictionary seems to rely on information provided by Power.
10. J.W. Power sketchbook, 1903–06, PIC.R8667-8733, National Library of Australia. Power's 54 sketchbooks, which span four decades of his career, testify to his skills as a draughtsman, as well as his appetite for travel and the study of museum collections.
11. Power became a member of the Royal College of Surgeons, England, and received the licentiate of the Royal College of Physicians, London, in 1908; he practised at 50 Harrington Gardens in south-west London. From April 1917 Power served in the Royal Army Medical Corps as a temporary lieutenant; he was promoted temporary captain on 25 April 1918. For biographical information see: Anthony Bradley, 'Power, John Joseph Wardell (1881-1943)', *Australian Dictionary of Biography*, Australian National University, http://adb.anu.edu.au/biography/power-john-joseph-wardell-8090/text14119, accessed 19 July 2012.
12. Power's own art collection included four of Araújo's paintings and a photograph of one of them, *Paysannes bretonnes*, among Power's collection is reminiscent of Marie Laurencin's stylised figures. On his return to Brazil, Araújo (1881–1955) undertook schemes for architectural decoration on several grand porticos in Rio de Janeiro in the 1930s, described as 'an unquestionable sign of the presence of indigenous inspiration in Brazilian art. Above the main door of the building, an indigenous-caryatid-mermaid in polychrome ceramic welcomes visitors. She is surrounded by crustaceans, such as crabs, sea horses, and algae, from the sea and Amazonian rivers.' Marcio Alves Roiter, 'Art Deco in Brazil: The Marajoara influence in Brazilian art deco', www.proec.ufg.br/revista_ufg/Revista_Deco_2011/arquivos_PDF/marcio_alves_roiter.pdf. accessed 19 July 2012
13. J.W. Power, *Eléments de la Construction Picturale*, Antoine Roche, Paris, 1932, p. 5.
14. 'Pedro Luiz Correia de Araújo' Itaú, *Cultural Encyclopaedia of the Visual Arts* http://www.itaucultural.org.br
15. Power's sketch books include gridded-up drawings of paintings after Gris, Braque, Ozenfant and Léger. Sketchbook 51, R8550, National Library of Australia.
16. Ludwig Hirschfeld Mack, *The Bauhaus: An Introductory Survey*, Longmans, Croydon, 1963, pp. 2-3.
17. Gladys Fabre, *Léger et L'Esprit Moderne: une alternative d'avantgarde à l'art non-objectif 1918-1931*, Musée d'Art Moderne de la Ville de Paris, Paris, 1982, p. 420. Power may well have found an affinity with the Swedish painter and fellow student Gosta Adrian Nillson, known as GAN, who wrote a thesis on *La Divine géométrie* arguing 'that since the universe was governed by geometric laws, these same laws should also govern the work of art ... He also showed how compositions could evolve through progressive generation.' pp. 420-421.
18. Gladys Fabre, 'Petite histoire illustrée de l'Académie Moderne – Liste des élèves de Léger entre 1924-1931', *Léger et l'esprit moderne: une alternative d'avant-garde à l'art non-objectif 1918-1931*, Musée d'art Moderne de la Ville de Paris, Paris, 1982, p. 493. Marie Laurencin, Alexandra Exter and Louis Marcoussis also taught classes in the 1920s. After the war Léger taught the Australians Ethel Cramp (c.1950–54), Eileen Mayo, Leonard Hessing (c.1949–51) and Jeffrey Smart (c.1948).
19. J.W. Power to Anthony Bertram, letter 1, 1926, RB Lib –Add. Ms120, Rare Books & Special Collections, Fisher Library, The University of Sydney. These 34 letters written between 1926-34 were acquired from Bertram in 1973 by Bernard Smith, then Director of the Power Institute. They were accompanied by Bertram's unpublished manuscript 'Memoirs of John Power', c.1973, now held in the Archives. Anthony Bertram, 'Memories of John Power', unpublished Manuscript, 1973, pp 3, 4, University of Sydney Archives, Department of Fine Arts Records: J.W. Power, G35/1/1.
20. *Bulletin de l'Effort Moderne*, October, 1925, No. 18, np. Power had showed a work called *Footballers* in the 1923 London Group exhibition.
21. Gladys Fabre and Marie-Odile Briot, 'Avant propos', *Léger et L'Esprit Moderne: une alternative d'avantgarde à l'art non-objectif 1918–1931*, Musée d'Art Moderne de la Ville de Paris, Paris, 1982, p. 25.
22. Jean Leymarie cites Léger's remarks in his essay, commenting that, 'The ruler, the set-square and the compasses, instruments which were necessary to the painter's precise manner of working, also appear as objects in his works,' in Jean Cassou and Jean Leymarie, *Fernand Léger: Drawings & Gouaches*, Thames & Hudson, London, 1973, p. 88.
23. Power collected mathematical models by the Cussons Company of Manchester and many are reproduced in his linocut *L'homme calculateur* (1939) in *XXe Siècle*, Vol. 5-6, Paris, 1939. All of his models have now been lost. Power was not alone in this interest. Man Ray's photograph of Kummer's model, a plane surface with sixteen points of which eight are true, for instance, was reproduced in Herbert Read's *Surrealism*, Faber & Faber, London, 1936, plate 94.
24. J.W. Power to Anthony Bertram, letter 1, 1926, RB Lib –Add. Ms120, Rare Books & Special Collections, Fisher Library, The University of Sydney.
25. 'Ogee' is a term used in architecture and mathematics to refer to the form of two arcs shaped somewhat like an S that curve in opposite directions, so that the ends are parallel.
26. Virginia Spate, 'Transformations: A short and belated note on the paintings of John Power', in *John Power 1881-1943: Artist and Benefactor*, Museum of Contemporary Art, Sydney, 1991, p. 36.

27. Anthony Bertram, 'Memoirs of John Power', unpublished manuscript, 1973, p. 8, The University of Sydney Archives, Department of Fine Arts Records: J.W. Power, G35/1/1.

28. J.W. Power, *Éléments de la Construction Picturale*, Antoine Roche, Paris, 1932, English translation, 1933, p. 26.

29. Juan Gris, response to a questionnaire on his art, *L'Esprit Nouveau*, Paris, No. 5, February 1921, pp. 533-534, republished by Herschel B. Chipp, in *Theories of Modern Art: A source book by artists and critics*, University of California Press, Berkeley, 1971, p. 274.

30. Denys J. Wilcox, *The London Group 1913-1939*, Scolar Press, Aldershot, 1995, p. 230.

31. Power was not the first Australasian artist to be a member of the London Group. Horace Brodzky had been elected in 1914, Frances Hodgkins would be in 1940-43 and Roy de Maistre in 1954.

32. Frank Rutter, *Sunday Times*, 28 March 1926, Ms.5761, Manuscripts, National Library of Australia.

33. Selections from press cuttings from J.W. Power's reviews, Ms 16/11/10 AJ are held in Manuscripts, National Library of Australia. It is interesting to note that Power was understood by most British reviewers to be an Australian artist. But Bertram is an exception. His 1926 exhibition was news, too, in his hometown, reported on under the headline 'Australian Artist Praised' in *The Sun*, 15.3.1926. The question of Power's nationality next arose in 1935 following the publication in *Abstraction-Création* of the results of a questionnaire. In the census-like 'Memorandum' at the front of the *cahier* Australia is not listed as a country with a member or friend, but neither is Ireland, the home of Hone and Jellett, the two countries apparently absorbed within the category 'Great Britain'. This same assumption underlies Power's inclusion in Basil Burdett's 1939 *Exhibition of French and British Modern Art* where his work was included in the section 'British Paintings'.

34. Anthony Bertram, *Saturday Review*, 26 March, 1926. That year Power's work was acquired by the Contemporary Art Society alongside that of John Nash and Duncan Grant. Muirhead Bone, Anthony Eden, Samuel Courtauld and Roger Fry were members of the committee that selected work on behalf of the Society in order to present it to the public collections of English museums. It seems likely that this was the mechanism by which the Nottingham Art Gallery acquired Power's work.

35. Anthony Bertram dedicated his book *Rubens* (1927) to J.W. Power.

36. Anthony Bertram, 'Memories of John Power', unpublished manuscript, The University of Sydney Archives, 1973, pp. 3, 4, The University of Sydney Archives, Department of Fine Arts Records: J.W. Power, G35/1/1.

37. J.W. Power to Anthony Bertram, letter 10, c.1929, RB Lib –Add. Ms120, Rare Books & Special Collections, Fisher Library, The University of Sydney.

38. Maurice Raynal, 'Au Salon des Surindépendants', *L'Intransigeant*, Paris, 27.10.1930, p. 9.

39. Reproduced in *Bulletin de l'Effort Moderne*, Paris, No. 18, 1925, np. Power had to correct his copy of the journal as his *Le Football* (1924) was mislabelled as the work of Max Ernst.

40. J.W. Power to Anthony Bertram, letter 11, April.1929, RB Lib –Add. Ms120, Rare Books & Special Collections, Fisher Library, The University of Sydney.

41. Anthony Bertram, 'Memories of John Power', unpublished manuscript, pp. 8-9, The University of Sydney Archives, Department of Fine Arts Records: J.W. Power, G35/1/1.

42. The first inventory of Power's art collection *Catalogue of Modern Paintings*, was done by Langlois, a Jersey auctioneer, following the death of his widow in May 1961. Six months later Sotheby's London published a more accurate *Catalogue of Modern Paintings, Drawings and Graphic Art: The property of the late Dr John Joseph Wardell Power*, 7 November 1962, republished in *Modernism & Australia: Documents on Art Design and Architecture 1917- 1967*, eds., Ann Stephen, Philip Goad, and Andrew McNamara, The Miegunyah Press, Melbourne University Publishing, Carlton, 2008, pp. 811-817.

43. Virginia Spate, 'Transformations: A short and belated note on the paintings of John Power', *John Power 1881-1943: Artist and Benefactor*, Museum of Contemporary Art, Sydney, 1991, p. 36.

44. Jocelyne Rotily, 'A picture of America by Gerald Murphy', *A Transatlantic Avant-garde: American Artists in Paris 1918-1939*, ed. Sophie Lévy, Musée d'art Américain, Giverny, 2003, p. 56; see also Gladys Fabre, *Léger and the Modern Spirit: 1918-1931*, Musée d'Art Moderne de la Ville de Paris, Paris, 1982, p. 153; see Fernand Léger, 'The Aesthetic of the Machine', *Bulletin de L'Effort Moderne*, Paris, Vol. I No. 1, January, No. 2, February, 1924, pp. 5-9, reprinted in *Theories of Modern Art*, ed. Herschel Chipp, University of California Press, Berkeley, 1971, p. 278.

45. J.W. Power, Notebook, c.1940, Ms. 5761, Manuscripts, National Library of Australia. This small notebook was written in his final years and reads as a philosophical reflection on his own work.

46. Power's unpaginated handwritten translation of Leopold Zahn, *Paul Klee: Leben, Werk, Geist*, Gustav Kiepenheuer, Postdam, 1920, is held in Ms. 5761, Manuscripts, National Library of Australia.

47. J.W. Power, Sketchbook No. 1, Switzerland, 1934, includes sketches from the surrounding towns of Berne. Accn. No 8500. Pictures, National Library of Australia.

48. J.W. Power to Anthony Bertram, letter 16, c. 1930, RB Lib –Add. Ms120, Rare Books & Special Collections, Fisher Library, The University of Sydney.

49. Anne Dangar to Grace Crowley, letter dated 23.6.1946. Reprinted in *Earth, Fire, Air, Water: The letters of Anne Dangar to Grace Crowley, 1930–1951*, ed. Helen Topliss, Allen & Unwin, St. Leonards, 2000, p. 263.

50. J.W. Power to Anthony Bertram, letter 12, April 1929, RB Lib –Add. Ms120, Rare Books & Special Collections, Fisher Library, The University of Sydney.

51. J.W. Power to Anthony Bertram, letter 12, April 1929, RB Lib –Add. Ms120, Rare Books & Special Collections, Fisher Library, The University of Sydney.

52. Kandinsky was still at the Bauhaus in 1929 when his first Paris exhibition was held. Christian Zervos featured Picasso's new works in the first issue of his magazine, 'Picasso at Dinard, Summer 1928', *Cahiers d'art*, N°. 1, 1929. Power's annotated set of *Cahiers d'art* are now held in the National Library of Australia.

53. J.W. Power to Anthony Bertram, letter 22, November 1931, RB Lib–Add. Ms120, Rare Books & Special Collections, Fisher Library, The University of Sydney.

54. Gladys Fabre, 'Abstraction-Création 1931–1936', *Abstraction-Création 1931–1936*, Musée d'Art Moderne de la Ville de Paris, Paris, and Westfälisches Landesmuseum, Münster, 1978, p. 5.

55. J.W. Power to Anthony Bertram, letter 17, c. 1930, RB Lib –Add. Ms120, Rare Books & Special Collections, Fisher Library, The University of Sydney.

56. J.W. Power to Anthony Bertram, letter 18, February 10, 1931, RB Lib –Add. Ms120, Rare Books & Special Collections, Fisher Library, The University of Sydney.

57. On the London art market see Andrew Stephenson "Strategies of Situation': British Modernism and the Slump c.1929-1934', *The Oxford Art Journal*, Oxford, 14.2.1991, p. 30.

58. Vantongerloo's annotated set of *Abstraction-Création cahiers* (reproduced in this catalogue) was acquired by the Marquand Library of Art and Archaeology, Princeton University in 2011. As treasurer, these were his defacto accounts book and they show Power to be a regular and generous *payeur*.

59. J.W. Power to Anthony Bertram, letter 25, 19 April 1932, RB Lib –Add. Ms120, Rare Books & Special Collections, Fisher Library, The University of Sydney.

60. J.W. Power to Anthony Bertram, letter 21, March or April 1931, RB Lib –Add. Ms120, Rare Books & Special Collections, Fisher Library, The University of Sydney.

61. See the table of artists in *Abstraction-Création 1931-1936*, Musée d'Art Moderne de la Ville de Paris, Paris, and Westfälisches Landesmuseum, Münster, 1978, pp. 304-306.

62. Bruce Arnold, *Mainie Jellett and the Modern Movement in Ireland*, Yale University Press, New Haven & London, 1991, p. 137. The story of Jellett and her friend and colleague Evie Hone, both students of Gleizes, has many echoes of the friendship between Dangar and Crowley.

63. Anne Dangar to Grace Crowley, letter 11.3.1934, Helen Topliss, *Earth Fire Water Air: Anne Dangar's letters to Grace Crowley 1930-1951*, Allen & Unwin, St. Leonards, 2000, p. 118.

64. Juliette Lavie, 'Alphabet d'Emmanuel Sougez: Une oeuvre manifeste?'in *Textimage*, No.3, Winter, 2009, p. 5. The year before publishing Power's book Roche published Picabia's *Le Peseur d'Ames* (The Weigher of Souls) with a text by André Maurois.

65. J.W. Power, *Éléments de la Construction Picturale*, Antoine Roche, Paris, 1932, English translation 1933, p. 31. Power's own copy of Ghyka's book is now held in the Rare Books collection at the National Library of Australia (RB MOD 1490). Adler may have owned a work by Power as he wrote her name beside the 1929 painting *Apollo and Daphne* on his 1934 exhibition plan, see page 44. Certainly in 1934 they met at Avenue de Wagram, their appointment recorded by Power in one of his sketchbooks. That same year in July Jeanne Bucher wrote to Power promising 'to send you proofs of the new prospectus (I will take a photograph of the cover) that Mlle. Adler and I have designed. You gave me the liberty.' Jeanne Bucher to J.W. Power, University of Sydney Archives, Department of Fine Arts Records: J.W. Power, G35/1/1.

66. J.W. Power, *Eléments de la Construction Picturale*, Antoine Roche, Paris, 1932, p. 7.

67. J.W. Power, *Éléments de la Construction Picturale*, Antoine Roche, Paris, 1932, English translation 1933, p. 17.

68. J.W. Power, *Éléments de la Construction Picturale*, Antoine Roche, Paris, 1932, English translation 1933, p. 14.

69. Power's *L'homme calculateur* was inserted in *XXe siècle*, Paris, No. 5/6, 1939. In his linocut Power included a number of images of mathematical models he had purchased from G. Cussons Ltd of Manchester, now lost.

70. As late as 1939 Boucher was still advertising Power's book in *XXe Siècle*, Paris, No. 5/6, 1939.

71. Paul Fierens, *Survage*, Éditions des Quatre Chemins, Paris, 1931. This book formed part of Power's library now held in the National Library of Australia.

72. Marcel Zahar, *The Studio*, London, Vol. CXVII No. 552, March 1939, p. 129.

73. Farner's 'bibliografie' from the 1935 exhibition *Theses, Antitheses, Syntheses* in Luzern is reprinted in *Hans Erni: Art Non-Figuratif 1933-1938 Abstraction-Création*, Musée Hans Erni, Luzern, 1982, pp. 69-72.

74. Lionello Venturi, *History of Art Criticism*, E.P. Dutton & Co., New York, 1936, p. 297.

75. André Lhote, *Treatise on Landscape Painting*, 1939, A. Zwemmer Limited, London, English translation 1950, p. 13.

76. Power's book was important to Victor Pasmore and his colleagues Adrian Heath and Kenneth and Mary Martin. In the art historian Alistair Grieve's view, Power's 'most noteworthy contribution is his exposition of the "moving format"', employed as it was by so many postwar English abstract artists. See Alistair Grieve, *Constructed Abstract Art in England After the Second World War: A Neglected Avant-garde*, Yale University Press, New Haven & London, 2005, pp. 59, 229-30. See also Alastair Grieve, 'Charles Biederman and the English Constructionists: An exchange of theories about abstract art during the 1950s', *The Burlington Magazine*, London, Vol. 126 No. 971, February 1984, p. 67. Power's book was influential, too, on subsequent generations, being an important reference point for Peter Lowe, Ann Monfort, 'Peter Lowe', *art concret*, l'Espace de l'Art Concret, Mouans-Sartoux, 2000, p. 251. On the influence of Power's theories into the 1960s see Jonneke Jobse, *De Stijl Continues: The Journal Structure (1958-1964) An Artists' Debate*, 010 Publishers, Rotterdam, 2001, p.392.

77. J.W. Power, *Abstraction-Création*, 1931, p. 28, translated by Antonia Fredman.

78. J.W. Power, *Abstraction-Création*, 1932, p. 36, translated by Antonia Fredman.

79. J.W. Power to Anthony Bertram, letter 15, November 1929 and letter 25, 19 April 1932, RB Lib –Add. Ms120, Rare Books & Special Collections, Fisher Library, The University of Sydney.

80. J.W. Power to Anthony Bertram, letter 33, c.1935, RB Lib –Add. Ms120, Rare Books & Special Collections, Fisher Library, The University of Sydney.

81. J.W. Power, Notebook, MS5761, Manuscripts, National Library of Australia.

82. J.W. Power, Notebook, MS5761, Manuscripts, National Library of Australia.

83. Rare images of the gallery space at 44 Avenue Wagram are reproduced in *Hans Erni: Art non-Figuratif 1933-1938 Abstraction-Création*, Musée Hans Erni, Luzern, 1982, pp. 9, 19.

84. A list of members and friends numbering some 400, half of whom lived in Paris was published in *Abstraction-Création*, 1935, pp. 2-3.

85. On the back of each of the works in his 1934 exhibition Power attached a red handwritten number corresponding to that work's number on his plan. The artist's own annotated photographic album indicates several works are missing, presumably sold.

86. George Baker, 'Leather and Lace', *October* 131, MIT Press, New Haven, Winter 2010, pp. 116-149.

87. J.W. Power to Anthony Bertram, letter 31, February 1934, RB Lib –Add. Ms120, Rare Books & Special Collections, Fisher Library, The University of Sydney.

88. As the large proportion of Power's work is undated, it makes it difficult to accurately say that the hanging of his 1934 exhibition is strictly chronological. The most reliable dating of certain paintings is confirmed by Power's annotations in his photographic album, RB 571.4/2, Rare Books & Special Collections Library, Fisher Library, The University of Sydney.

89. Lesley Harding observes 'A preliminary modello shows the picture's debt to dynamic symmetry: the golden points (GP) are marked on the sides of the rectangle, and the transference points (TDP) calculated with a compass and ruler.' 'Australia in the World and the World in Australia 1930-1939', in Lesley Harding and Sue Cramer, *Cubism & Australian Art*, The Miegunyah Press, Melbourne University Publishing, Carlton, Australia, 2009, pp. 66-67.

90. Aby Warburg, 'Sandro Boticelli's *Birth of Venus* and *Spring*' cited in Philippe-Alain Michaud, *Aby Warburg and the Image in Motion*, Zone Books, New York, 2004, p. 69.

91. Stephen Phillips, 'Toward a Research Practice: Frederick Kiesler's Design-Correlation Laboratory', *Grey Room*, Winter 2010, No. 38, Pages 90-120, posted Online February 22, 2010. (doi:10.1162/grey.2010.1.38.90) © 2010 by Grey Room, Inc. and the Massachusetts Institute of Technology, uploaded March 30, 2012.

92. J.W. Power to Anthony Bertram, letter 32, late September 1934, RB Lib –Add. Ms120, Rare Books & Special Collections, Fisher Library, The University of Sydney. Coincidentally, in 1924 Eluard, escaping the Parisian hothouse for the South Pacific, had passed through Sydney.

93. J.W. Power, Notebook MS5671, Manuscripts, National Library of Australia.

94. Jennifer Mundy writes that Grigson 'had been to Paris at the suggestion of Ben Nicholson to see an exhibition by the group, and knew that the majority of its members practiced a straight-line, "pure" abstraction of the sort he disliked so strongly'. Jennifer Mundy, 'The naming of Biomorphism', *Biomorphism and modernism*, eds., Oliver A Botar and Isabel Wünsche, Ashgate, Surrey, 2011, note 8, p. 73. Grigson's essay 'Comment on England' appeared in *Axis*, January 1935, p. 8. It is not known whether Grigson ever met Power. In 1934 Power wrote to Bertram that 'I must get hold of "Axis" also Reades (sic) Book – he writes very well but I did hear that he was not quite so successful at the Burlington. Perhaps he is too "1934" for the likes of Tatlock. I heard about Barbara Hepworth & the trio what a disgusting finale to a romance!!', J.W. Power to Anthony Bertram, letter 32, late September 1934, RB Lib –Add. Ms120, Rare Books & Special Collections, Fisher Library, The University of Sydney.

95. Jennifer Mundy, 'The Naming of Biomorphism', in *Biomorphism and Modernism*, eds., Olivar A.I. Botar and Isabel Wünsche, Ashgate, Surrey, 2011, p. 65-67.

96. Bernard Smith 'The role of an institution of Fine Arts', *ARTS: The Journal of the Sydney University Arts Association*, Vol., 6 1969, p. 5.

97. It is interesting to note that *Marine* was cut out from Power's plan. This may have been because it could not fit under the ceiling or because he needed to use the drawing for some other plan or work.

98. Mark Antliff, 'Organicism among the Cubists: The case of Raymond Duchamp-Villon', in *Biomorphism and Modernism*,

eds., Olivar A.I. Botar and Isabel Wünsche, Ashgate, Surrey, UK, 2011, p. 170. Antliff concludes that Duchamp-Villion looks to 'works such as Rubens's *Susanna and the Elders* of 1620, which in turn is modeled after Greek statues of Aphrodites.'

99. Spyros Papapetros, 'On the biology of the inorganic: Crystallography and discourses of latent life in the art and architectural historiography of the early twentieth century', *Biomorphism and modernism*, eds., Oliver A Botar and Isabel Wünsche, Ashgate, Surrey, 2011, p. 79.

100. Power's unpaginated handwritten translation of Leopold Zahn, *Paul Klee: Leben, Werk, Geist*, Gustav Kiepenheuer, Postdam, 1920, in Ms. 5761, Manuscripts, National Library of Australia.

101. J.W. Power, Notebook, c.1940, MS5761, Manuscripts, National Library of Australia, unpaginated.

102. J.W. Power to Anthony Bertram, letter 32, c. 1934, RB Lib –Add. Ms120, Rare Books & Special Collections, Fisher Library, The University of Sydney. Power wrote to Bertram that 'Lecherche Barbe & Rowley were both very interested in the chart and took all my remaining stock but the big firms like Windsor & Newton, Rowney and Co etc. would not take it'. Power produced more than 200 oil sketches of his work in which he experimented primarily with various colour schemes.

103. J.W. Power, Notebook MS5671, Manuscripts, National Library of Australia, unpaginated.

104. J.W. Power, Notebook MS5671, Manuscripts, National Library of Australia, unpaginated.

105. J.W. Power to Anthony Bertram, letter 12, c.1930, RB Lib –Add. Ms120, Rare Books & Special Collections, Fisher Library, The University of Sydney.

106. J.W. Power, Notebook MS5671, Manuscripts, National Library of Australia, unpaginated.

107. J.W. Power Notebook, MS5761 Manuscripts, National Library of Australia, unpaginated.

108. J.W. Power to Anthony Bertram, letter 34, c.1938, RB Lib –Add. Ms120, Rare Books & Special Collections, Fisher Library, The University of Sydney.

109. Power exhibited alongside the American artists John Ferran, the Canadian Alfred Pellan and the Scotsman J.D. Fergusson, with the Groupe d'artistes Anglo-Americains

110. It was Saint-Maur who proposed the so called 1% law, the legislative requirement that the budget for new buildings allocate 1% of their budget to artists, craftspeople and tradespeople for the construction of new works of art, a proposal that was eventually adopted after the war under the aegis of the then Culture Minister André Malraux.

111. Georges Vantongerloo, 'Le groupement Abstraction-Création et L'Art Mural', *Edition Catalogue Critique du Salon de L'Art Mural*, L'Art Mural, Paris, 1938, unpaginated. Power next showed in the third salon in 1938 when his work could be found in Salle IV together with Jacques Villon, Yan Bernard Dyl, Gleizes and Herbin. Matisse, Picasso, Lhote, Survage and Robert Delaunay were next door in Salle V. See also Sarah Wilson, 'Die Kunst und die Französische Volksfront', *Die Olympiade unter Diktatur: Rekonstrucktion der Amsterdamer Kunst Olympiade 1936: Kunst im Widerstand*, Gemeentearchief Amsterdam, Stadtmuseum Berlin, 1996, p. 37.

112. An initiative of the committee Bescherming van de Olympische gedacte, BOG, founded in 1935 by sportsmen, workers and intellectuals, and of the largely communist artist's organisation Bond van Kunstnaars, the BKVK, founded the year before as a united front for cultural workers against Nazism.

113. D.O.O.D was not the only time Power exhibited in Amsterdam. In 1933 he contributed work to the *Exposition Internationale des Natures Mortes*.

114. Power was thanked for his contribution to the exhibition where he was identified as an 'abstract' artist. John Steen, '"D.O.O.D." 1936: Der internationale Hintergrund', *Die Olympiade unter der Diktatur- Rekonstruktion der Amsterdamer Kunstolympiade 1936, Kunst in Widerstand* Gemeenterarchief Amsterdam and Stadtmuseum Berlin, 1996, p. 25.

115. *Entartete Kunst* toured Germany after its initial airing in Munich in 1937.

116. Leo Klaster in André Swijtink, 'The Netherlands: In the shadow of Big Brother', eds Arnd Krüger, William J. Murray, *The Nazi Olympics: Sport, Politics and Appeasement in the 1930s*, University of Illinois Press, 2003, p. 220. Though the exhibition ultimately had little effect, Klaster observed that 'the most important thing was that something was done, irrespective of what could possibly be achieved'.

117. Willy Rotzler, *Constructive Concepts: A History of Constructive Art from Cubism to the Present*, ABC Edition, Zurich, 1988, p. 120. The American Abstract Artist's first yearbook was published in New York in 1938.

118. J.W. Power, Sketchbook 52, PIC.R8667-8733, Pictures, National Library of Australia.

119. Alfred Barr, *Cubism and Abstract Art*, Museum of Modern Art, New York, 1936, pp. 130-200.

120. Both independently wealthy, Power and Wadsworth seem to have been particularly close. In his bequest there are four photographic reproductions of Wadsworth paintings.

121. See 'New Exhibitions', *The New York Times*, 22.4.1934.

122. Édouard Joseph, *Dictionaire Biographique des Artistes Contemporaines 1910-1930*, Librarire Grund, Paris 1934, pp. 158-159.

123. Sophie Lévy, '"Sympathetic Order"', *The Transatlantic Avant-garde: American artists in Paris, 1918-1939*, Musée d'Art Américain, Giverny, 2003, p. 20.

124. Power, in his photo albums, indicates that the painting *Tête* (1931), reproduced in the first *Abstraction-Création cahier*, belonged to Foltyn. J.W. Power, Photo Album, RB 571.4/2, Rare Books & Special Collections Library, Fisher Library, The University of Sydney.

125. Power appears to have owned at least two Ozenfant paintings. Ozenfant's *Verres et bouteilles* (c.1922–26) was bought by the Tate Gallery from the auction of Power's collection in 1962. Ozenfant's *Still Life* (1923) reproduced in Maurice Raynal, *Modern French Painters*, Tudor Publishing, New York, 1934 is labelled 'Collection Power'. Power's purchase of Ozenfant's work is the subject of a letter from Ozenfant to Rosenberg, 12.1.1928, Fonds Léonce Rosenberg, Bibliothèque Kandinsky, Paris. *Still Life* (1923) is also reproduced in an article on Ozenfant by S. John Woods in *The Studio Burlington Magazine* p. 33, held in the Jean Appleton Papers, Box 1. Power's Gleizes, *Tableau* (1921), was also bought by the Tate Gallery in 1962 and is now part of their collection.

126. *The Sun Herald*, 1962, press clippings, University of Sydney Archives, Department of Fine Arts Records: J W Power, G35/1/1.

127. Samuel Beckett to Tom McGreeny, 15.6.1936, quoted in James Knowlson and John Haynes, *Images of Beckett*, Cambridge University Press, 2003, p. 151.

128. Otto Freundlich to J.W. Power, letter dated 12.2.1938, translated by Chris Andrews. *The Sun Herald*, 1962, press clippings, University of Sydney Archives, Department of Fine Arts Records: J W Power, G35/1/1.

129. Power also supported, for instance, the New Zealand poet A.R.D. Fairburn. In the early 1930s he bought six copies of Fairburn's first volume of poetry *He shall not rise* (1930) and passed them around amongst his friends. J.W. Power to Anthony Bertram, letter 7, c.1930. RB Lib –Add. Ms120, Rare Books & Special Collections, Fisher Library, The University of Sydney.

130. Paul Rosenberg, 'French artists and the war', *Art in Australia*, Sydney, Series 4 No. 4, December 1941, pp. 19, 29.

131. Robert Hughes, 'Bequest and behest', *Nation*, Sydney, 28.7.1962, p. 16.

132. Gladys Fabre, 'Qu'est ce que l'École de Paris?' in *L' École de Paris 1904-1929, Le part de l'autre*, Musee d'Art Moderne de la Ville de Paris, 2000, p. 34 note 31, quoted by Lévy, p. 16. *A Transatlantic Avant-garde: American Artists in Paris 1918-1939*, ed. Sophie Lévy, Musée d'art Américain, Giverny, 2003.

133. The art historian and critic Dave Hickey has made this point in relation to under-recognised post-war West Coast abstract painters. See for instance his 'Karl Benjamin: A new past is now available', *Dance the Line: Paintings by Karl Benjamin*, Louis Stern Fine Arts, West Hollywood, 2007, pp. 8-13. The architectural historian Joan Ockman, too, has written on the retrospective understanding of modernist culture. In her view 'its ultimate aim is nothing less than a redemption of humanity through the recuperation of history's disenfranchised.' See Joan Ockman, 'Reinventing Jefim Golyscheff: Lives of a Minor Modernist', *Assemblage*, 11, 1990, p. 97.

Plan of exhibition and plates

Power, invitation, Paris, 1934

du 14 au 28 avril 1934

EXPOSITION

POWER

vernissage

le 14 avril, de 16 à 19 h.

ABSTRACTION-CRÉATION

exposition permanente

de 10 h. à midi et de 15 h. à 19 h., 44, avenue de wagram

paris (8e)

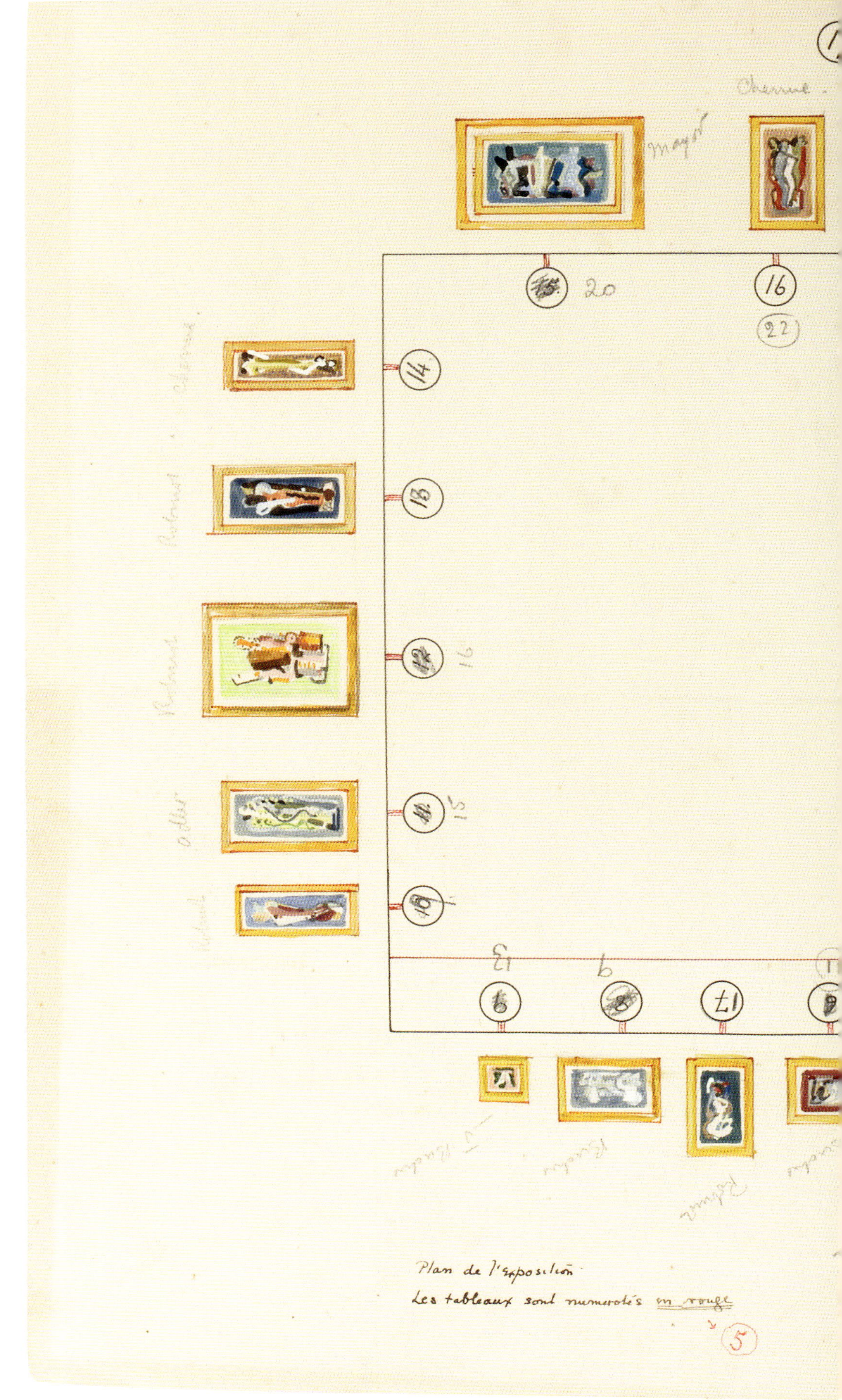
Plan de l'exposition
Les tableaux sont numerotés en rouge

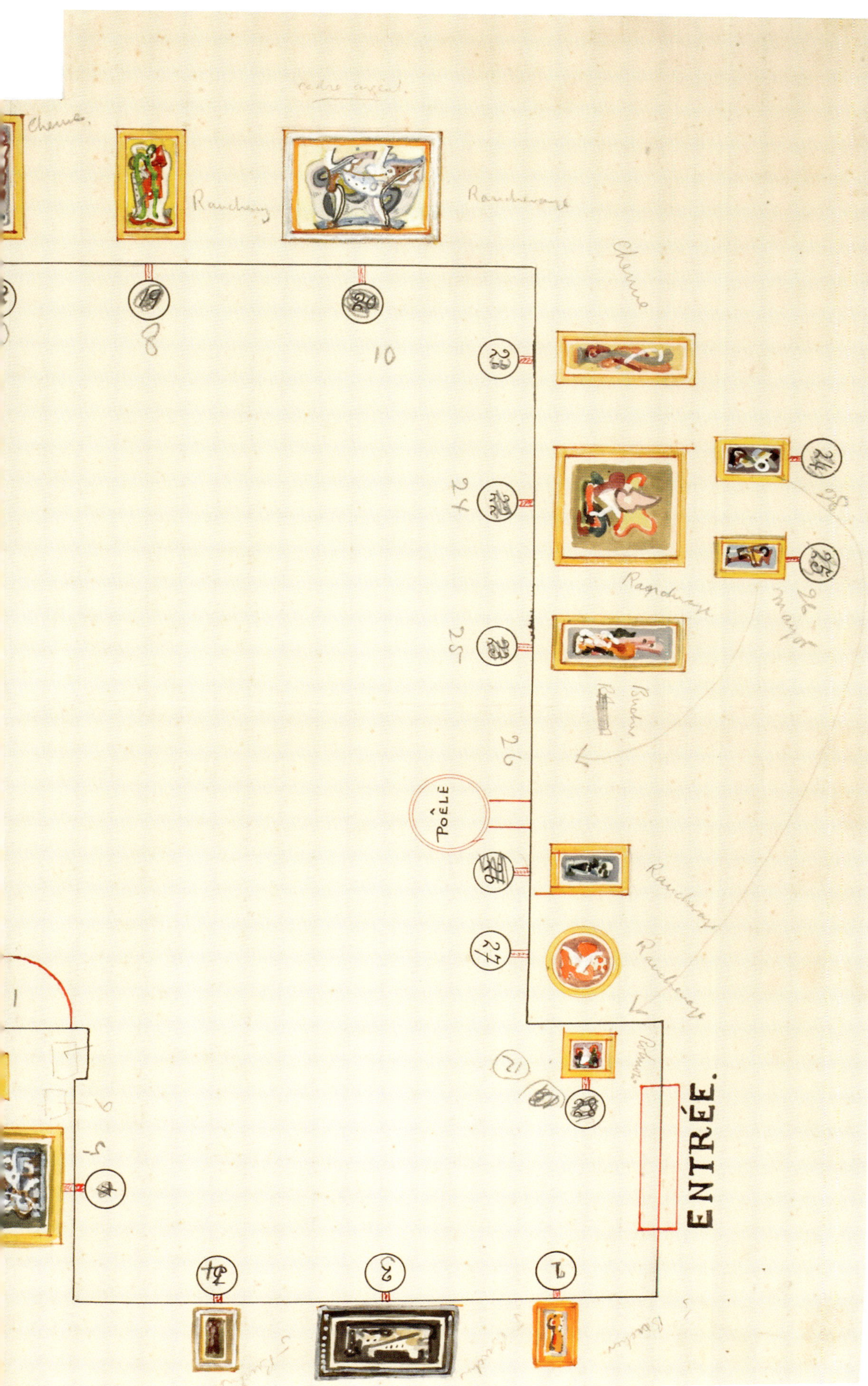

J.W. Power, Plan de l'Exposition 1934
gouache, pencil and ink on paper,
62.8 x 50 cm, PW1961.1177

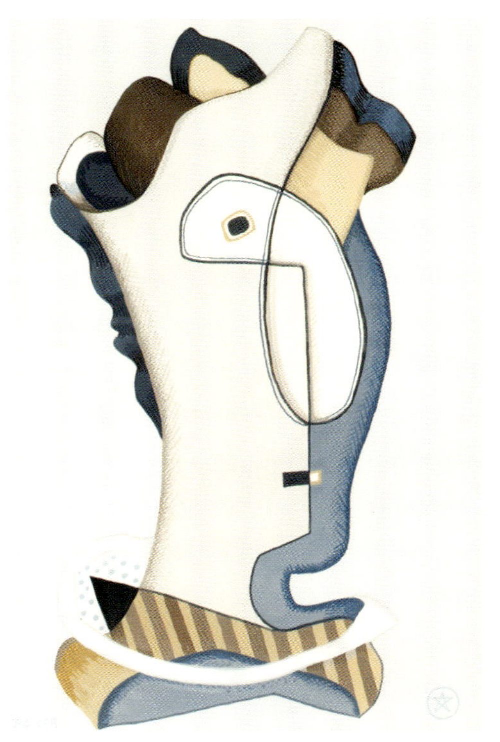

PLATE 1

Tête (Head), c. 1929
gouache, 34.7 x 22.5 cm, PW1961.38

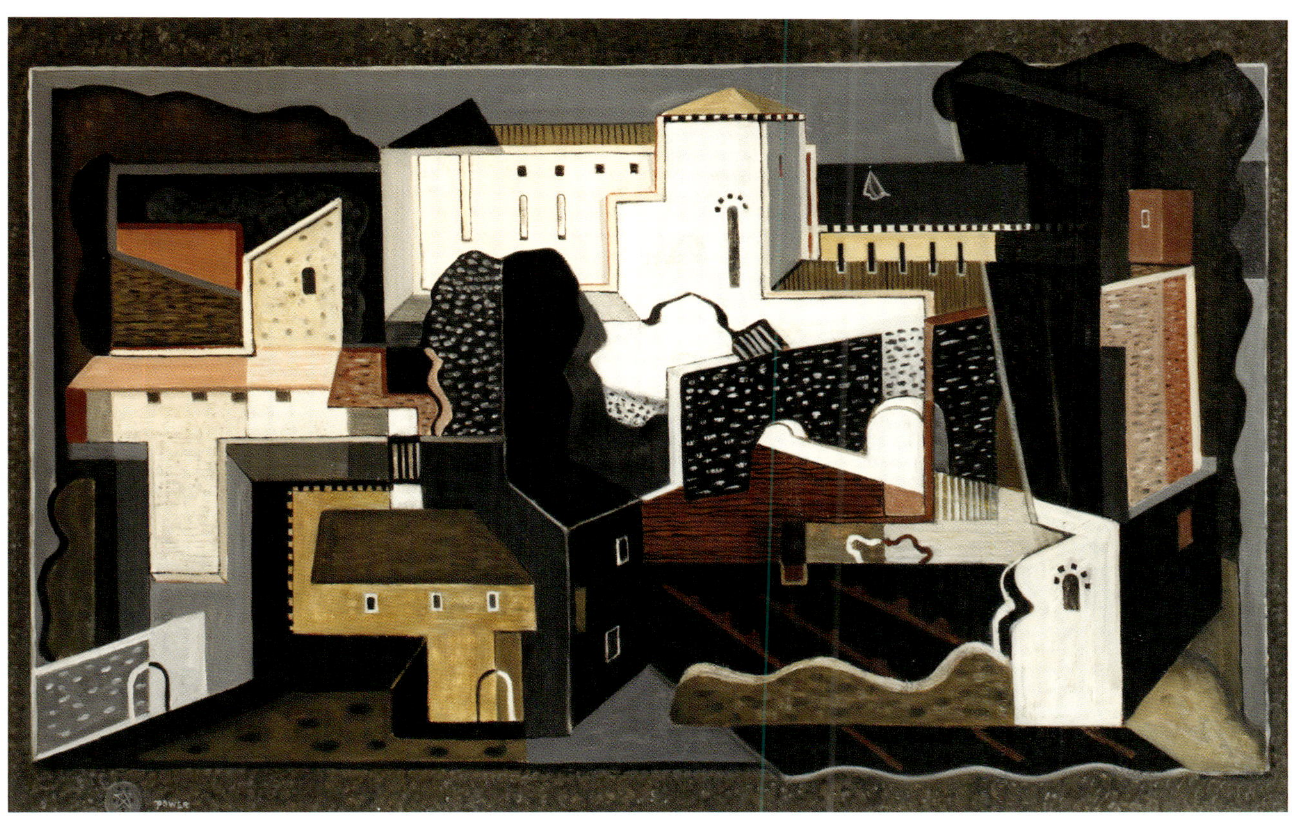

PLATE 2

Paysage Cannes, (Landscape Cannes) 1927
oil on canvas, 91.4 x 60.9 cm, PW1961.34

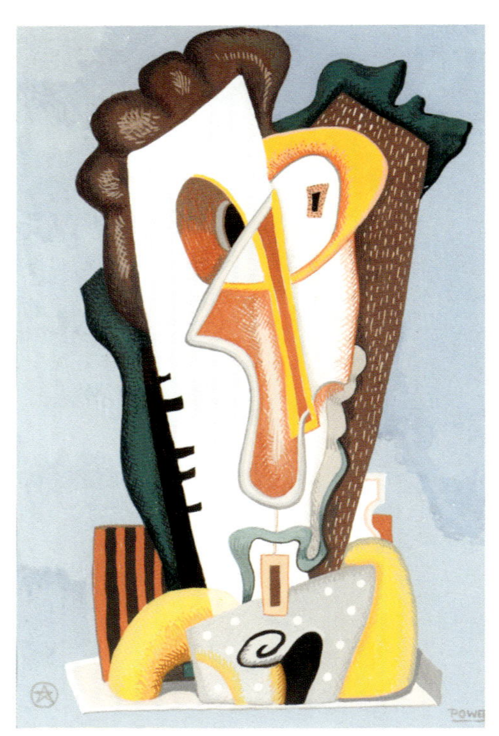

PLATE 3

Tête (Head), c. 1929,
gouache, 34.7 x 22.5 cm, PW1961.39

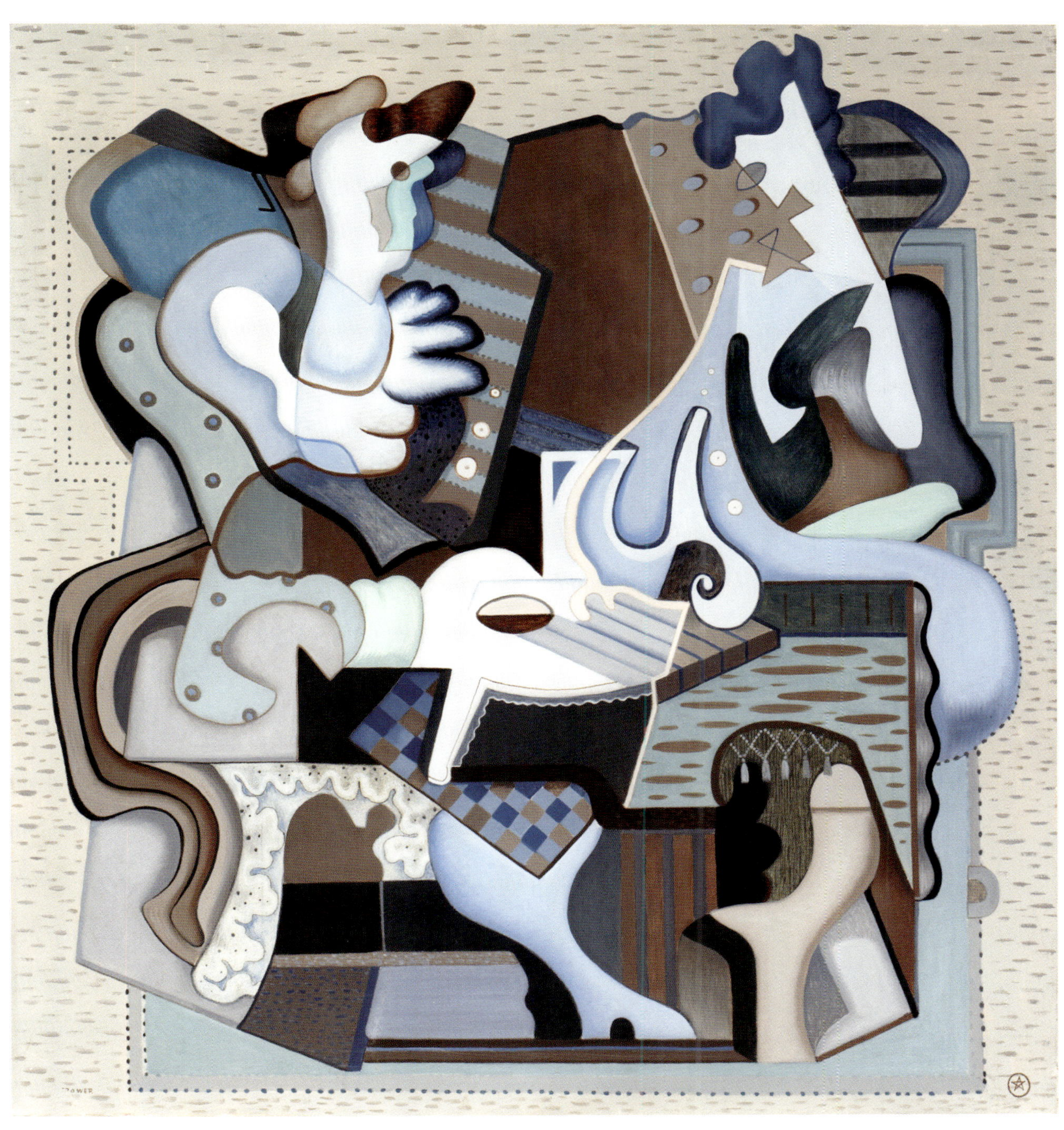

PLATE 4

Commerages (Gossipers), c. 1929
oil on canvas, 96.7 x 89.1cm, PW1961.78

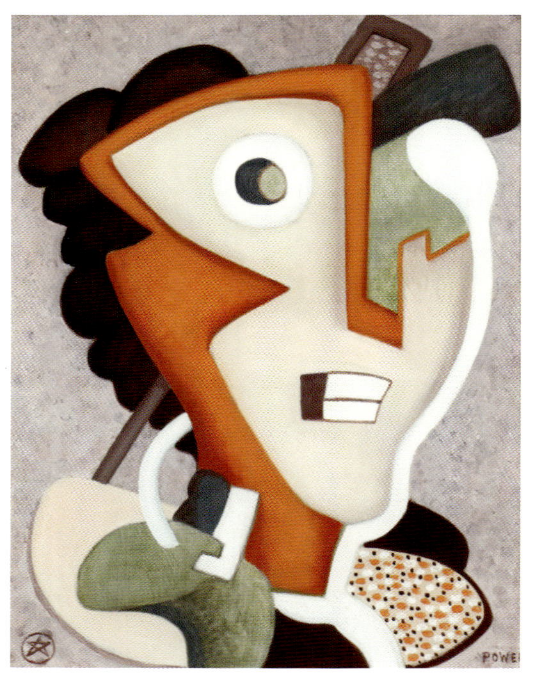

PLATE 5

Tête (Head), c. 1930
oil on canvas, 34 x 25.7 cm, PW1961.10

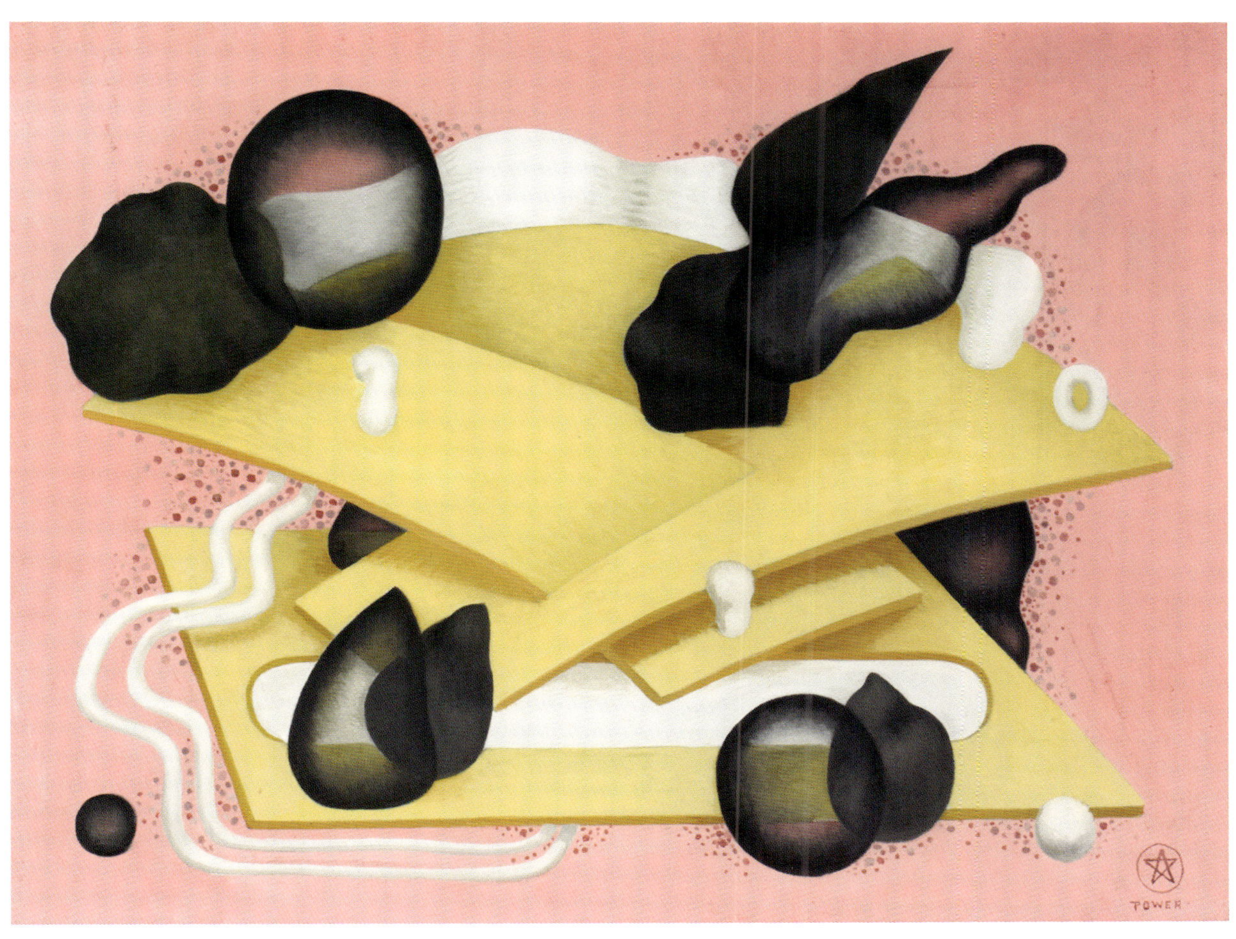

PLATE 6

Paysage (Landscape), 1934
oil on canvas, 50.9 x 66.3 cm, PW1961.24

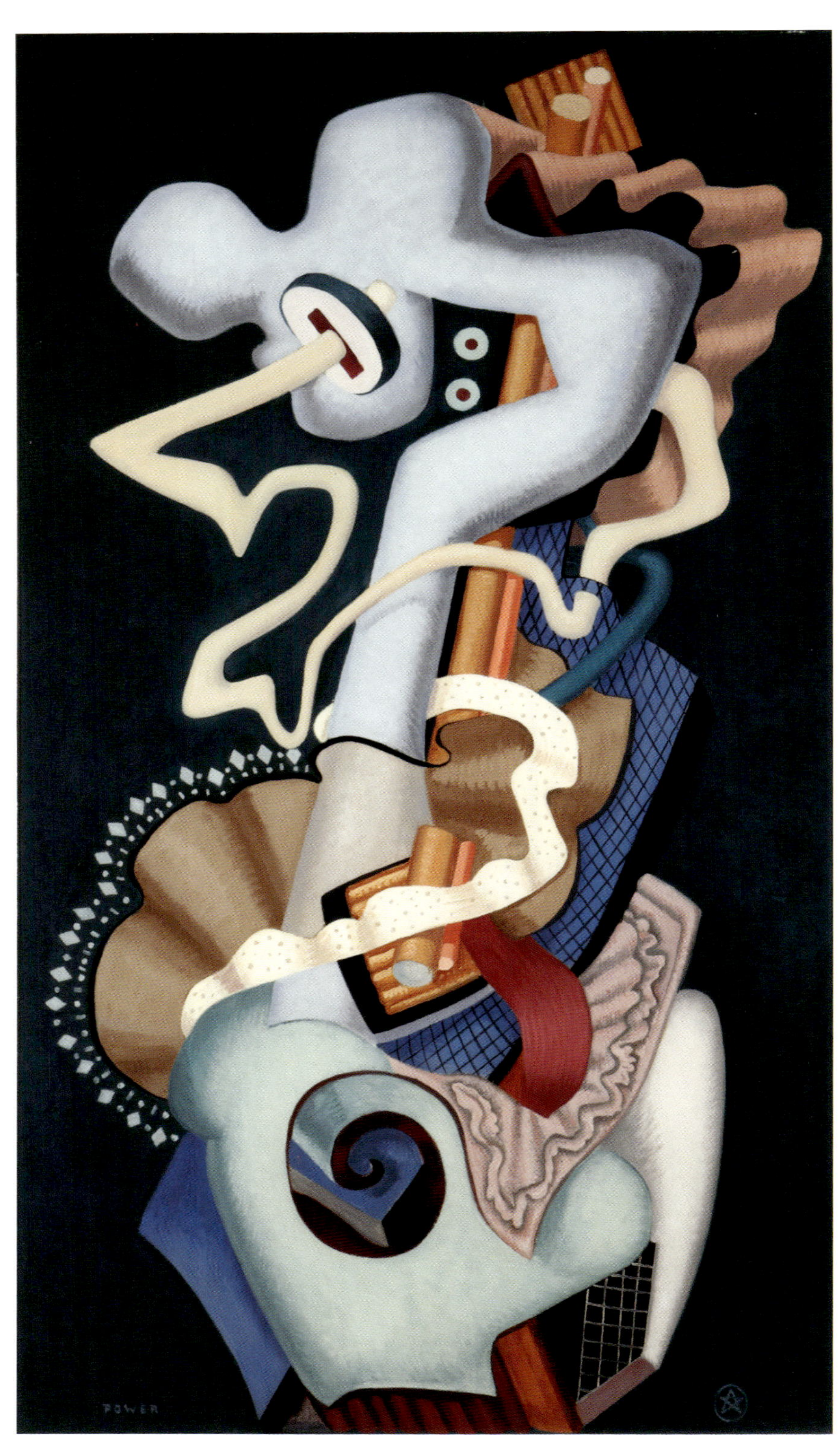

PLATE 7

Tête (Head), c.1930
91.4 x 55.9 cm, oil on canvas, PW1961.65

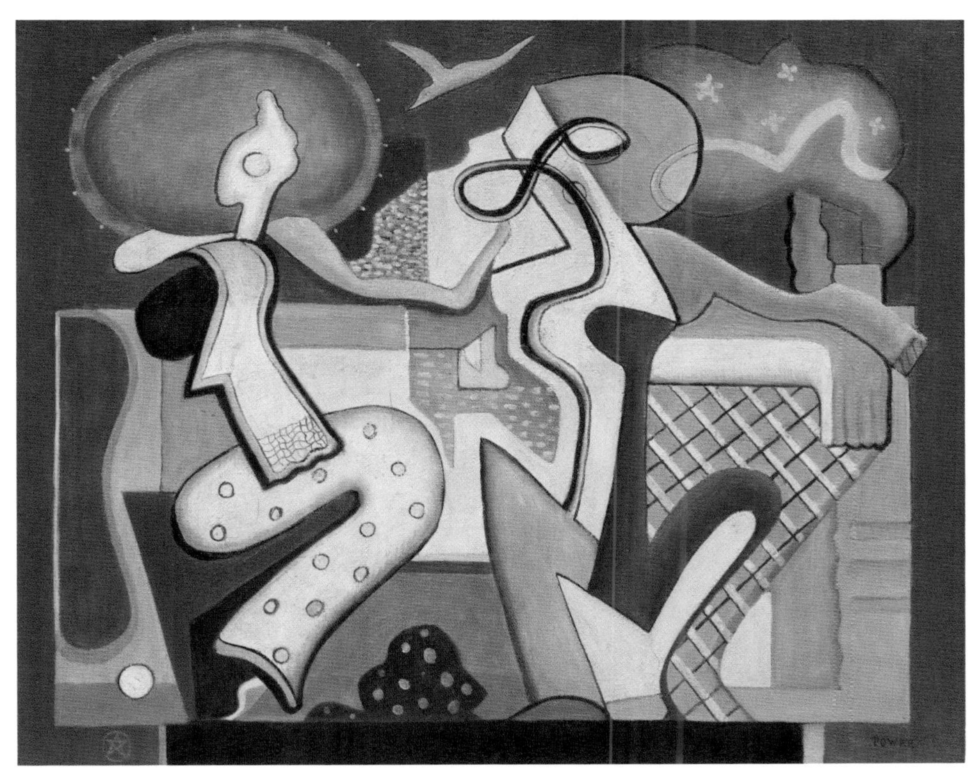

PLATE 8

Moonlight Flirtation, 1930-31
oil on canvas, 50 x 60.1 cm, PW1961.57

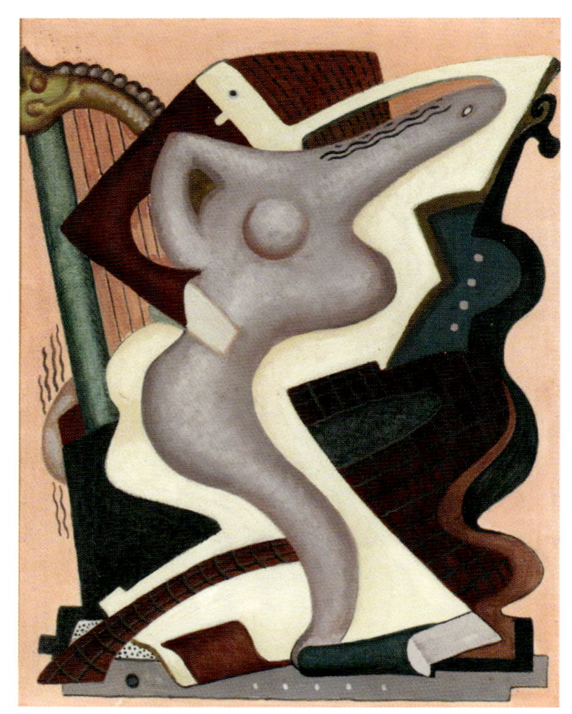

PLATE 9

Danseuses à la Harpe (Harp dancers), 1929
oil on canvas, 34 x 26 cm, PW1961.12

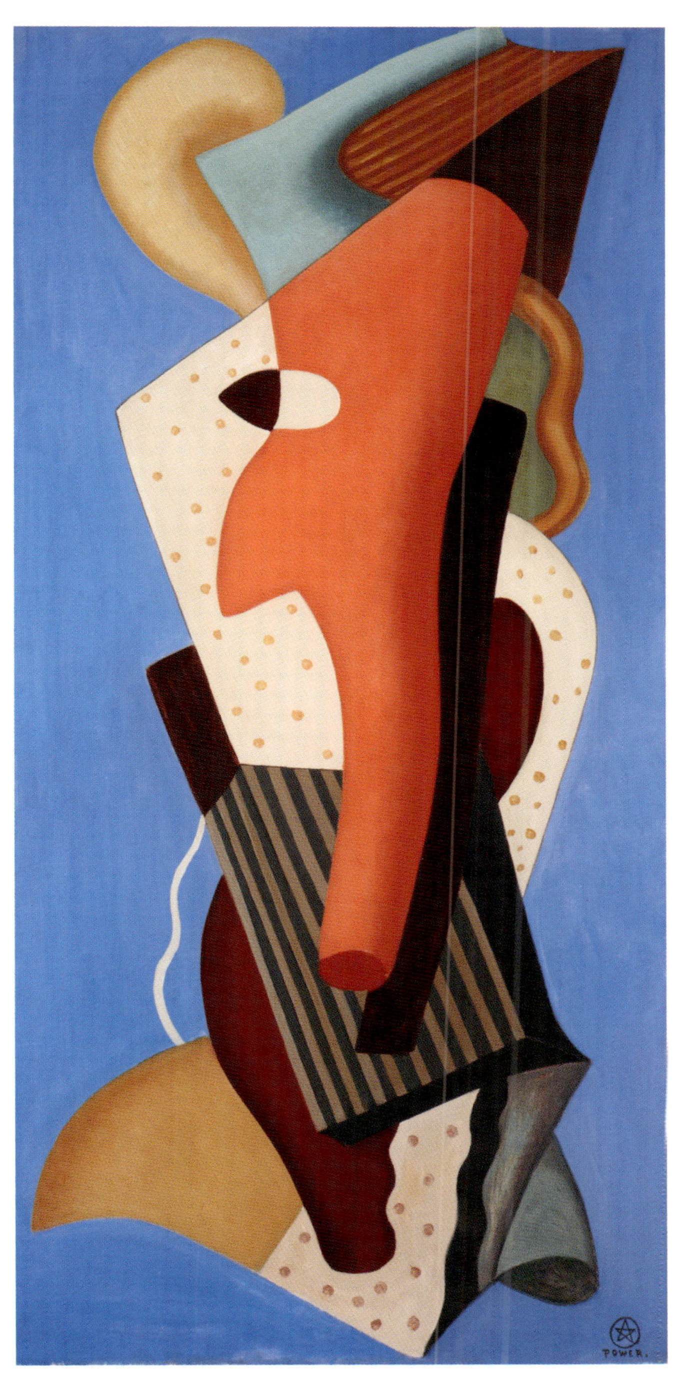

PLATE 10

Tête (Head), 1931
oil on canvas, 94 x 45.8 cm, PW1961.66

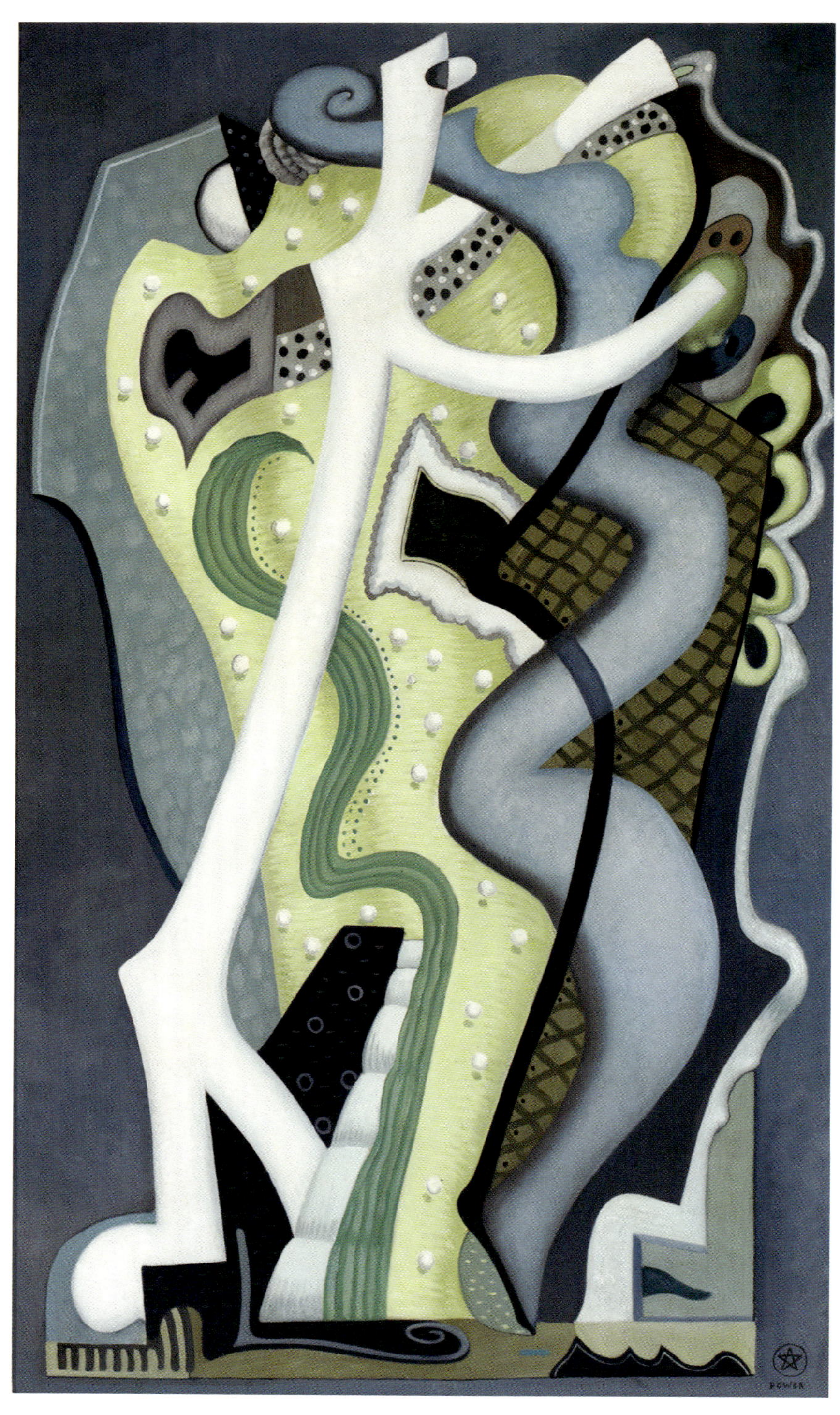

PLATE 11

Apollon et Daphné (Apollo and Daphne), 1929
oil on canvas, 109 x 63.9 cm, PW1961.86

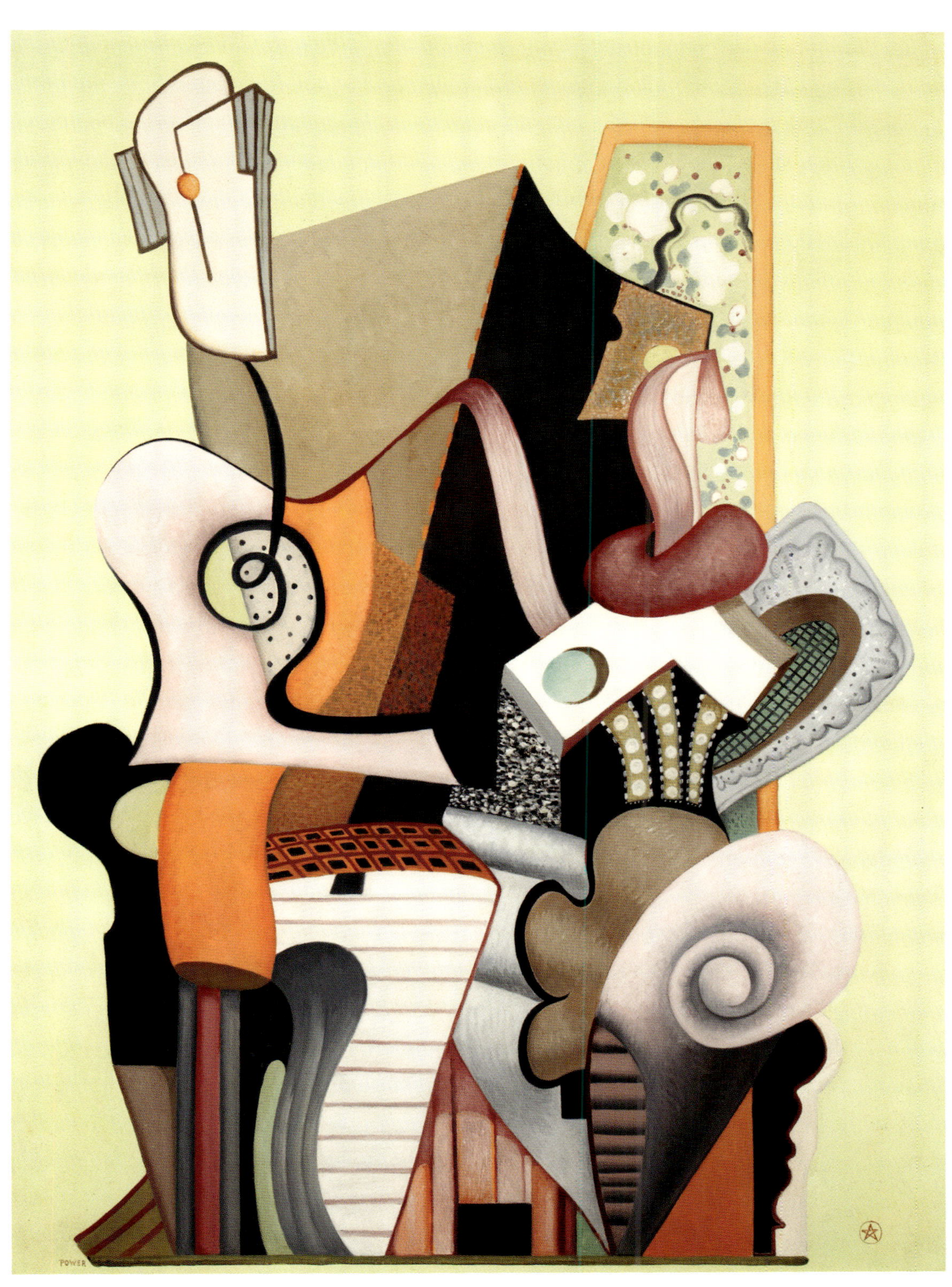

PLATE 12

Conversation, 1931-32
oil on canvas, 112.5 x 84.2 cm, PW1961.88

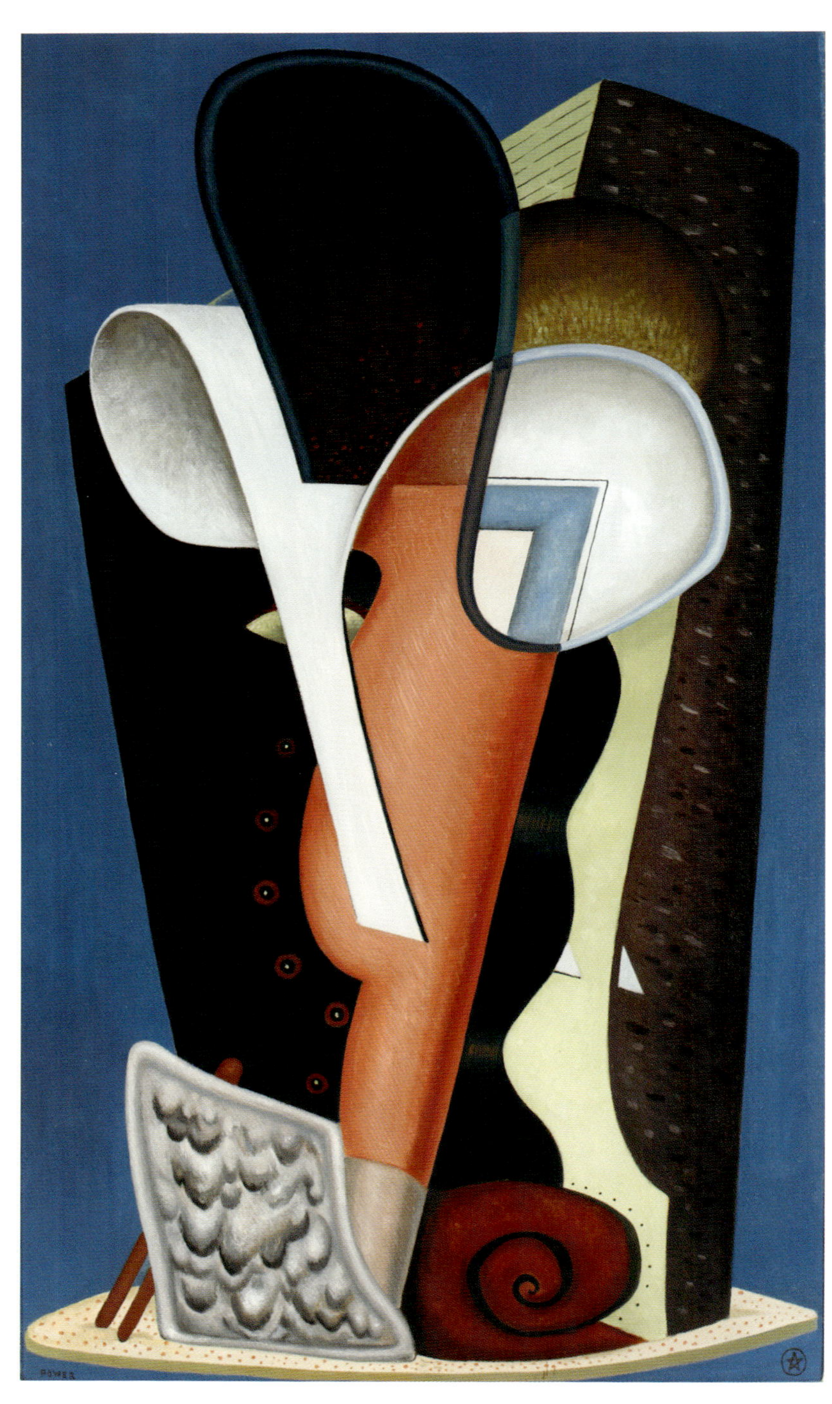

PLATE 13

Tête (Head), c. 1931-2
oil on canvas 110 x 63.5 cm PW1961.87

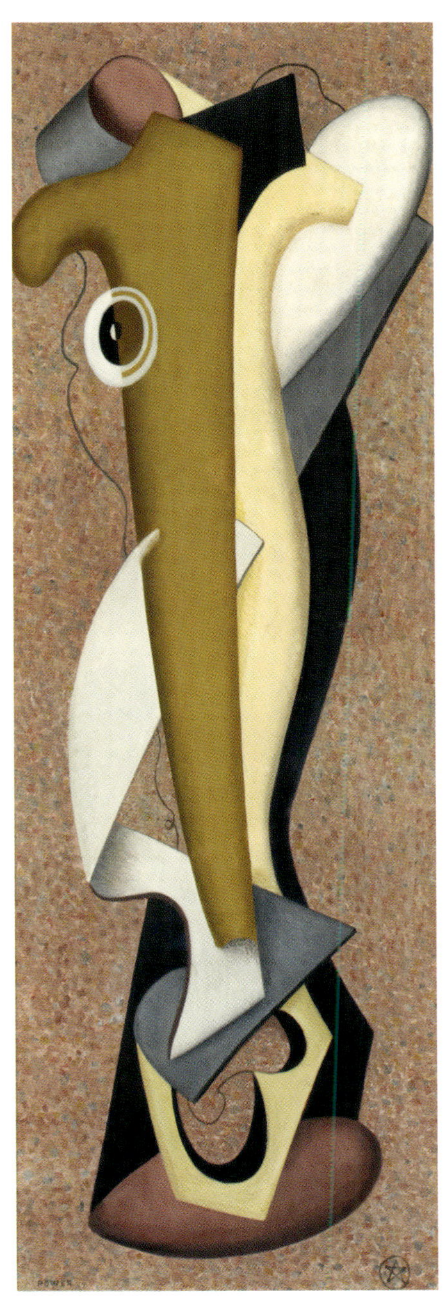

PLATE 14

Danseuse (Dancer), 1933
oil on canvas, 91.4 x 33 cm, PW1961.69

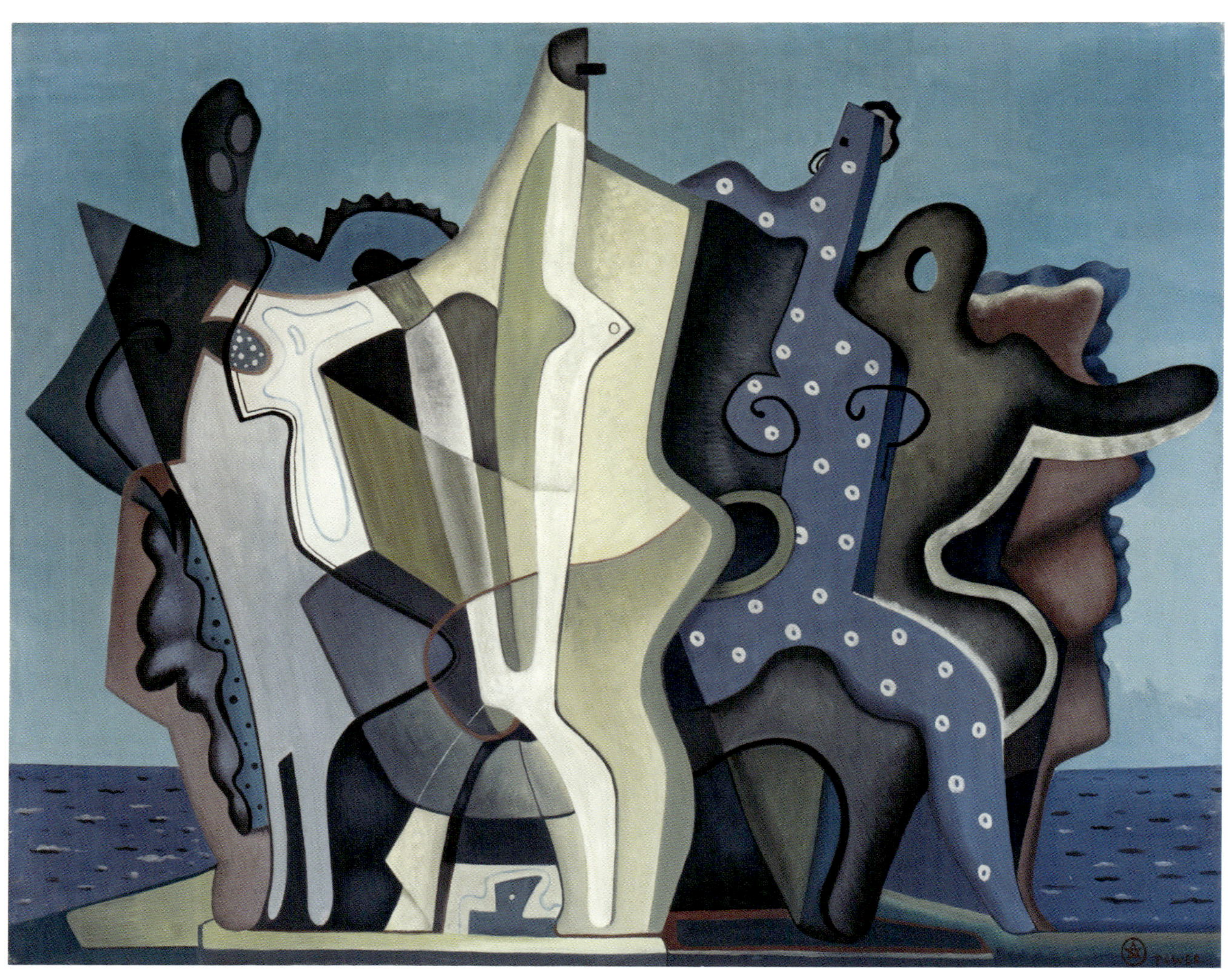

PLATE 15

Groupe or *Baigneuse* (Group or Bathers), c. 1931
oil on canvas, 101.6 x 83.8 cm, PW1961.84

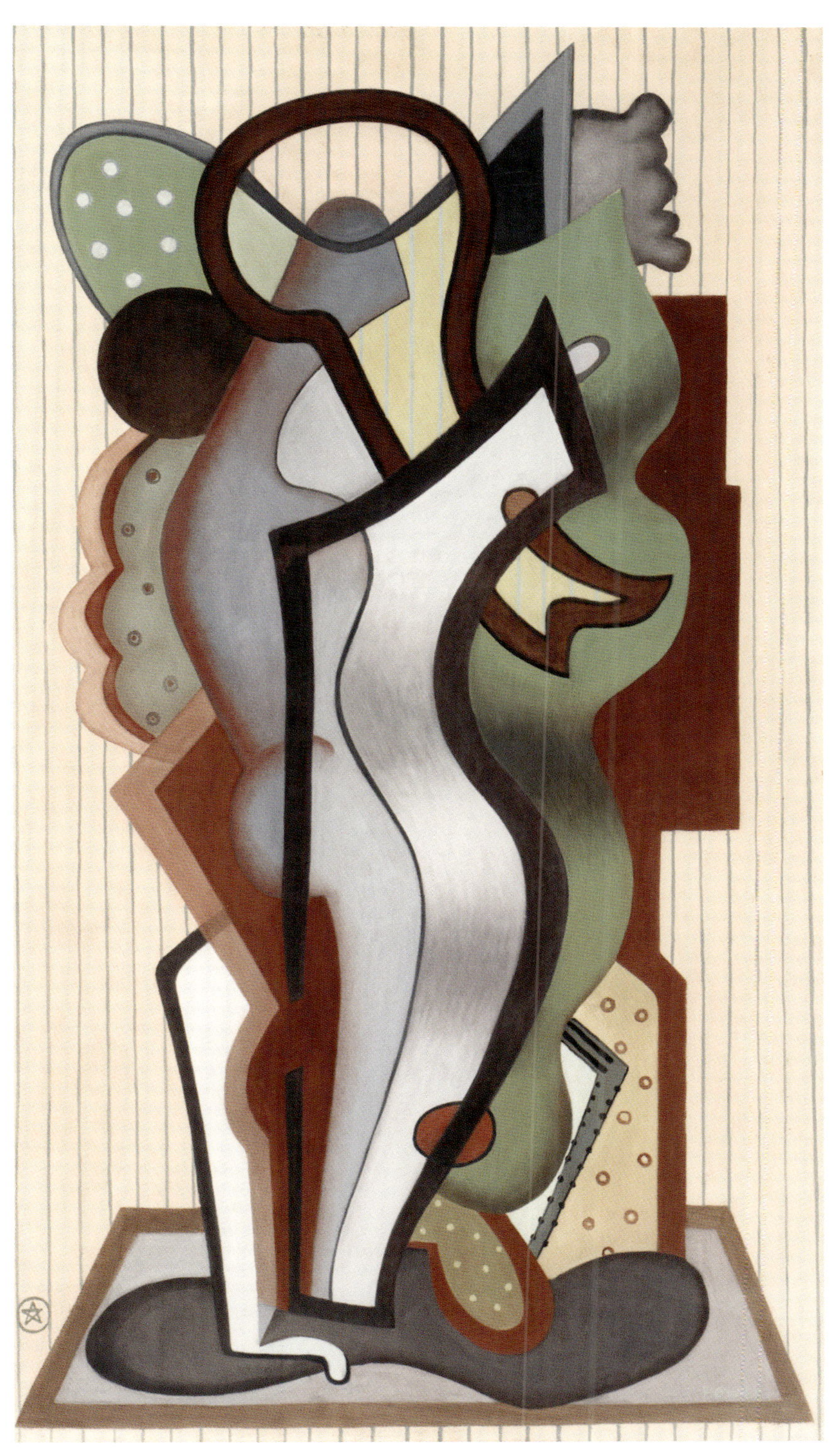

PLATE 16

Untitled, c. 1931
oil and egg tempera on canvas, 88.9 x 50.7 cm, PW1961.27

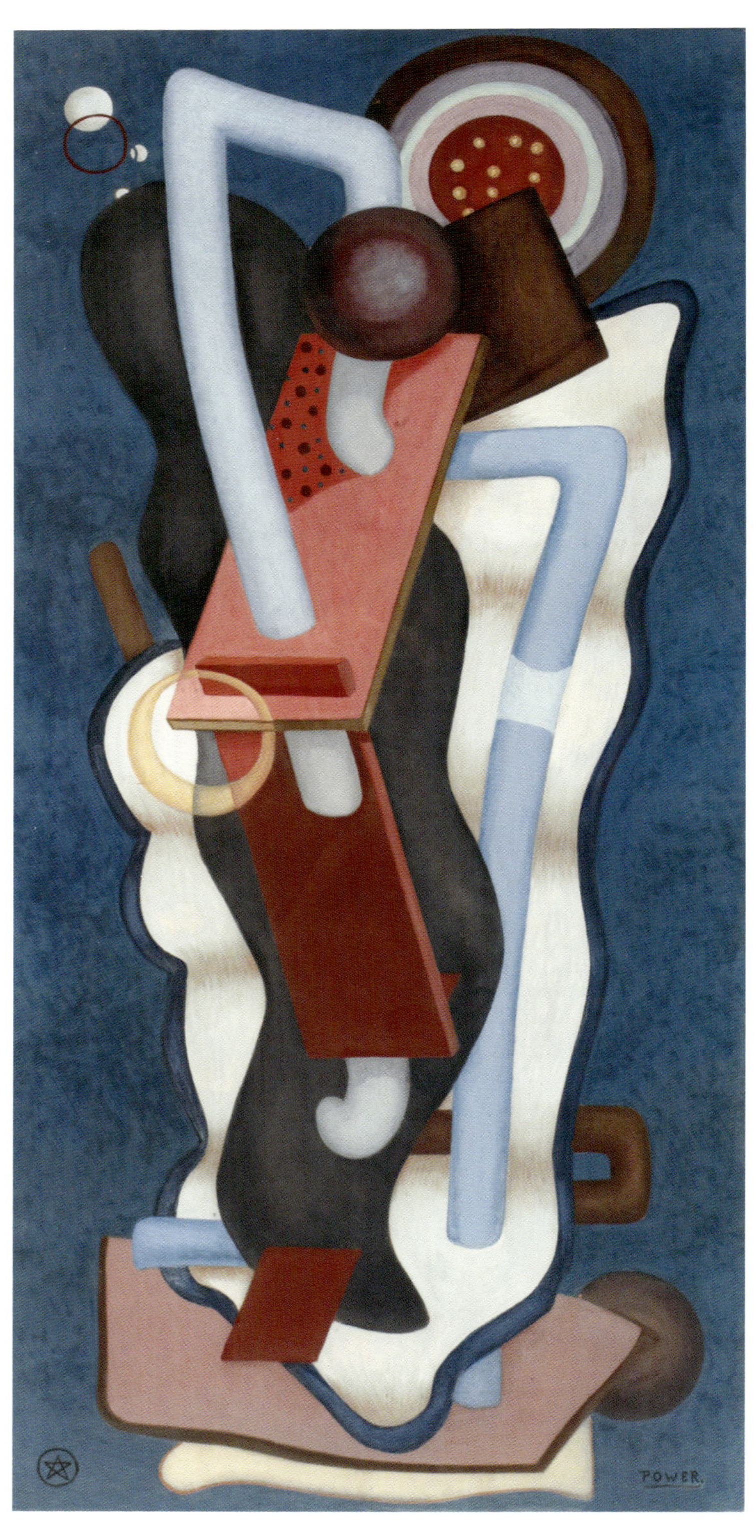

PLATE 17

Abstraction, 1932
egg tempera and oil on canvas, 94.5 x 46.3 cm, PW1961.33

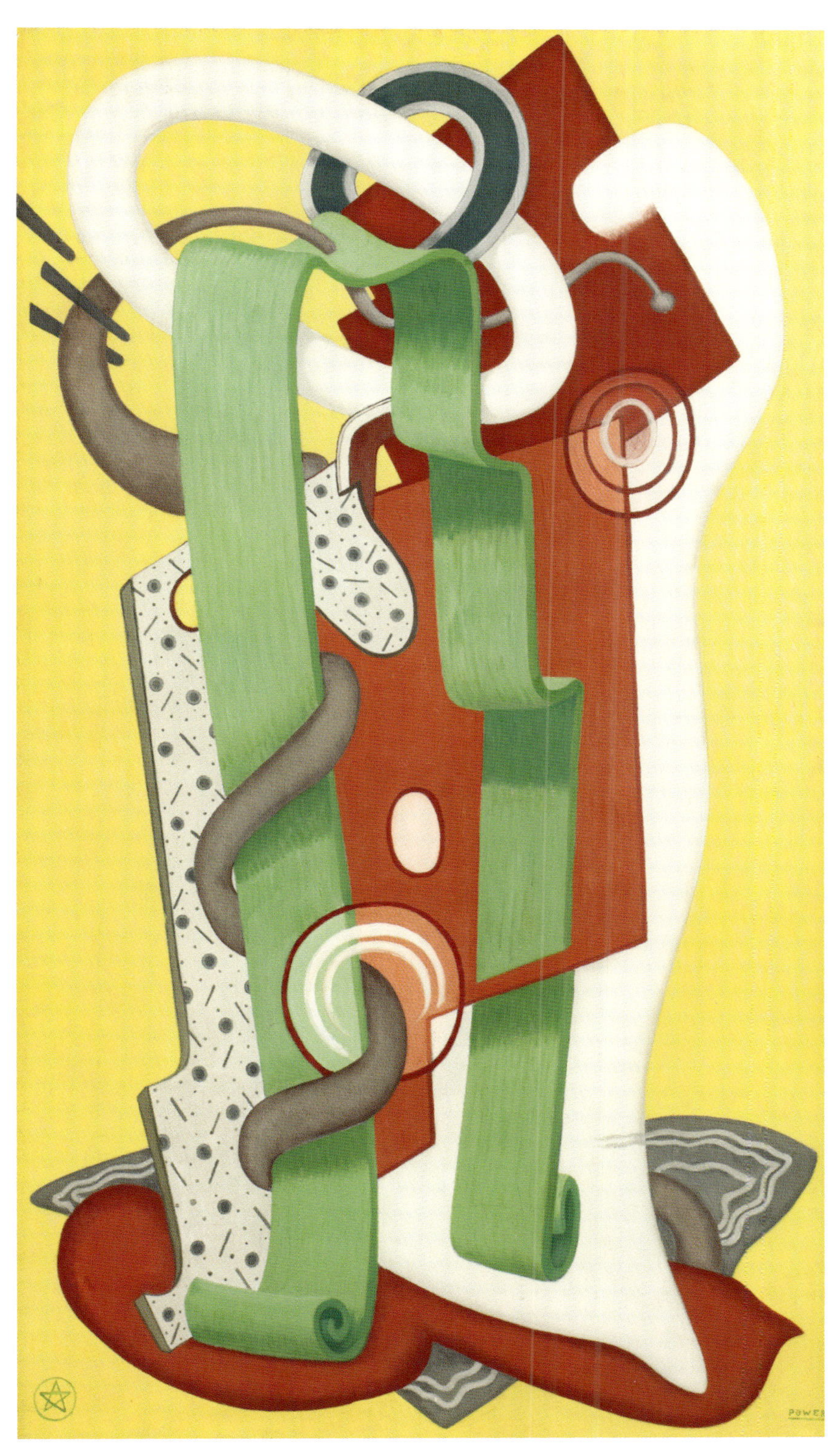

PLATE 18

Abstraction, c. 1932
oil on canvas, 89.3 x 51 cm, PW1961.68

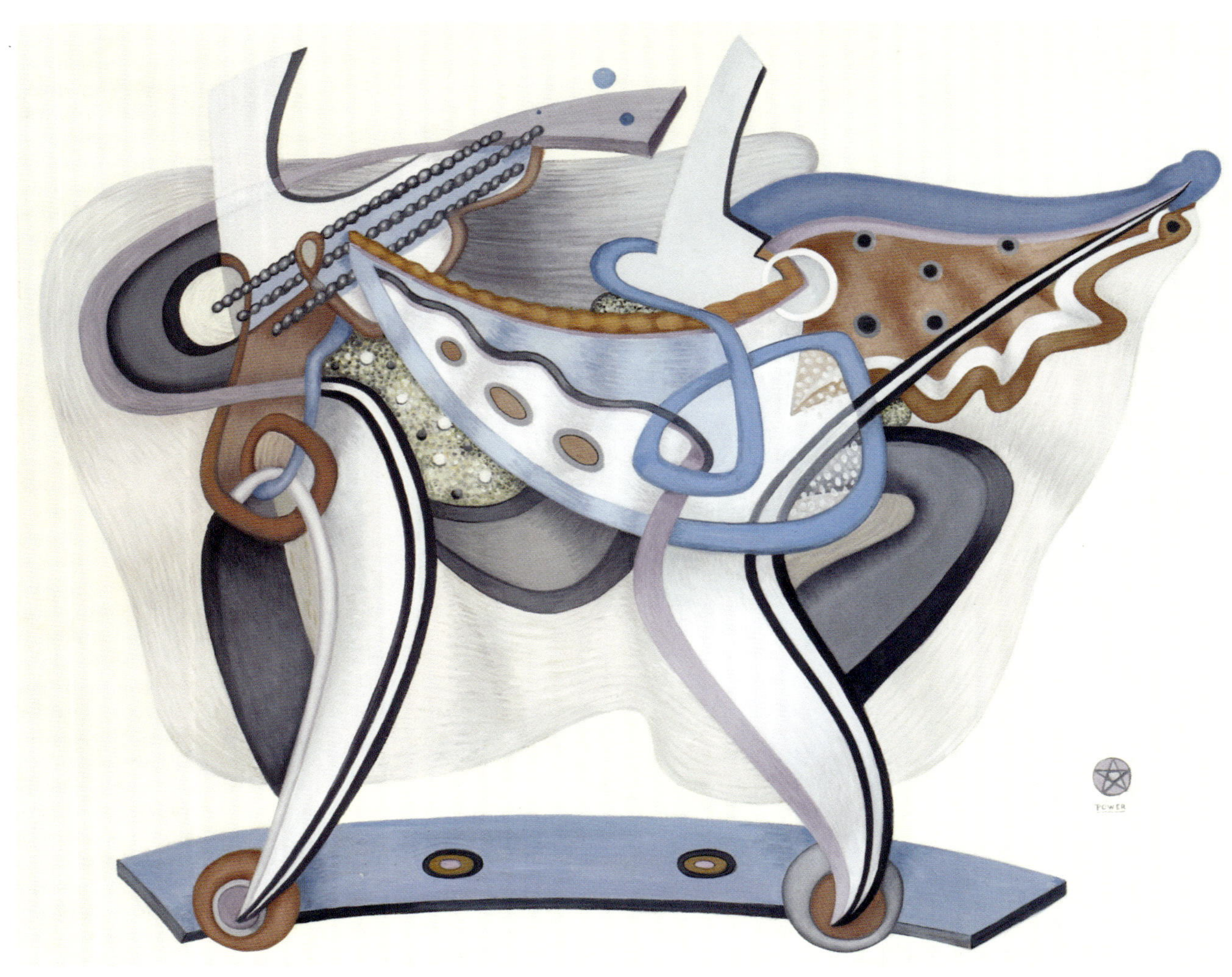

PLATE 19

Danseurs (Dancers), 1934
egg tempera and oil on canvas, 81.5x 100.3 cm, PW1961.70

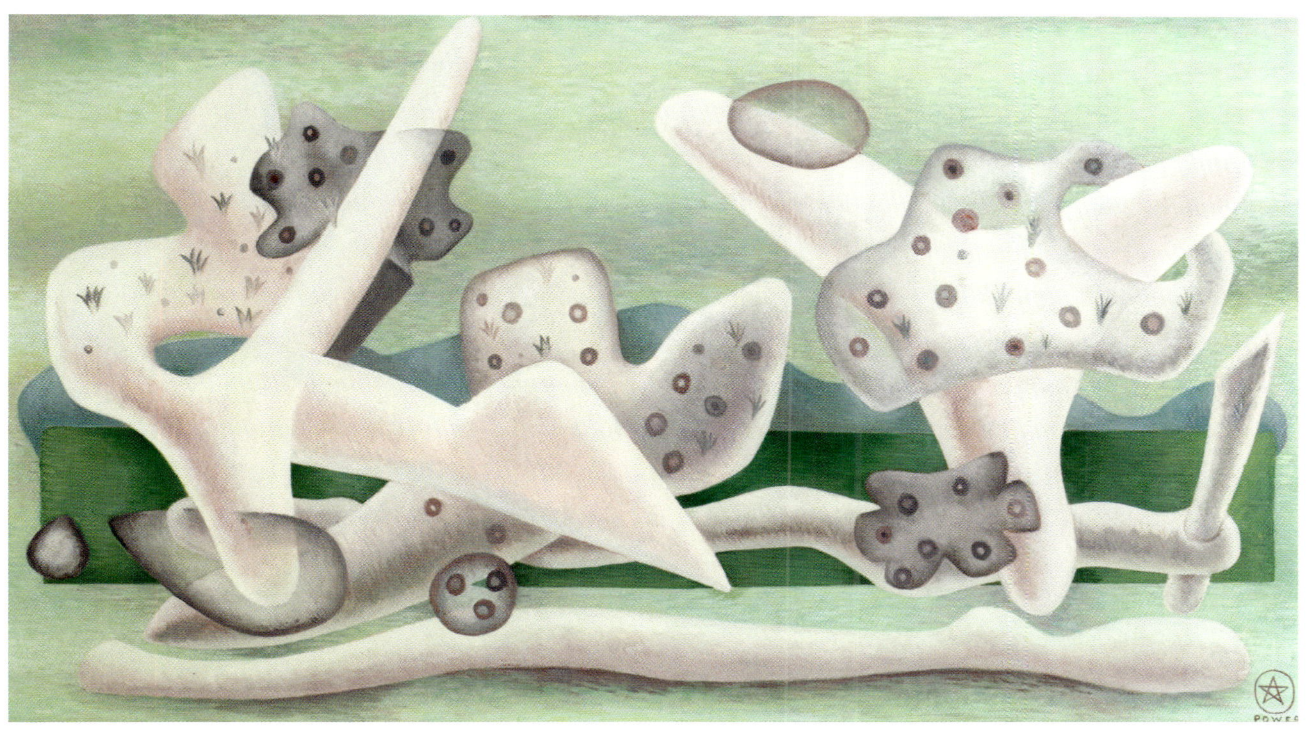

PLATE 20

Marine, c. 1933
oil on canvas, 50.8 x 89.3 cm, PW1961.31

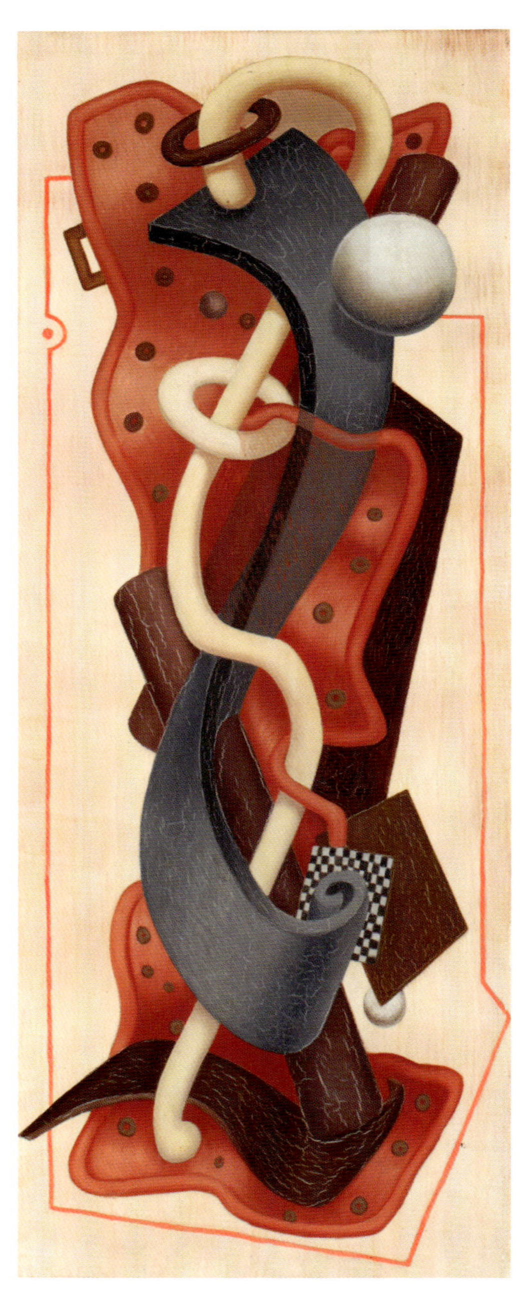

PLATE 21

Abstraction, 1931
oil on canvas, 92.5 x 35.5 cm, PW1961.64

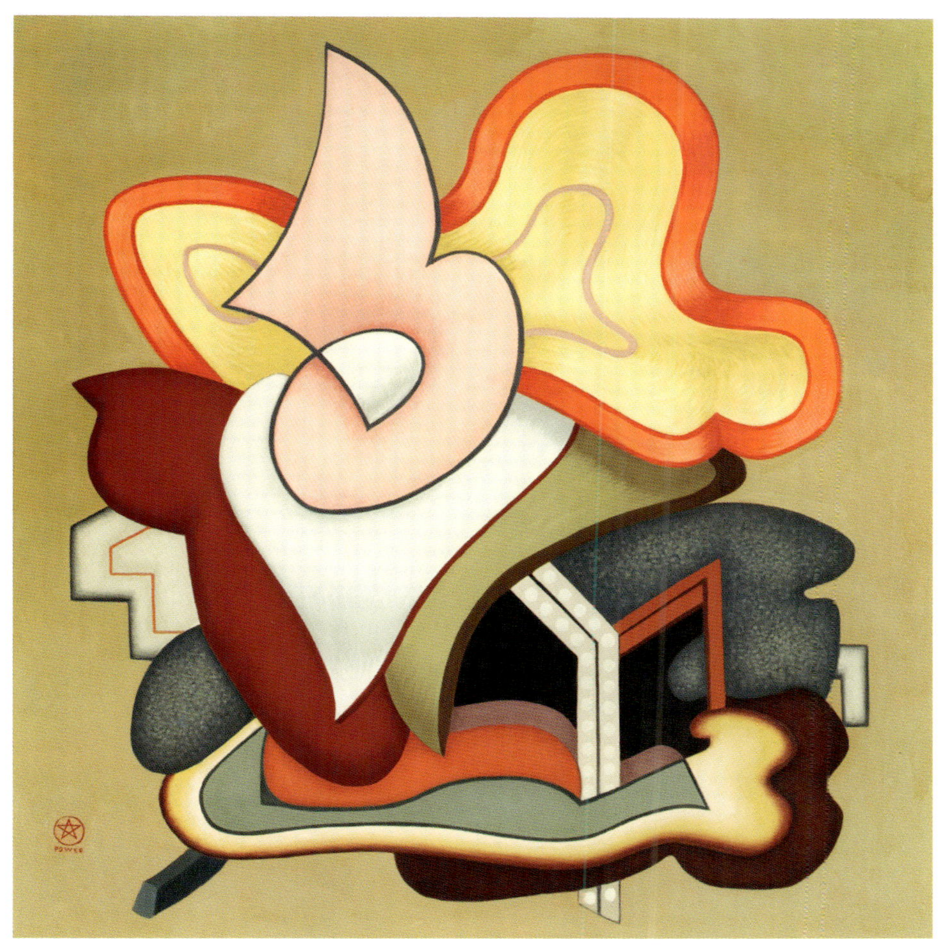

PLATE 22

Flower in parenthesis, c. 1933
oil on canvas, 96.3 x 93.7cm, PW1961.73

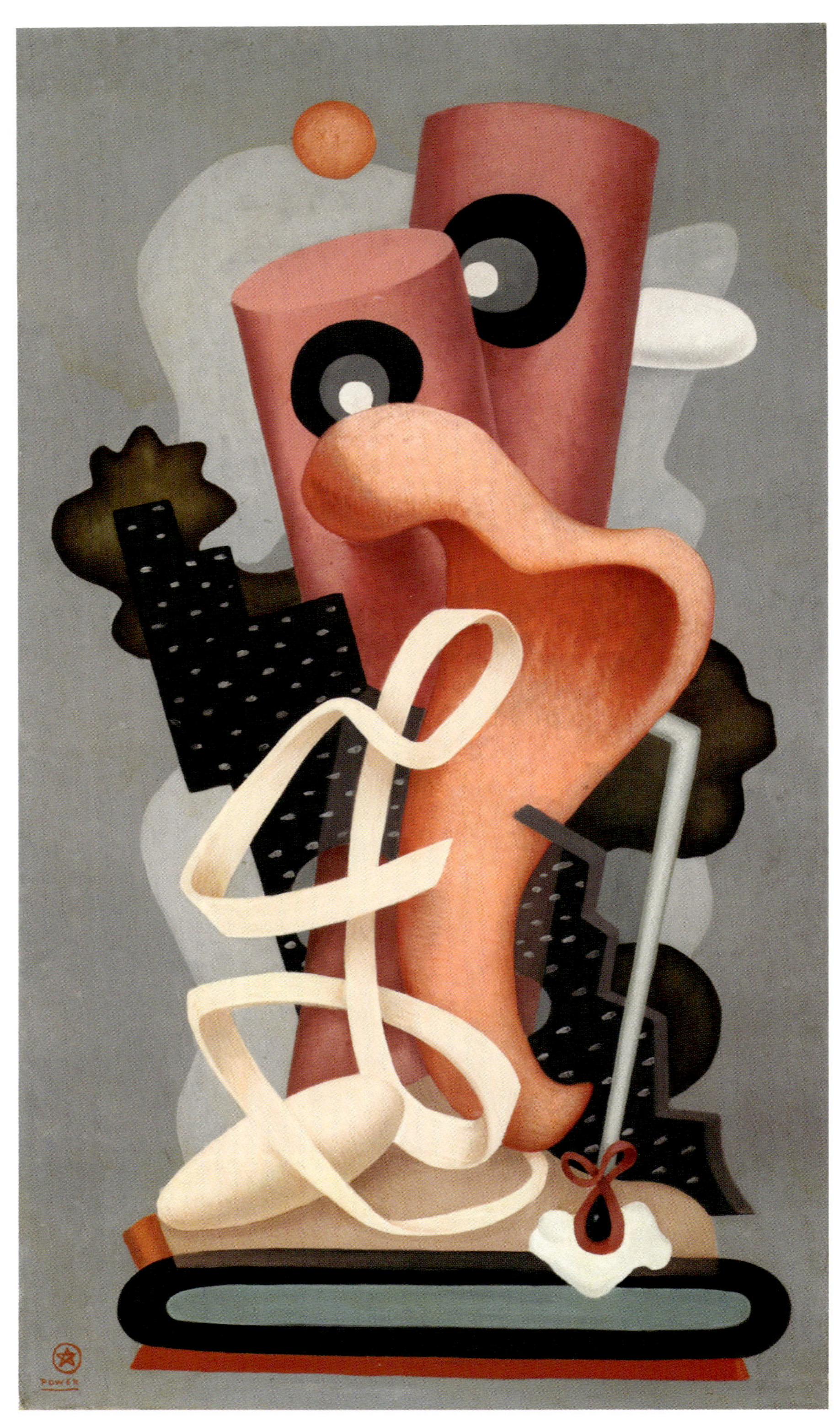

PLATE 23

Susannah and the Elders, 1931-32
oil on canvas, 88.9 x 50.7 cm, PW1961.25

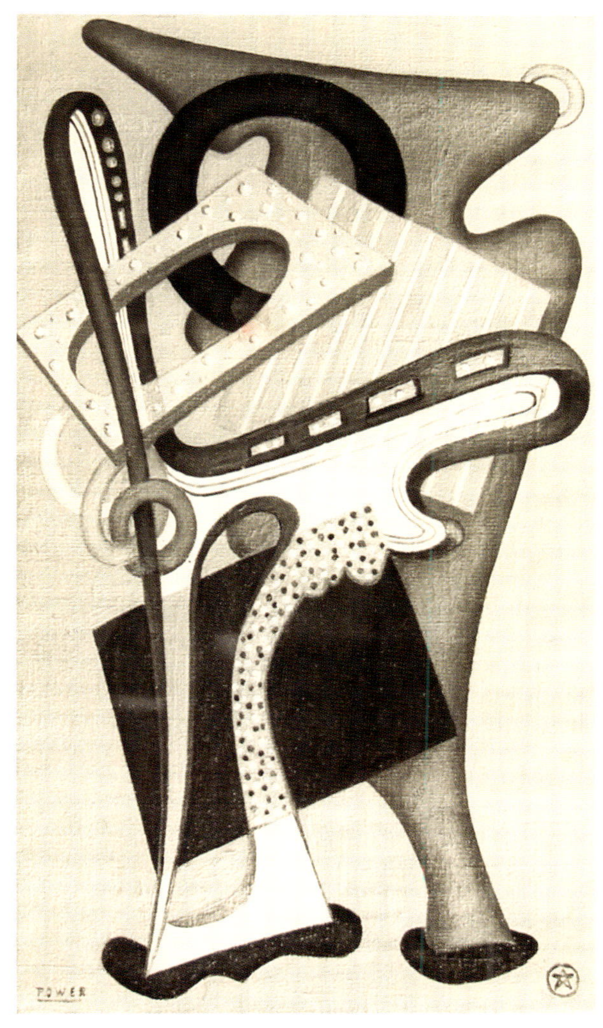

PLATE 24

Abstraction, c. 1934
present location unknown,
photograph from J.W. Power photo album, Fisher Library RB571.4/2

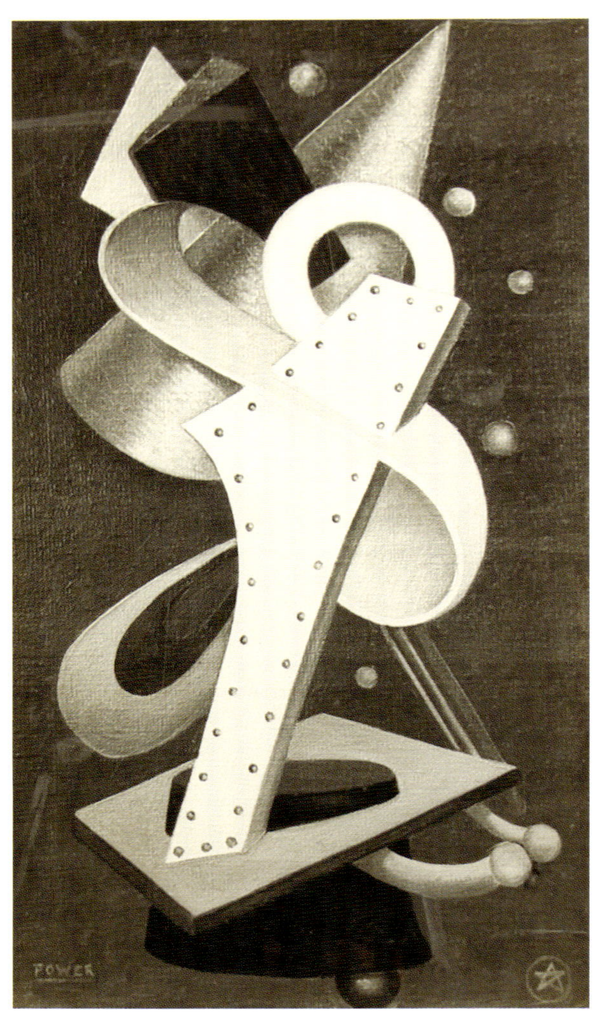

PLATE 25

Abstraction, c. 1934
55 x 31 cm, collection Léonce Rosenberg, present location unknown, photograph from J.W. Power photo album, Fisher Library RB571.4/2

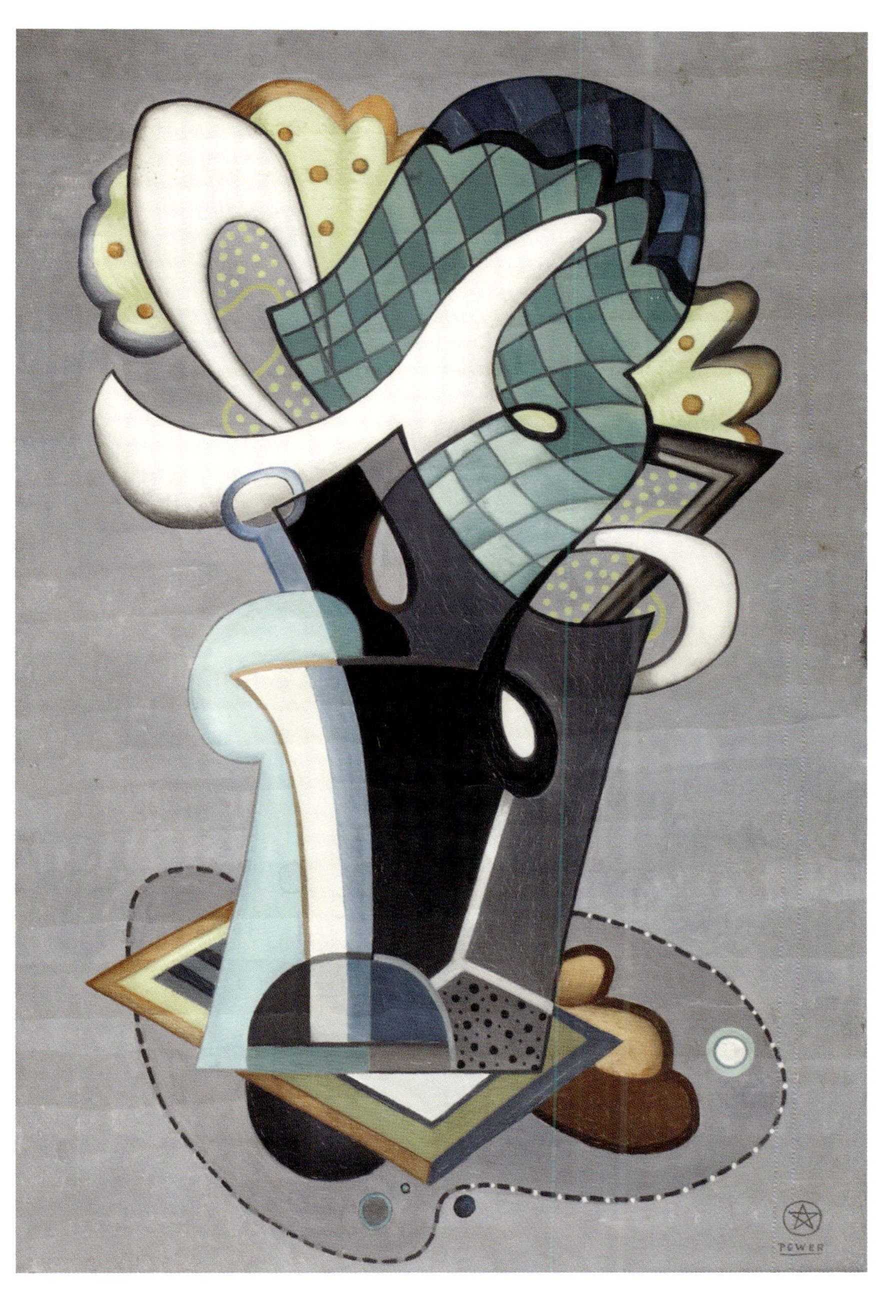

PLATE 26

Flowers c. 1933
oil on canvas, 76.4 x 51 cm, PW1961.1134

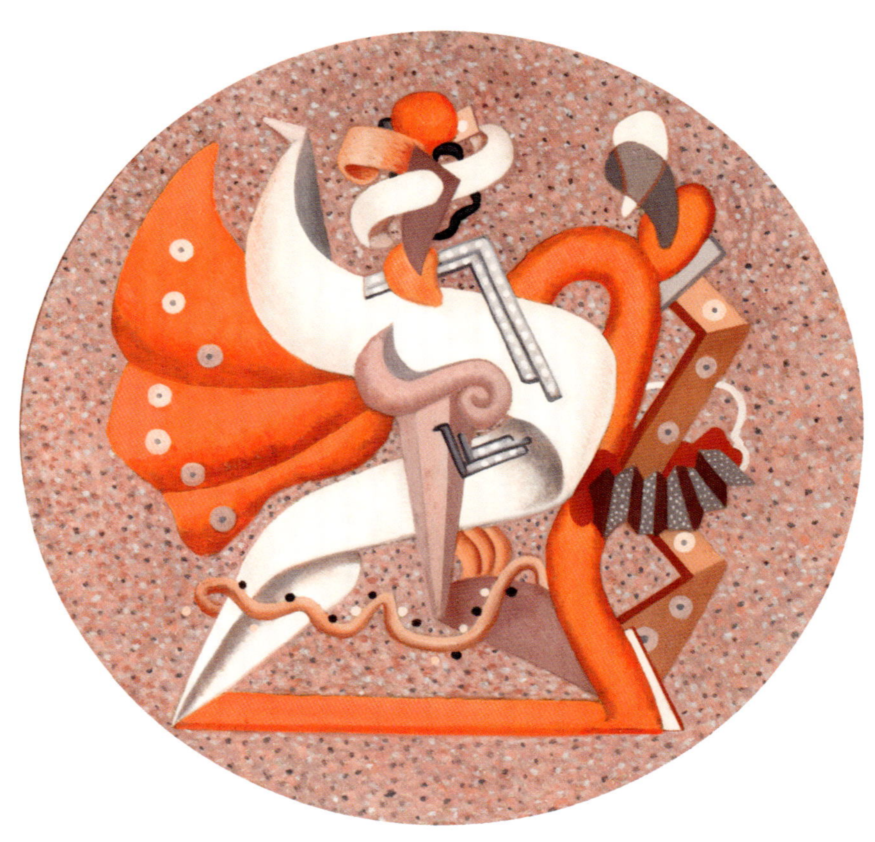

PLATE 27

Danseurs (Dancers), 1933-34
egg tempera and oil on canvas, 50.7 cm diameter, PW1961.89

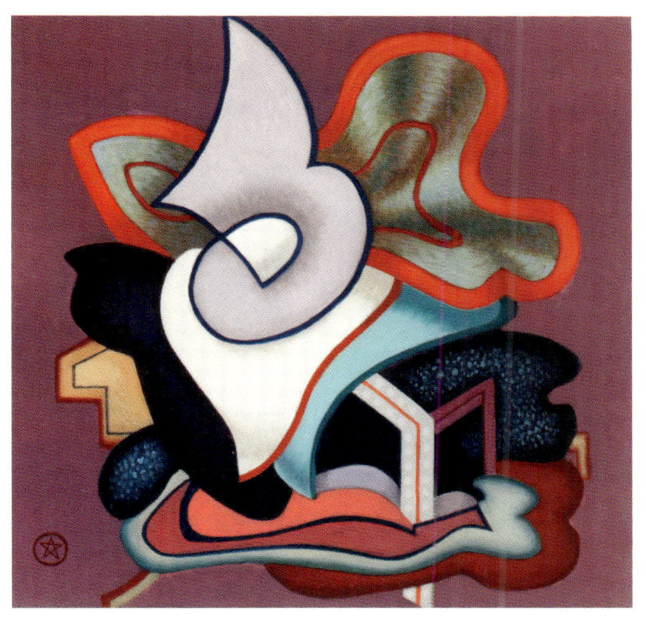

PLATE 28

Flower in parenthesis, 1933
egg tempera and oil on wooden panel, 36.2 x 36.2 cm, PW1961.115

Apollo and Daphne The enigmas of J.W. Power

VIRGINIA SPATE

Fig. 1.

J.W. Power, study for *Apollo & Daphne*, 1929
oil on wood panel, 34.5 x 26.4 cm, PW1961.306A

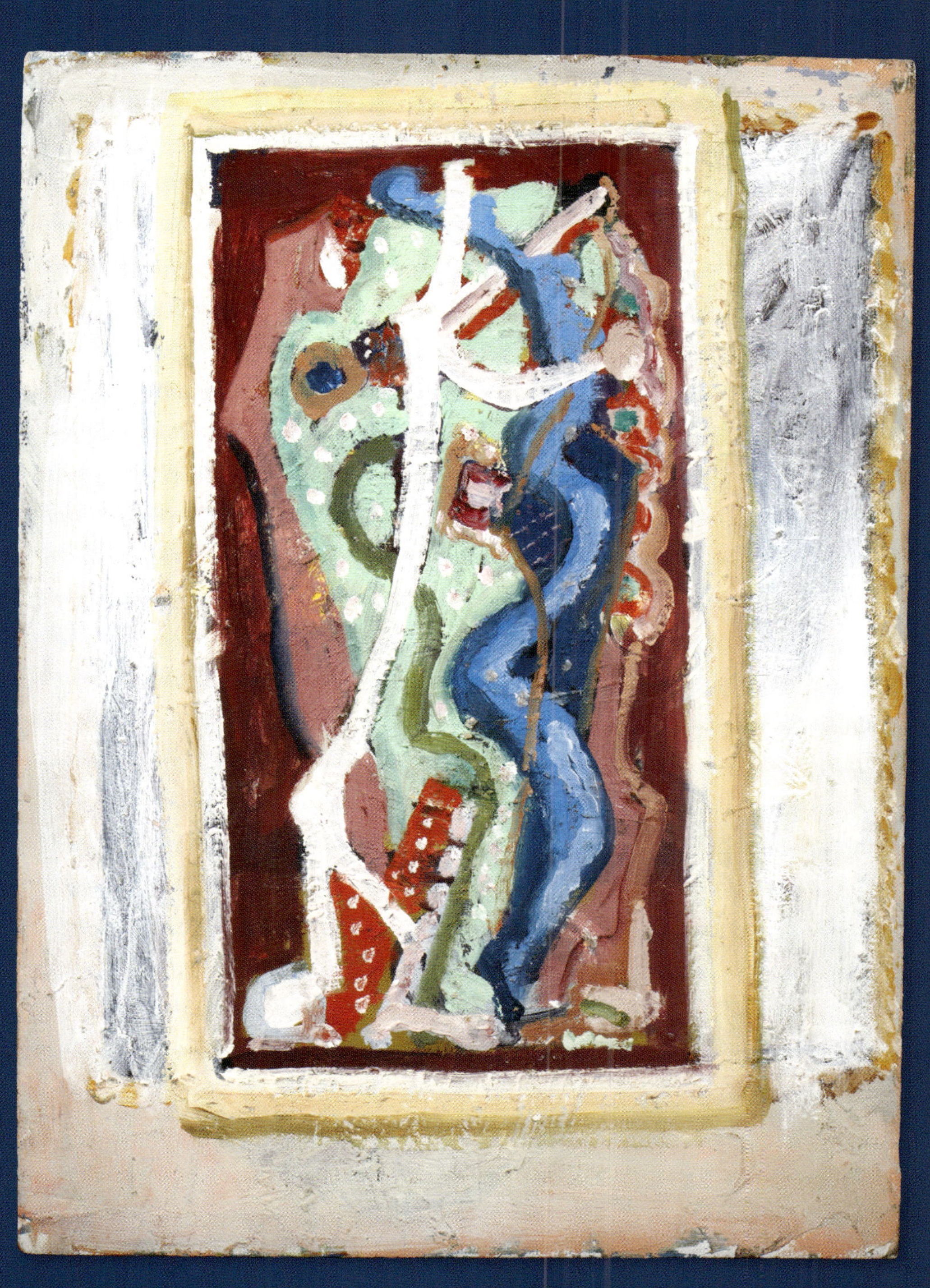

IN HIS 1934 EXHIBITION, J.W. Power showed two paintings whose subjects derived from centuries-old literary sources, one a classical myth, *Apollo and Daphne*, the other, *Susannah and the Elders*, biblical (Plates 11 and 23).[1] One depicts a nymph trying to escape an amorous god; the other, a woman spied on by two old men as she bathed in her garden and who tried to blackmail her into having sex with them. Both subjects go back to the Renaissance tradition, and one has only to think of Bernini's *Apollo and Daphne* or Tintoretto's *Susannah and the Elders* to be aware of the content of these powerful narratives.[2] Power was however dedicated to modernist art and undoubtedly shared its central tenet that form, not subject matter was the essence of the visual arts. Nevertheless he was tempted by subject matter, but transformed it into something quite different.

The explicit titles of many of Power's paintings were unique in the exhibitions of Abstraction-Creátion, the important group of painters and sculptors of which he was a member in the 1930s. The artists who created the group in 1931 stated unequivocally that 'non-figuration' was 'a purely plastic culture, *which excludes every element of explication, anecdote, literature, naturalism, etc.*'[3] (my emphasis). The double title, Abstraction-Création, made it clear that the participating artists could attain non-figuration by abstracting from the observed world or through the creation of a purely geometric concept of order. The latter found its purest form in the paintings of Mondrian – a member of the group – composed only of horizontal and vertical black lines and rectangles of white and three primary colours, red, yellow and blue. There is no invitation to seek meaning. Instead, as one gazes at the painting, the mind empties and one can enter a meditative state.[4]

In contrast, the title *Apollo and Daphne* lures the viewer to search for the figure of the god and the nymph, but, repeatedly, just as one is about to see a recognizable subject, it slips into abstraction.

Here is the story as narrated in the *Metamorphoses*, Ovid's great poetic compendium of the Greco-Roman myths. He told of Apollo's passion for the nymph Daphne, but she spurned love and, preferring 'the

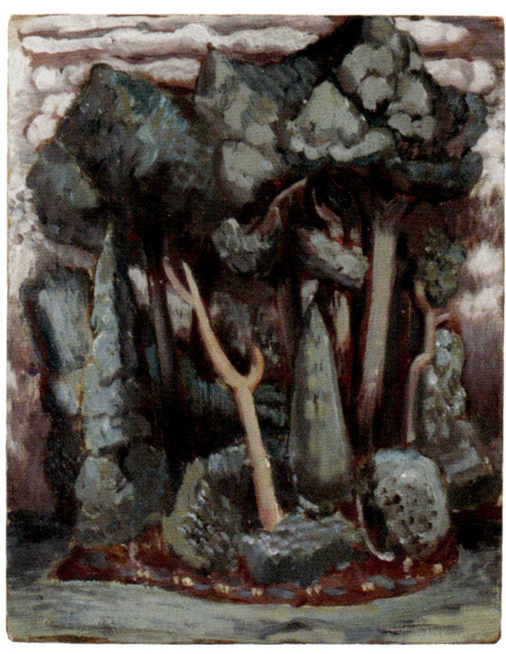

Fig. 2.

J.W. Power, study for *Trees*, 1929
oil on wood panel, 28.2 x 36.5 cm, PW1961.325A, reverse of Fig. 9. study for *Apollo and Daphne*

forest's secret depths', she begged her father, a river god, to allow her 'to enjoy Virginity forever...' But Apollo was soon in hot pursuit and Daphne fled from him, 'her slender limbs/ Bare in the breeze, her fluttering dress blown back/Her hair streaming behind her as she ran'.[5] As the god was about to grasp her, Daphne entreated her father to save her by transforming her body into another form. Her prayer was granted: her body was covered with bark; her arms became branches, her hair became leaves, her feet roots, and her head 'the crown of a green tree'. But Apollo still desired her: he held the tree-trunk and 'felt her heart still beat under the bark; he embraced the branches. He kissed the tree, but, even now, it recoiled from him'. Even so, the god preserved her as the laurel, his sacred tree.

Not only the title, but also the composition invites the spectator to seek out the narrative. The curving forms 'stand' on a sort of plinth that establishes a ground plane for the vertical shapes that suggest at least one human form, and that also creates a narrow space in which beings can move.[6] The pale, angular figure that seems to run towards the right probably stands for Apollo. The figure of Daphne is less legible – she is after all being metamorphosed into a plant –but Apollo's outstretched arms close around a strange, blue, snake-like form. Its lower half is strongly modelled as if to suggest an opulent body with hints of a heavy thigh and even curving buttocks. It is poised on one foot as if in flight, but its upper part appears to turn on its axis, stretching to the left, under then over Apollo's arms, and seemingly turns into a form that is part arm, part breast. Two black circles suggest eyes in a tiny face turned in terror towards the god (who has another kind of eye at the top of his stump of a head). Is this strange, twining creature the nymph Diana as she is being absorbed into 'the forest's secret depths'? Greenness begins to close over her face, as a green plant sprouts up from the ground plane, echoing the upward thrust of the form that I imagine may be changing from nymph to vegetation.

In addition to over 300 finished oil paintings, Power's great bequest contains about 200 very small works painted on wooden or canvas-covered boards. Most are preparatory studies for the larger, finished paintings. Power followed

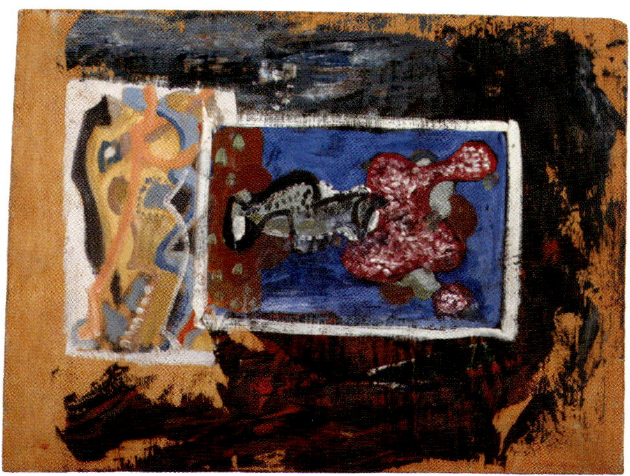

Fig. 3.

J.W. Power, (left) study for *Apollo & Daphne*, 1929
oil on wood panel 28.2 x 36.5 cm, PW1961.340A

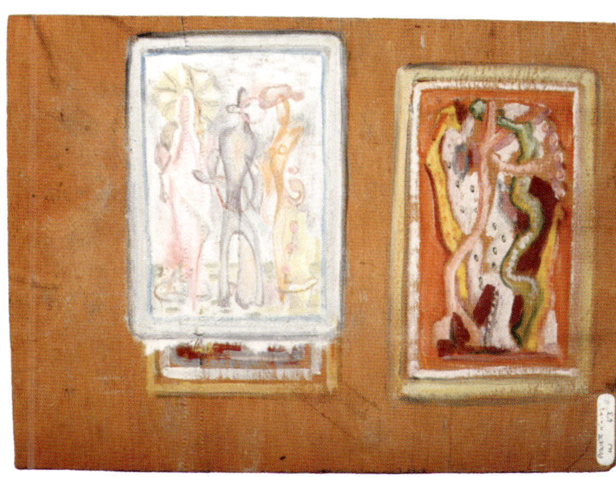

Fig. 4.

J.W. Power, (right) study for *Apollo & Daphne*, 1929
oil on wood panel, 35 x 26.8 cm, PW1961.340B

traditional practice in using a number of oil-sketches to work out his compositions. Usually a painter would begin with a rough sketch and would then clarify the composition, shaping the forms and experimenting with structures of line and colour. In the final study, these components would be drawn into a coherent whole, close to the final work.[7] But there is no such final study in Power's preparatory work for his major paintings, and there is a curious gap between his sketchy studies and the precision of the finished paintings. Given his meticulous technique, I doubt if he prepared them by a loose preparatory sketch on the canvas itself.[8]

There are eleven little oil sketches for *Apollo and Daphne* (1929) on seven panels. Power painted one or two little paintings on each panel, eight of which were surrounded by a 'gilded' frame.[9] Some share space with other subjects, and one even has a framed painting of a curiously shaped vase of flowers that overlaps a tiny sketch of the Apollo and Daphne theme [Fig. 3.]. The pairs of studies were not necessarily executed at the same time, but they were all painted quickly with fairly dilute paint that dried fast and allowed him to move from panel to panel without mixing layers of paint.

It is probably impossible to establish a firm sequence of studies, but I think that the five panels painted in rather chalky pastel colours were probably the first. In the first the loosely sketched Apollo and Daphne theme might best be deciphered by comparing it with subsequent studies, such as the framed painting on the reverse of this panel [Fig. 4.], in which one can see most of the components of the finished painting: the flat, vertical plane over which curves a fleshy pink figure about to embrace a green snake-like shape coiling up the painting, with what looks like an arm thrusting sideways and a pink and white blob that could stand for a head. In the next three paintings [Fig. 5. and 6.], Power broadened the vertical planes behind the figures, experimented with warm and cool colour schemes, and transformed 'Apollo' into a white shape more like a stick insect than a fleshy god.

In two unframed studies [Fig. 7.], Power left parts of the panel uncovered, giving him space to strengthen the dynamics of the composition, before developing the dense planes of colour. The painting on the left gives a clearer image of the plinth that creates space and establishes a ground plane for the figures. The colours are much brighter than the first

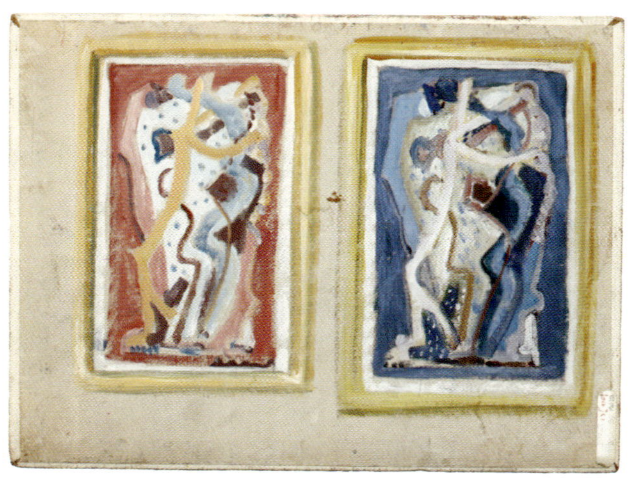

Fig. 5.

J.W. Power, studies for *Apollo & Daphne*, 1929
oil on canvas board, 26.4 x 34.5 cm, PW1961.233B

group of studies—indeed those in the tiny painting on the right are almost iridescent, particularly in the vivid pink fleshiness of the snake-nymph.[10]

In three little studies [Fig. 1 and 8.], Power painted Apollo a clear white silhouetted against a bright lime-green plane that would be crucial to the finished painting. In Fig. 1., the nymph is painted an intense blue, strongly modelled with a darker blue, and her 'head' is absorbed by two strokes of vivid green. Most of the details of the finished painting—the writhing green plants and the grids, spots and curls—are now in place. The last little painting [Fig. 9.] takes on its cooler colours, and the final shape of the figures.

There is a considerable difference between the studies and the suave and elegant finished painting. This indicates that Power would have spent intense care working out the subtle linear structure and refined tonalities and colour relationships. These create a mobile surface in which the pale, angular male figure with its curved arms, the cool, blue, rounded female form, the whiplash green plant and other linear forms ceaselessly weave in and out of vertical planes. The sleek paint surface formed by delicate brushstrokes, makes the figure of Daphne sensuous. The subtle tonalities of the deep blue background and the blue-greens, blues and violets are animated by the edginess of the lime green plane, the bright green of the plant, and the multiple angles and curves of the white shapes, all seem to be in movement. This is fitting, if we recall the myth: the chase; the moment the god is about to capture the nymph; the moment she is changed into another being.

Most of Power's paintings reveal his enjoyment of patterning and of detail. In this painting, we find forms that had already appeared in the studies: spirals, brown grids like nets, many different kinds of dots, strange, round shapes like pearls casting shadows on the lime-green plane. Power also created dark shapes that make holes in the green plane, as well as a white line that coils from the top to the bottom of the painting, curling around four green and black shapes to an inexplicable structure on the plinth. These inventions animate the painting, but also invite us to share Power's sheer pleasure in painting.

Like many of his works, *Apollo and Daphne* is enigmatic. Its wit and playfulness suggest that Power may have chosen the story of

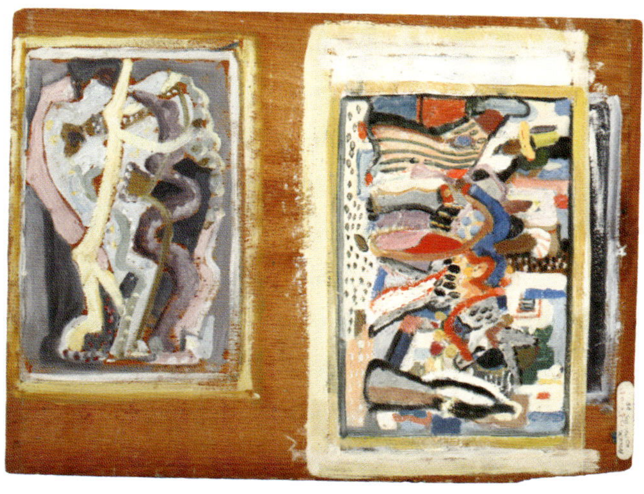

Fig 6.

J.W. Power, (left) study for *Apollo & Daphne*, (right) study for *North African Scene*, 1929
oil on wood panel, 26.4 x 34.5 cm PW1961.335.

Apollo and Daphne simply as a pretext for the creation of a painting, but I cannot help wondering why he should choose to paint a god seeking to rape a nymph, or why he represented the nymph as a repulsive, snake-like creature rather than the tree into which she was transformed. For Power, however, the concept of metamorphosis was probably profound for it enabled him to use the story of Diana's metamorphosis to create a strange new world for the imagination.

In both London and Paris, Power could have seen small museums created by painters who had bequeathed their homes and their works to their city or nation, thus ensuring a form of immortality. The modernist J.W. Power probably detested Gustave Moreau's academic and Symbolist paintings, but he may have been interested in his museum with its huge collection of oil paintings and hundreds of watercolours and drawings that enable one to examine his painting practice from its first idea to its realisation.

Perhaps such museums inspired Power's great gift to 'the people of Australia', but the outbreak of war made this impossible. In 1939 he wrote his will on the island of Jersey, eight months before it was occupied by Germany, and where he died two years before the war ended.

The fact that Power preserved two hundred and fifty panels when he and his wife were constantly moving from place to place suggests that he believed them to be an integral part of his legacy, and they do indeed allow us to participate in his creative process.

The little paintings are not, I think, simply studies. Power's habit of painting gilded frames around them was very unusual, if not unique (painters who wanted to indicate the boundaries of a composition would simply do so by painting or drawing lines). Many of these 'framed' pictures are superimposed over other paintings, sometimes up to three layers deep. Sometimes one can discern only a golden frame beneath roughly brushed, translucent white paint over which he painted one or more framed pictures. These partly revealed, partly concealed paintings are like ghosts of lost works. Could Power bear to lose any of them?[11] Did he wish to retain something of their living presence? Did they, like most abstract painting, have some spiritual resonance?[12] These are not the least of J.W. Power's enigmas.

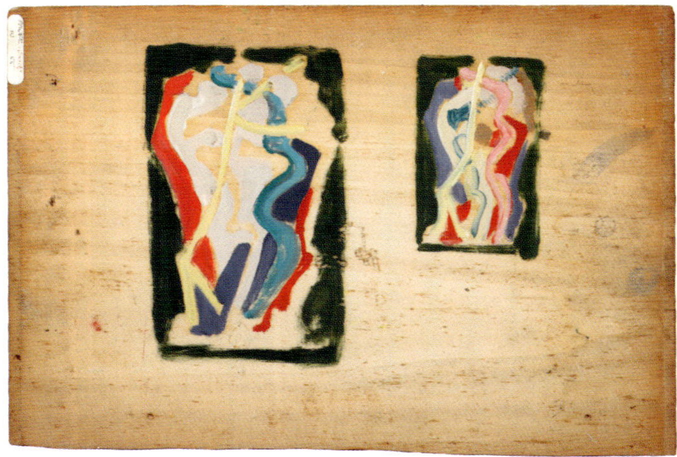

Fig. 7.

J.W. Power, studies for *Apollo & Daphne*, 1929
oil on wood panel, 26.4 x 34.5 cm, PW1961.342

Notes

1. My mother's name was Daphne; she always loved the flowers. I dedicate these few pages to her.
2. Bernini, *Apollo and Daphne* (1622-25), Rome, Villa Borghese; Tintoretto, *Susannah and the Elders*, Musée du Louvre, Paris, Kunsthistorisches Museum, Vienna.
3. Extract from the group's first *Cahier* in 1932, repr., eds. Charles Harrison and Paul Wood, *Art and Theory 1900-2000. An Anthology of changing ideas*, Blackwell, Oxford, 1992, p. 357.
4. In the Abstraction-Création group, Hans Arp's biomorphic sculptures were closest to Power's works, but Arp's titles are poetic, dream states rather than suggested narratives.
5. Ovid, *Metamorphoses*, trans. A.D. Melville, Oxford University Press, Oxford, New York 1987, p. 14-18.
6. This gravitational structure probably derived from Braque and Picasso's Cubism. The plinth can be seen more clearly in the preparatory studies.
7. Painters often made a grid over the drawing to assist in its enlargement to the final painting. I cannot find any evidence of this in Power's paintings.
8. In his book, *Éléments de la construction picturale*, 1932 and in some loose drawings, Power did elaborate diagrams of proportional structures, based on horizontal and verticals grids, but their relationship to his paintings has not been closely analysed.
9. Power was fascinated by frames and was rich enough to have very grand frames for his paintings, although he had to be more modest after the Depression in the 1930s, when many fellow artists found it difficult to survive.
10. These bright colours can be seen in the North African scene (Fig. 6.).
11. Power assembled two albums of photographs of his finished paintings Rare Books & Special Collections, Fisher Library. RB571.4/2 They make it clear that Power bought back some of his paintings from collectors.
12. I expected to find some sense of spiritual meaning in Power's *Eléments de la construction picturale* with its elaborate diagrams of proportions, but it does not contain a hint of their meaning.

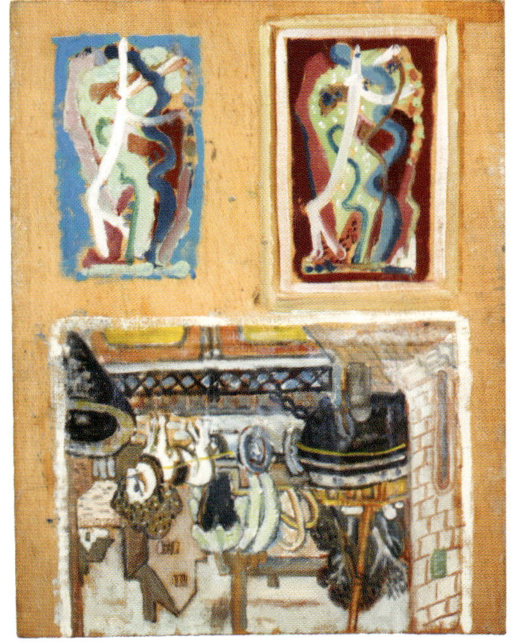

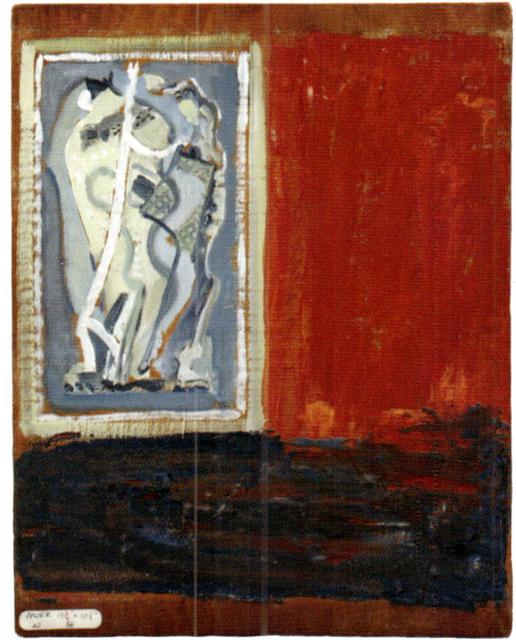

Fig.8.

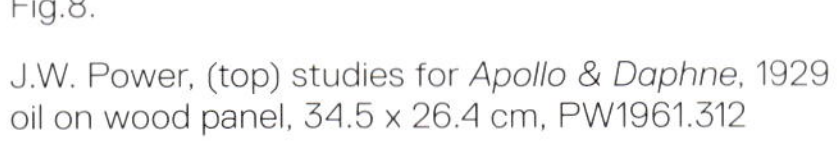

J.W. Power, (top) studies for *Apollo & Daphne*, 1929
oil on wood panel, 34.5 x 26.4 cm, PW1961.312

Fig. 9.

J.W. Power, study for *Apollo & Daphne*, 1929
oil on wood panel, 26.4 x 34.5 cm, PW1961.325B

Abstraction-Création cahier Nº 1–5

Abstraction-Création cahiers Nº 1-5, Paris 1932-36
28 x 22.5 cm, annotations by Georges Vantongerloo,
collection: Marquand Library of Art and Archaeology,
Princeton University

abstraction création art non figuratif 1932

prix 15 francs

abstraction création art non figuratif 1933

2

prix .. 15 francs
étranger 20 francs

abstraction création art non figuratif 1934

3

prix .. 15 francs
étranger 20 francs

abstraction création art non figuratif 1935

4

prix .. 15 francs
étranger 20 francs

abstraction création art non figuratif 1936

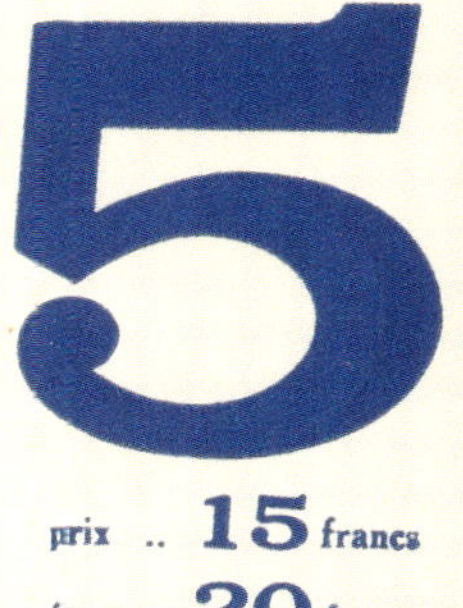

prix .. 15 francs
étranger 20 francs

Abstraction-Création 1931–36

GLADYS FABRE, TRANSLATED BY ANTONIA FREDMAN*

Gladys Fabre, *Abstraction-Création 1931-1936*, Paris and Münster, 1978, book, with Jean Hélion *Tensions Circulaires* (1931-32).

Westfälisches Landesmuseum für Kunst und Kulturgeschichte Münster

Musée d'Art Moderne de la Ville de Paris

abstraction création 1931·1936

DURING THE YEARS 1928–30, Paris became the capital of the international artistic avant-garde, taking over from Germany, in particular from Berlin, which had held this leading position in the early 1920s. The *Exposition Internationale des Arts Décoratifs* of 1925 heralded the awakening of the French capital, despite the conservative displays of many pavilions, with the exception of those by Russia, the Esprit Nouveau and Holland (the theatrical section designed by Friedrich Kiesler). The success of this Exposition restored the vitality Paris had lost in the immediate aftermath of the war. After a stay of one or two years in Berlin, artists came to know the diverse currents of the avant-garde abroad, notably those of Russian Constructivism and Suprematism. Having profited from the rampant devaluation of the mark, which boosted their modest purchasing power, they progressively abandoned Germany in favour of France, attracted by other tendencies, notably those derived from Cubism.[1] They were accepted into the schools and studios of Lhote and Calorossi, and the Académie Moderne of Leger and Friesz, who was later replaced by Ozenfant. During the years 1924–25, the Académie Moderne alone included artists from Scandinavia (Carlsund, Osterblom, Keyser, Clausen, Kaarbo, Wankel, E. Olson), Poland (Wlodarski, Grabowski, Nadia Grabowska), the United States of America (Essel Garderen, Florence Henri, M. Cowles), even Romania (Bratachano), Australia (Power) and Japan (Sakata). Gleizes himself recruited two young Irish students, M. Jellet and E. Hone, and another Australian, Anne Dangar. From 1927, the community of artists he established in Moly-Sabata was a hub of activity. Similarly, the presence in Paris of the Surrealist movement, and of well-known personalities such as Mondrian (from 1919 onwards), and Robert and Sonia Delaunay, attracted numerous visitors, some of whom eventually settled in Paris. Kassak, Janco, Lissitzky, Marinetti, Prampolini, J. Peeters and Michel Seuphor, like many of the other creative forces behind avant-garde magazines, came into contact with the leading figures of the Parisian artistic scene.

Thus during the second half of the 1920s, the colonies of foreign artists expanded and grew. Pevsner arrived in Paris in 1922, and Pougny in 1923, joining Sonia Delaunay, Goncharova and Larionov. The Hungarians Béothy and Henri Nouveau (1925), along with Martyn, Tihanyi and Bela Voros, followed the example of Miklos and Csaky, who were established in Paris before the First World War. The presence of Mondrian in Paris encouraged an understanding of Dutch Neoplasticism, which became the most influential of all the non-figurative tendencies to reach France. With the support of Léonce Rosenberg, the driving force behind the gallery and revue *l'Effort Moderne*, and of Badovici, director of *Architecture Vivante*, and of the painter

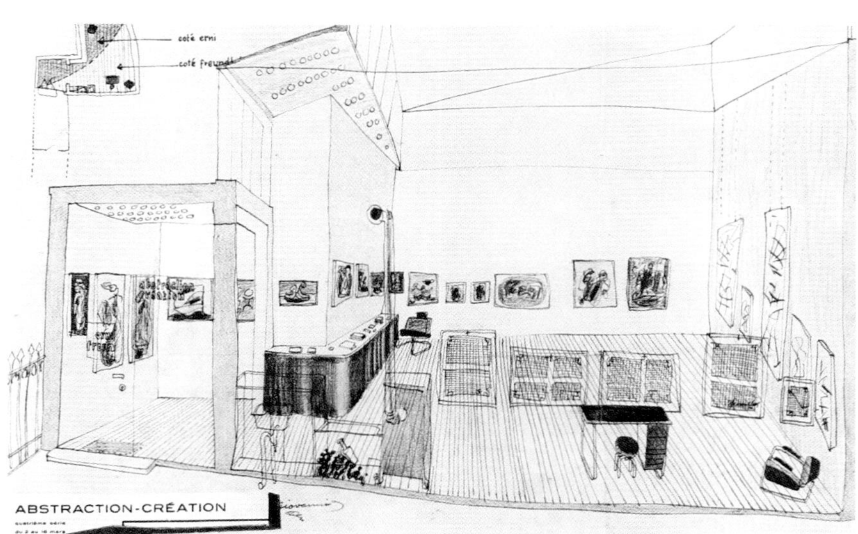

Hans Erni, sketch for 'Erni, Freundlich' exhibition, Abstraction-Création, 1934.

Del Marle, editor of *Vouloir*, Neoplasticism was further reinforced by the presence of Vantongerloo (1920 Menton, 1927 Paris), and van Doesburg, who having designed the interior of the Strasbourg café l'Aubette (1927) with Arp and Sophie Täuber, settled in Meudon in 1929.

Less well known, but equally active, the Polish artists in Paris demand our attention. Poznanski, a student of Gleizes, organised the first major international avant-garde exhibition *l'Art d'Aujourd'hui* in 1925, a precursor to *Cercle et Carré* in 1930. It was there that Katherine Dreier selected works by Carlsund, Keyser and Kaarbo for the collection of the Société Anonyme. Another Polish expatriate, Povolozky, publisher and owner of the bookstore La Cible, became the advocate of the only Parisian non-objective artists of the immediate postwar period: Kupka, Gleizes and Gallien. In 1929, Povolozky also showed Vordemberge-Gildewart and Flouquet, while the following year, the Galerie Zak promoted the work of Kandinsky. At the Galerie Sacré du Printemps in 1928, Jan Sliwinski exhibited works by Boeck, Flouquet, Shwab and Béothy. In the same premises, Seuphor and Paul Dermée organised events for *Documents Internationaux de l'Esprit Nouveau*, which were attended by numerous Polish artists: Alexandre Rafalowski, M. Stazewski, Zamoyski, the poets Choumoff and Brzekowski, the painters Grabowski and his wife Nadia Grabowska (later Nadia Léger). Along with Brzekowski – who organised cultural activities for the French-Polish association – Nadia Grabowska edited the bilingual journal *l'Art contemporain*, of which only two issues appeared. The intense activity of the Polish colony in Paris earned them a room at the *Salon d'Automne* in 1928, in which Nicz-Borowiakowa, Stazewski and Strzeminski also exhibited. However, their most significant act was the creation of the Muzeum Sztuki (Museum of Art), in Lodz, Poland. Three-quarters of the collection comprises gifts of the Parisian artistic avant-garde collected by Brzekowski, Nadia Léger, Seuphor and Stazewski. The remainder was assembled in Poland by Strzeminski.

In France, the non-figurative artists of the 1920s had the opportunity to exhibit at the Salon des Surindépendants. A dissident faction, made up of the most progressive elements of the Salon, organised the exhibitions "1940", in 1931 and 1932, which brought together numerous future members of Abstraction-Création, and which dedicated a retrospective to van Doesburg immediately after his death.[2] Finally, the exhibitions *l'ESAC (Expositions Sélectes d'Art Contemporain)*, organised by Nelly van Doesburg in Amsterdam in 1929, and the *Internationell Utställning av Post-Kubistisk Konst* (International Exhibition of Post-Cubist Art), put together by Carlsund in Stockholm in 1930, could equally be considered steps leading to the formation of the Abstraction-Création movement.[3]

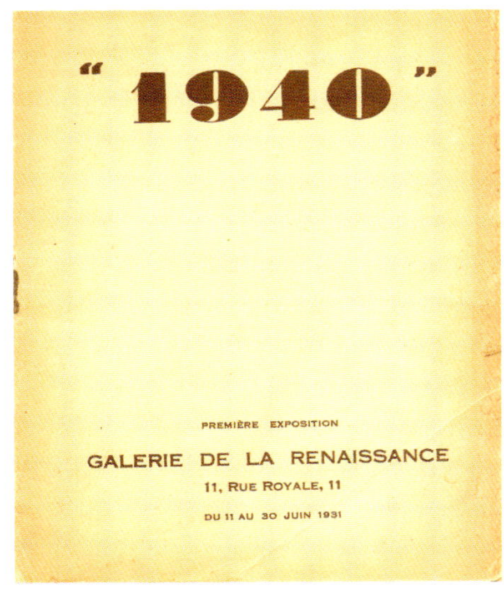

"1940", Paris, 1931, catalogue.

Formation and history of the movement

IN THIS FERVENT ARTISTIC climate, Michel Seuphor and Torrès Garcia decided to form a group, Cercle et Carré, which in March 1930 first published a journal that was to last three issues and presented a major exhibition on rue de la Boëtie.[4] Despite the emphasis placed on non-figurative art, with representatives of Neoplasticism such as Mondrian, Vilmos Huszár, Huib, Hoste, Vantongerloo, Gorin and Vordemberge-Gildewart, and figures such as Kandinsky, Schwitters, Buchheister, Pevsner and Stazewski exhibiting, some participants worked in a mixed style of figuration, combining Cubism, Futurism and Purism. In *Art Concret* (April 1930), the group's *revue*, Hélion opposed those artists who sought 'to humanise geometry and to make geometric the human' which was, despite van Doesburg's denials, a true challenge to Cercle et Carré:

> 'Some painters squeeze their characters into a square and a circle in order to wrap them up in it. Others strangle a cube to give it a waistline, cap it with a sphere, attach some cylinders and call it both man and machine. Others construct the picture with geometric elements and stabilise it in this state, then pepper it with a little humanity, inserting here and there a tiny bit of face, opening an eye, drawing out a hand, a jaw, a known object in order to give the viewer that little thrill of kinship which will help him, they believe, to assimilate the painting.'

Art Concret was born of an obscure conflict between Seuphor and van Doesburg.[5] Their difference of opinion renewed old tensions between the rigorous Neoplasticism of Seuphor, Mondrian and Vantongerloo and van Doesburg's new theories on Elementarism. According to Seuphor, van Doesburg was officially invited on 7 January 1930 to participate in Cercle et Carré, but declined the invitation in order to form his own movement.[6] In a letter to Thijs Rinsema, dated 2 February 1930, van Doesburg complained of not having been approached. He wrote with insight, 'This is about the politics of the self and each fears the dominance of the other.' In fact, not content with playing a supporting role and not having initiated Cercle et Carré, Van Doesburg no more wanted to participate in the group than Seuphor was willing to invite him.[7]

The 'barrowful of money' that van Doesburg needed to start his own movement was promised by Carlsund, who committed to financing the publication of *Art Concret*. In fact, Carlsund paid for half of the first issue. The financial collapse and scandal of the Post-Cubist Art exhibition in Stockholm left Carlsund unable to settle his account with the printer, let alone publish another issue. Embarrassed, he dared not return to France nor did he feel able to take up the invitation to participate in Abstraction-Création.

Despite its ephemeral nature, the importance of Art Concret lies in the rigour of its theories

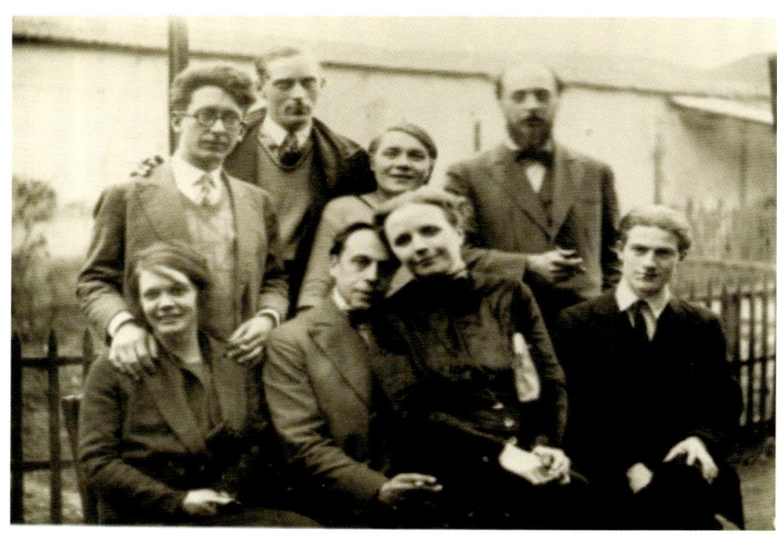

The Art Concret group, with Jean Hélion standing on the left with Otto Carslund, on the right; seated on the right, Marcel Wantz with Théo and Nelly Van Doesburg, centre; photo by Leon Tutundjian.

and in the homogeneity of the group: van Doesburg, Carlsund, Hélion, Tutundjian, Wantz and Shwab.[8] Its hard-line program rejected all symbolism, all extra-pictorial references, asserting that the pictorial element has no significance beyond 'itself'. 'A square, a circle, a colour are concrete elements, just as a cow or a tree. They are an optical realisation of thought.' This formalist approach was accompanied by an almost minimal severity in the decisions about form and colour, by anonymity in the treatment of surface, and by the use of mathematics and optical laws in laying out elements of their work. In fact, the theoretical impact of this manifesto, which served as a reference point for the most extreme tendencies in European non-objective art from 1935 to 1950, has proved far more influential than the works themselves, which largely remain tied to the non-objective aesthetic of the 1920s.[9]

Abstraction-Création rose from the ashes of Cercle et Carré and Art Concret. Seuphor fell ill, and the enterprise of Cercle et Carré, robbed of its driving force, faced an uncertain future. Aware that Art Concret was not financially viable, depending as it did upon five or six people of limited means, van Doesburg brought Hélion, Tutundjian, Arp, Herbin, Kupka, Gleizes, Valmier and Delaunay together in his studio, shortly before his death, to create a new, more open group.[10] The sole criteria was that the work be non-figurative. On 15 February 1931, Abstraction-Création was born. Among the participants, thirteen artists had belonged to Cercle et Carré and two members of the organising committee came from Art Concret.

Abstraction-Création thus brought together all the different non-figurative currents of the avant-garde. In its preface, the committee explained the dichotomy apparent in the title: abstraction and concrete art (creation) are presented as the two possible alternatives.

> 'Abstraction because certain artists have arrived at the conception of non-figuration through the progressive abstraction of natural forms. Creation because other artists have directly reached "non-figuration" through a conception of pure geometric order or through the exclusive use of elements collectively called abstract, such as circles, planes, bars, lines, etc.'

Kupka later wrote that even the title of the review was extensively debated, that it was not the best choice, but a compromise.[11] It allowed for the integration of multiple tendencies of non-figurative art, but its very existence would give rise to numerous discussions at the heart of the movement.

The incorruptible champions of non-objective art were Herbin and Vantongerloo. Hélion and Arp, among others, criticised them for this dogmatism, which led them, for example, to reject a painting by Valmier where one could discern a 'fish', and on the other hand, to admit very mediocre canvases on the pretext

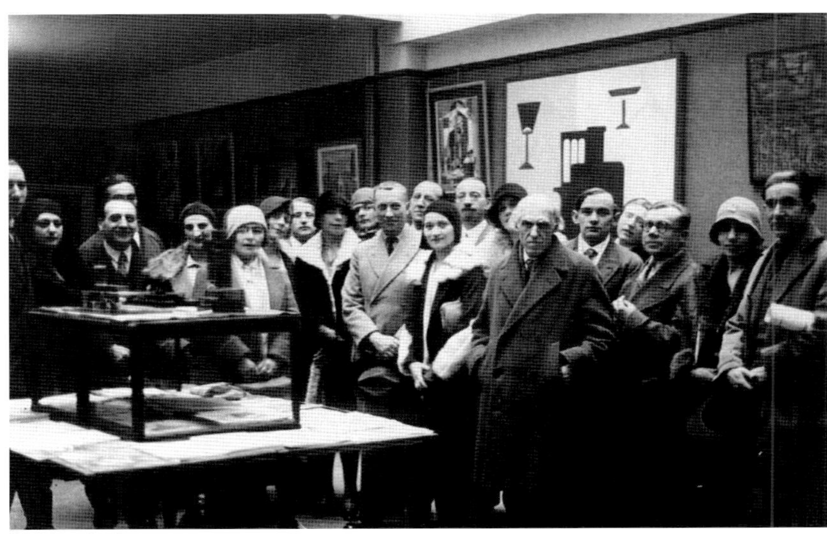

Exhibition *Cercle et Carré*, Galerie 23, 1930: includes Marcelle Cahn, Franciska Clausen, Nadia Léger, Florence Henri, Sophie Täuber, Torrès Garcia, Mondrian, Ingelard H. Bjarnason, Michel Seuphor, Vordemberge-Gildewart, Luigi Russolo, Gorin and Frau Torrès-Garcia.

that they adhered to the single strict view of non-figuration. This policy, at once liberal and sectarian, lacked clear guidelines and irritated some members, including Pevsner, Gabo, Freundlich, Delaunay, Valmier, Arp, Sophie Täuber-Arp and Hélion, who all withdrew in 1934. The reasons for these resignations are outlined in two letters signed by Hélion, Täuber-Arp, Fernandez, and Freundlich. Financial problems were contributing factors to this decision.[12] For lack of finances, only one issue a year could be published, whereas the initial project envisaged the release of eight issues with much more ambitious content. In the end, only two monographs were published. The first, on Herbin, was financed by the painter Power, who had a personal fortune. As guarantee for the sum advanced to Herbin, each member of the committee gave a work to Power. Other monographs on Delaunay, Kupka, Mondrian, Pevsner, Gabo, Schwitters, Valmier, Vantongerloo, Arp, Villon, Freundlich were to follow, but not one of them saw the light of day. Only the Swiss painters Erni, Schiess, Seligmann, Täuber-Arp and Vulliamy succeeded in gathering the funds to produce a second publication.

The poverty of these artists, many of whom lived on unemployment benefits, did not allow them to keep their premises at 44 avenue de Wagram for longer than 18 months. However, begining in late 1933, the group organised a series of events. It required the perseverance and dynamism of a figure like Herbin to maintain some cohesion between these individual personalities, who were not only influenced by different ideologies and aesthetics, but were faced with economic crises. Herbin's beautiful letter to Freundlich of March 1934, offering comfort and suggesting financial solutions (raffles, selling cards) which would allow Freundlich's continued participation as a core member of Abstraction-Création attests to his unceasing efforts to maintain the association. In his autobiography, Calder recalls this endless search for funds which, while running counter to the aesthetic puritanism of Herbin and Vantongerloo, obliged the committee to make the now well-known concessions to Surrealism, indeed even to figurative art.

> 'At the end, they were hard up for funds and it was suggested they invite some successful artists to have their pictures printed alongside our own – they'd pay a bit more than we to carry the publication along. Somebody suggested inviting Picasso, and Delaunay became furious. They did invite Brancusi. He sent a photograph, but no funds.'[13]

On the other hand Brignoni and Glarner, who exhibited as members of the group, never featured in the *cahiers*, undoubtedly as they lacked money. Pierre Antoine Gallien and Henri Nouveau, though invited to the first meetings, do not seem to have joined.

Such anomalies, as the figurative artists Brancusi and Picasso, and those who participated but were not referenced in the *cahiers*, make it difficult to give an exact figure to the membership of Abstraction-Création. As indicated in the preface of No. 4, the number of members varied, but was around fifty each year and about one hundred overall. The figure of 416 put forward by most historians is absurd.[14] This number stems from the simplistic addition of members and friends listed by arrondissement of Paris and by nationality, also in No. 4. It is obvious that these two statistics overlap and that the term 'friends' encompasses a very marginal public. This error has given credence to the idea that Abstraction-Création was a *pot-pourri* of non-figurative tendencies. Dora Vallier, in her work *l'Art Abstrait*, comments on these inexact figures: 'From that moment on, the artists converting to abstraction counted in their hundreds: 416 (painters and sculptors) at the 1935 exhibition, of whom 251 were French... This sudden expansion would have us believe in the triumph of abstraction.'[15]

Most retrospectives of non-figurative art have similarly contributed to a misunderstanding of the art of the 1930s, representing the closure of the Bauhaus in 1933 as the end of earlier avant-gardes and symbolic of European aesthetic decline. Yet it was precisely the decline of the avant-garde in Russia, Hungary, Austria and Germany that set the circumstances for the artistic expansion first in France, then in Switzerland, England, Italy, Scandinavia, and finally in the United States and Brazil.

Abstraction-Création bore witness not only to Parisian cosmopolitanism in the early 1930s, but also to different perspectives on a society in crisis and to the renewal of non-figurative art across generations. One of the legacies which remains poorly understood, though essential in the evolution of this non-objective art, came from a minority of artists who sought a difficult synthesis with aspects of Surrealism. Although hardly a rigorous selection, based as it was on friendship, these relationships brought to light some real talent. Some artists, such as Tutundjian, have been able to escape from oblivion thanks to their association with Abstraction-Création. Others, such as Max Bill, became leaders of postwar European art. Moreover, Abstraction-Création promoted young artists of all nationalities and made possible various artistic renewals outside France.

ANATOLE JAKOVSKI

HERBIN

Editions " Abstraction-Création "
26, Boulevard Masséna, PARIS-13e

Anatole Jakovski, *Herbin*, Paris, 1933, book.

Abstraction-Création, an open forum for aesthetic, political and social ideas

ABSTRACTION-CRÉATION consciously disseminated a heterogeneity of styles and theories. From 1933, it affirmed the individual expression of each non-figurative artist, without any censorship based on ideology, race or nationality: 'we devote *cahier* Nº 2 to the total opposition to all oppression, of whatever order it might be.' The politics of Freundlich, Hélion and Herbin, all members of the Association des Artistes et Ecrivains Révolutionnaires, never undermined their tolerance for conflicting opinions.[16] The *cahiers* of Abstraction-Création became an open forum for different tendencies and nationalities across generations. Their content reflected not only the group's aesthetic conflicts, but also diverse and contradictory views about the artist's role in modern society. One cannot mention here all these differing points of view, but the following example will give the tone of the journal's pages.

The simplistic formulation of the questionnaire published in *cahier* Nº 2 that asked, 'Why do you not paint nudes?... Is a locomotive a work of art?...' immediately irritated several artists who believed, along with Delaunay, that this discussion had the 'aim of enlightening an evening class.' In fact, these questions, which were prepared by Herbin and submitted to the approval of the committee, reflected above all the preoccupations of French abstraction. The confrontations between Art/Nature and Art/Machine, phrased in such terms, already appeared obsolete to younger followers of a non-objective art, as evidenced by numerous responses, notably those of Kobro and Moholy-Nagy.

From the very first edition, an article by Paul Vienney, a lawyer and Communist, belonging to the same cell as his friend Herbin, questioned the future of abstract art in a socialist society. He concluded that abstraction is divorced from the people and incapable of action. In his opinion, the artist escapes the sensory world without contesting the old order and, furthermore, conveys no absolute values appropriate to modern civilisation. To these attacks based on historical materialism, other artists responded with utopian idealism. Gorin and Vantongerloo saw the world economic and social crisis as the endpoint of a cycle and the beginning of a new era. For them, *Art plastique* was entirely appropriate for collectivist society, through its relationship with science (mathematics) and through its anonymity, as it dealt only with universal laws of reason. '"I, myself, me" are the signs of the old civilisation. Anonymity will be the sign of the new era. All work will be for the benefit of society.'[17] While Gorin and Vantongerloo believed that individualism led to anarchy, Herbin, in contrast, considered it to be the guarantee of creative freedom. 'Must we destroy the official art of capitalism to replace it with another official art?' he wrote. 'The Revolution and its final outcome, communist society, cannot to any degree adopt a stance which is contrary to its essential aim of freedom... Art remains based on character and the artist is still, first and logically, alone against the world.'[18] As for Gleizes, collectivism lay within the framework of a *retour à la terre* (return to the soil), a return to artisanship and to a spiritual quest. The community he founded in Moly-Sabata in 1927 lived according to these principles. For them, mechanisation had destroyed the spark of spirituality within man, and consequently the artist's duty was to search both within himself and within the grand tradition of painting (notably the Roman fresco) for the means to embody a sense of the Divine.

A conversation at cross-purposes, indeed, which makes clear that the path from abstraction to concrete art led to an evolution in the religio-philosophical principles of art. The theosophy which permeated the thinking of older artists was replaced by materialism. The work of art no longer responded to divine principles and universal laws, but reflected the demands of science, technologies and optical laws. For a minority of non-figurative artists, just as for the Surrealists, art was in the service of revolution.[19] For others, the work of art had no significance or sense beyond itself. This evolution of aesthetic ideas and the emergence of a pure formalism would have pictorial and material consequences.

Abstraction-Création, a renewal of the avant-garde of the 1920s

THE SPECIFICALLY FRENCH core of Abstraction-Création came for the most part from Cubism, which during the 1920s hovered between abstraction and a return to figuration, as in the work of Gleizes, E. Hone and M. Jellet, Herbin, Valmier, Villon, Reth and Delaunay. This current had been supported in *l'Effort Moderne*, the gallery and journal run by Léonce Rosenberg, which explains why the first committee, including among others Herbin and Valmier, had published a text by Rosenberg in *cahier* Nº 1 of Abstraction-Création.

The work of J.W. Power, supported by Léonce Rosenberg since 1924, belonged in this post-Cubist camp, combining abstraction with a 'surreality of the modern spirit', not dissimilar to Valmier and Prampolini. In Rosenberg's view, 'abstract art, figurative or not, is the highest point in the spiritual evolution of a civilisation, and cannot, as all other authentic expressions of the past, live in the love of men except through humanity, science and the imagination of the worker.'[20] Nevertheless, this 'in-between aesthetic' which sought a balanced humanist expression by resisting the extremes, evolved significantly. The year 1930 marked a turning point. Through contact with the increasing number of foreign artists in Paris, this tendency became more radical, as it abandoned abstraction in favour of non-objective art (without reference to nature or to the object). It did so through the use of pure colours applied in solid areas without gradation; the geometric rendering, simplification and precision of forms; a renunciation of the illusion of depth and an affirmation of the picture plane; and a rhythmic emphasis on line or the adoption of biomorphism to express movement or living forms. This belated evolution of French abstraction, in comparison to international non-figurative tendencies,

auguste herbin .

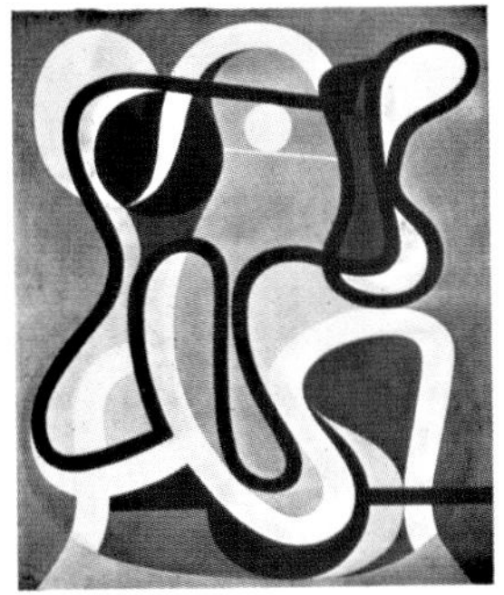

herbin a . 1931 .

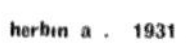

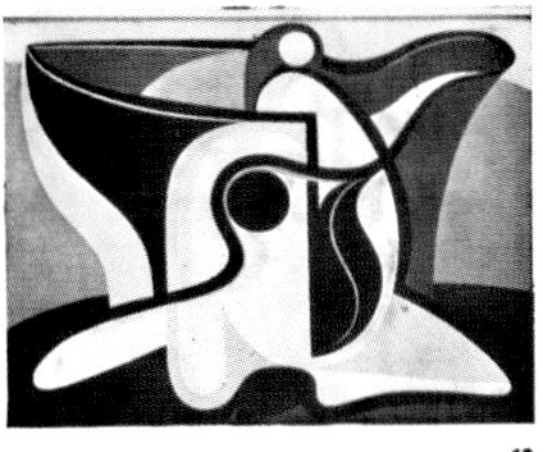

19

Abstraction-Creation cahier Nº 1, 1932

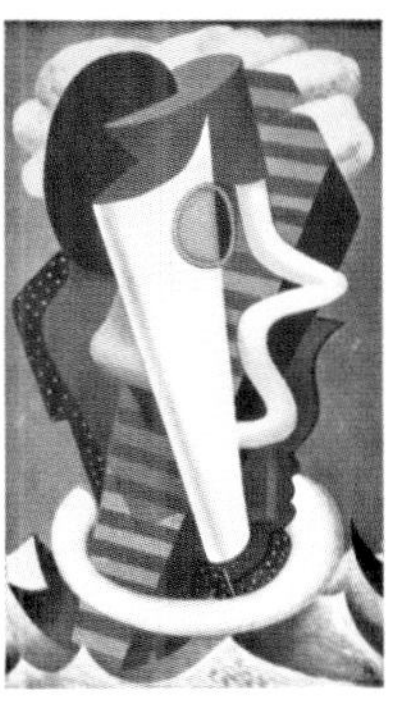

power j . 1931 .

john w . power .

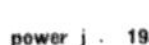

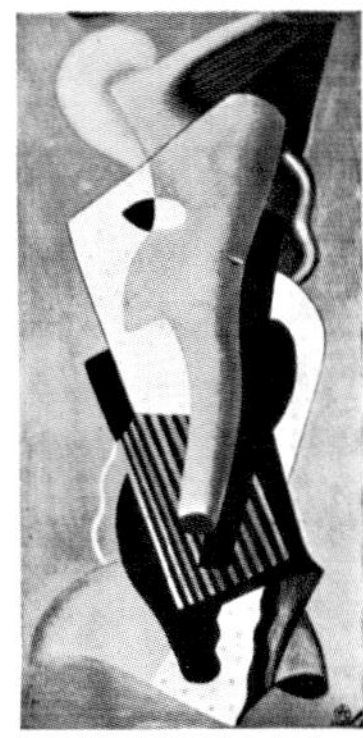

28

Abstraction-Creation cahier Nº 1, 1932

entailed a profound originality as each work is an individual expression, uncompromised by a collective style, school or movement. Such was the case in the linear Vitalism of Herbin's *Volutes*, in Power's arabesques, Prampolini's cosmic trajectories, and Villon's spiraling lines superimposed onto the 'splitting' of planar surfaces. Gleizes simply added rhythmic lines in white, black or grey to the 'translations and rotations of the plane' that he had first undertaken in 1924.

With *Rythme, Joie de Vivre* (1930), Robert Delaunay ushered in a new era. In his *Journal*, this painter summed up in a single pithy sentence his output of the 1920s. 'The human figure reclaims its rights. Portraits.' In other words this decade was not crucial for him. The *retour à l'ordre* (return to order) and financial necessities of the postwar period had pressured Delaunay to undertake portraits of numerous well-known personalities such as Soupault, Tzara, Hélène Marre and Madame Heim, while his wife Sonia Delaunay devoted herself to the decorative arts, which she continued to pursue in the 1930s. In contrast with Abstraction-Création, Delaunay broke with Cubist figuration and concerned himself with translating rhythm into clear, precise circular geometric forms, pure colours and diverse materials. His research would be applied to mural painting, following the recent work of De Stijl, the Bauhaus and the Constructivists, a current reinforced by the *Salons de l'Art Mural* and the *Exposition Internationale* of 1937.

This transformation was also apparent in Kupka. As he wrote in *cahiers* N° 1 and 2, 'A lesson in mechanisation, and I am back to where I was in 1912. New spirit, new technique.' Henceforth, the Czech painter looked less towards nature than to his own history of painting which would serve him as a basis of experimentation. 'The refinement of the initial concept involves that of working on a building site, so that legibility becomes easier, at the cost of abstracting all that is extraneous to organic unity... keep only the

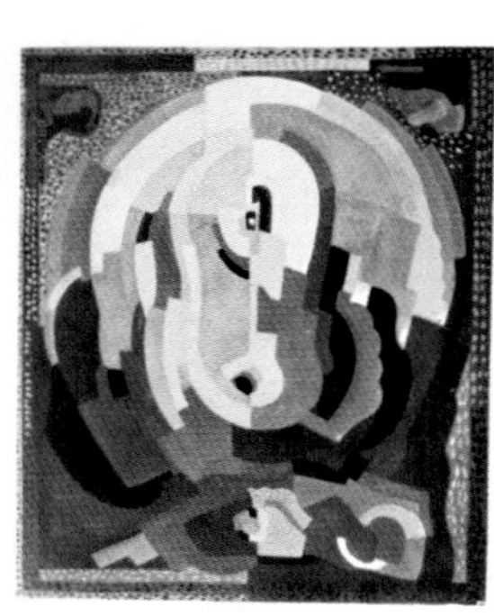

Hone 1932

Hélion

Comparer les tableaux aux arbres ? Il est grand temps de le faire. Nous avons trop aisément prétendu à la justification des grands mots. L'universel, le général, le permanent, etc., ne signifient rien de bien clair. N'en parlons plus pour quelque temps.

L'arbre est le type même de toute œuvre. Il commence dans le sol, masse opaque et lourde. Il croît dans l'espace, masse transparente et légère. Il naquit d'un point qui fut la graine et qui contenait le module et le schéma de son devenir. Il pousse, tâte le sol aux environs, tâtonne et tout de même prend de la vitesse, sort, monte, se répand et suit, dans l'espace, toutes sortes d'attractions et de répulsions qui rectifient sa forme élémentaire.

Il s'efforce de faire face le plus largement possible à l'espace. Il s'arrête de croître lorsqu'il a atteint l'équilibre entre la force projetante qu'il avait reçue de sa graine et l'inertie du sol.

L'aventure d'un tableau n'est-elle pas à cette image ? Le sol est à la fois la surface et les couleurs : l'espace est à la fois celui que le peintre réussit à développer entre les couleurs celui qui fait face à la toile et celui qu'embrassent les idées de son temps.

Le tableau naît, comme l'arbre, de l'action de l'attraction de l'espace sur l'idée-graine initiale. Le peintre s'efforce de développer sa petite idée première devant l'espace. Elle est à son image, grande ou petite, mais chacun peut reconnaître si le tableau qui en est issu a été mené aussi loin qu'il pouvait aller dans le triple espace des couleurs, des regards et des idées.

Il ne s'agit pas de copier l'apparence des arbres ni d'imiter leur façon de pousser. Pourtant, c'est dans la mesure où l'artiste s'efforce de maintenir entre ce triple espace, son tableau et son idéologie une continuité aussi profonde que celle qui unit la graine, l'arbre et l'espace ambiant, que son travail risque d'être plus qu'un hasardeux coloriage.

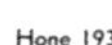

Hone 1932

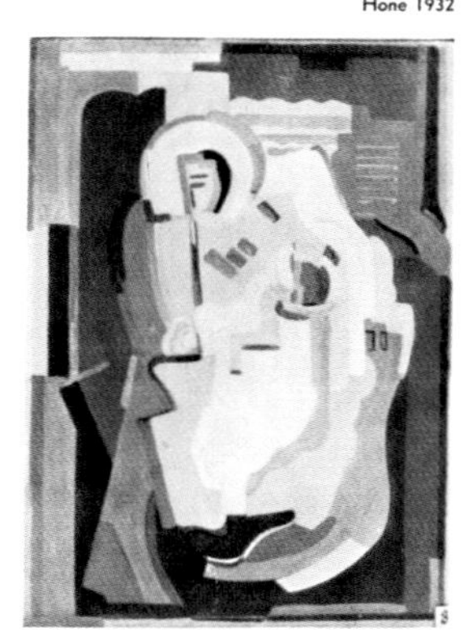

20

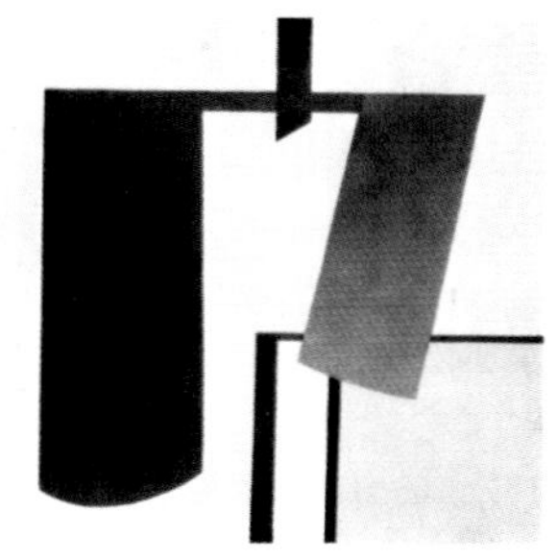

Hélion 1933

Hélion 1933

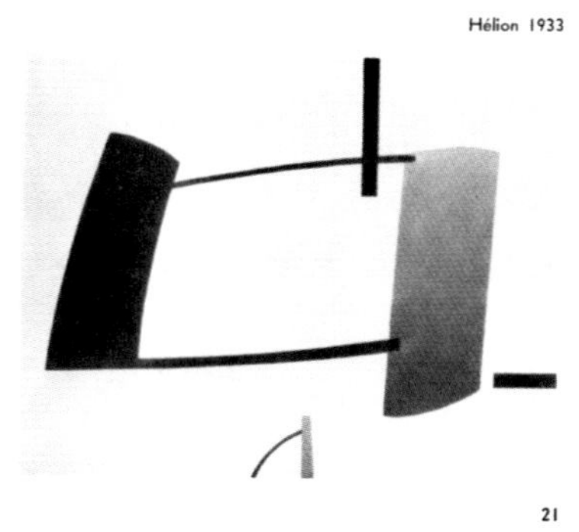

21

Abstraction-Creation cahier N° 2, 1933

elemental qualities...' This idea of stripping back was applied by Kupka through his palette and by his use of a kind of impasto. Aided by his cold and precise technique, he moved towards the simplification and geometric rendering of forms that had, until then, often been baroque. The illusion of the third dimension was rejected in favour of an affirmation of the picture plane. Finally, this was the period when Kupka turned from Hinduism to study Greek philosophy: Plato and Pythagoras. The titles of his works *Eudia* (1933) and *Equation des bleus en mouvement* (1929–31) attest to this change of direction, an influence not unknown among Neoplasticist artists in France. Kupka knew how to adapt certain characteristics of international non-figurative art to his work. Indeed, he pushed it to its most absolute and most innovative in *Peinture abstraite* (1930–32) as illustrated by the twelve black-and-white gouaches reproduced in *cahier* N° 2, remarkable for their minimal formalism and organisation of open space.

As is seen in Kupka's evolution from 1930 onwards, the new direction taken by non-figurative painting drew on aesthetic ideas long advocated by Neoplasticism, the most established of the foreign movements in France. At the heart of Abstraction-Création, the devotees of Neoplasticism and Elementarism consequently formed a group with Mondrian, van Doesburg, Vantongerloo, van der Leck and their young followers: Domela, Vordemberge-Gildewart, Gorin, Moss, Hélion and his American friend Einstein (1930-32). Once again, the art of the 1930s was not content with the slavish repetition of its precursors, but found new and sometimes revolutionary solutions. Shortly before his death, van Doesburg began developing an art based on seriality – as in *Composition arithmétique* (1930) – which had previously been explored in the abstract cinema of Hans Richter. At the same time, he ushered in a concept of open space that would later be pursued by Vordemberge-Gildewart.

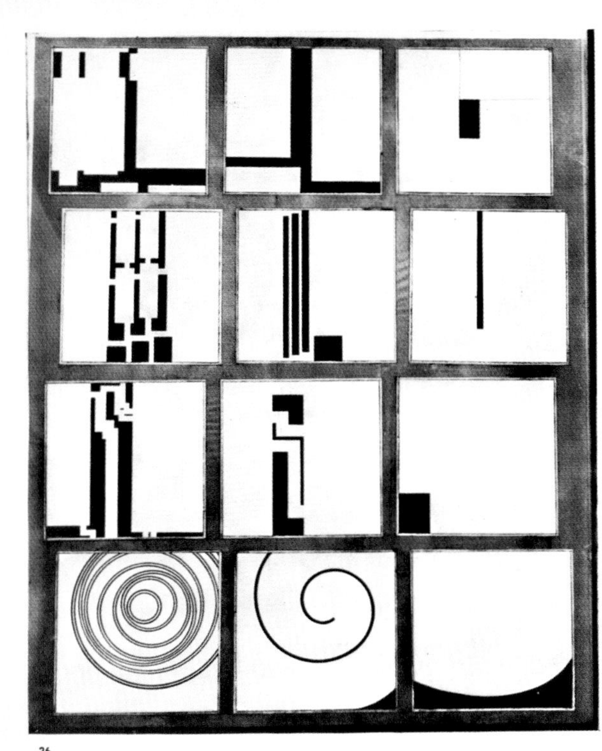

26

Kupka. Abstractions.

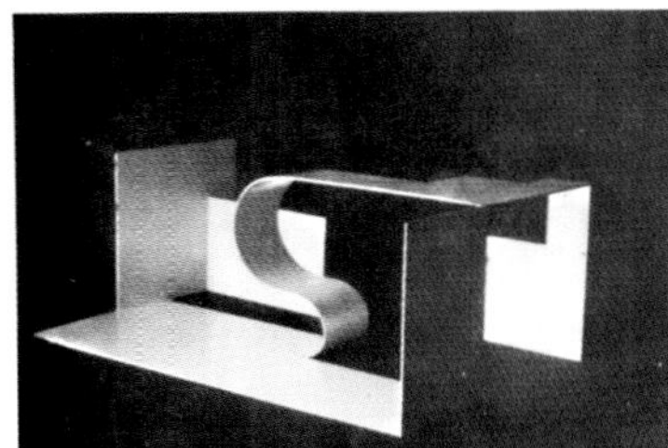

Kobro 1930

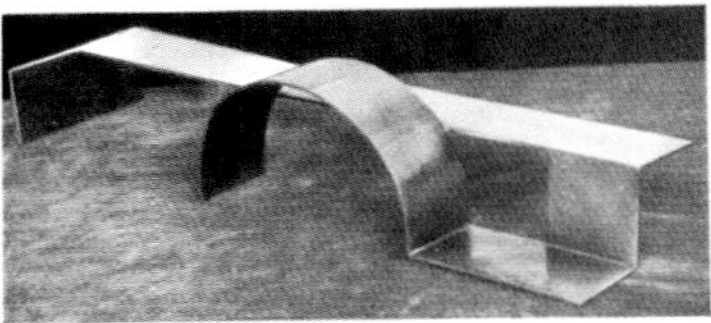

Kobro 1931

Kobro

1. L'action de sculpter un nu donne des émotions d'ordre physiologique ou sexuel. Je sculpte d'après nature, comme on va au cinéma pour se mieux reposer. J'aime m'amuser, en corrigeant ce qui n'était pas terminé dans n'importe quel mouvement de l'art ancien.

2. Un arbre a une forme inexacte et due au hasard. Puisque je tends vers le concret, les arbres n'ont aucune influence sur mon travail.

3. La locomotive n'est pas une œuvre d'art, puisque, lors de sa construction, on a voulu son bon fonctionnement et non pas l'harmonie de la forme. La locomotive n'est pas une œuvre d'art, si ce n'est que pour cette raison que pour être utile, elle est symétrique. Cela n'empêche que, pour un artiste, elle peut donner davantage qu'un arbre. La locomotive a une forme plus humaine, c'est l'œuvre de l'homme.

4. La valeur d'une œuvre d'art ne dépend pas de sa ressemblance à un produit de la technique, mais de la perfection de forme artistique. Toute machine atteint son but au moyen du mouvement, qui coupe l'espace. La tendance de la composition dans l'espace est de s'unir avec l'espace.

5. L'imitation de la machine est aussi nuisible, que l'imitation du monde animal. L'une et l'autre empêche le développement d'une forme purement plastique et abstraite.

27

Abstraction-Creation cahier N° 2, 1933

Hélion justified this new aim in *Art Concret*: 'The notion of the infinite universe negates the "enclosure" of the picture in its frame, to replace it with a picture that continues indefinitely, both within and beyond the frame.' Domela focused on works in relief, in which he played with the effects of materials and colour, utilising different metals, and occasionally electric light. In the late 1930s, both he and Vantongerloo began incorporating curved lines into their Neoplastic worlds. Moss gradually freed herself from the influence of Mondrian. In 1931, she preceded him in adopting "the double line" to add dynamism to her compositions. Then in 1936, she completed a white monochrome relief structured with string.

Polish Unism, developed by Strzeminski and his wife, the sculptor Katarzyna Kobro, emerged as a uniquely innovative expression. It advocated a materialist formalism founded on both 'the eye and the spirit'. Physiology and optical laws were combined with an historical awareness of perception. Strzeminski's Unist painting aimed to abolish oppositions between the figure and background, composition, dynamic tension or colour contrast, in favour of the organic unity of the work, grasped in its totality through an immediate reading, without extra-pictorial interpretations based in spirituality or idealism. This radical artistic autonomy became an important achievement of the 1930s.It allowed the younger generation of artists to work from exclusively formal, even optical, criteria, while taking into consideration the visual and cultural aspects of reception and the creative role of the viewer.

Faced with the dangers of excessive ornamentation, as previously condemned by Le Corbusier and Ozenfant in *Après le cubisme* (1918), advocates of formal autonomy sought to justify their art by drawing on the sciences, as in the fourth dimension, Gestalt or the theory of form, and on mathematical laws,

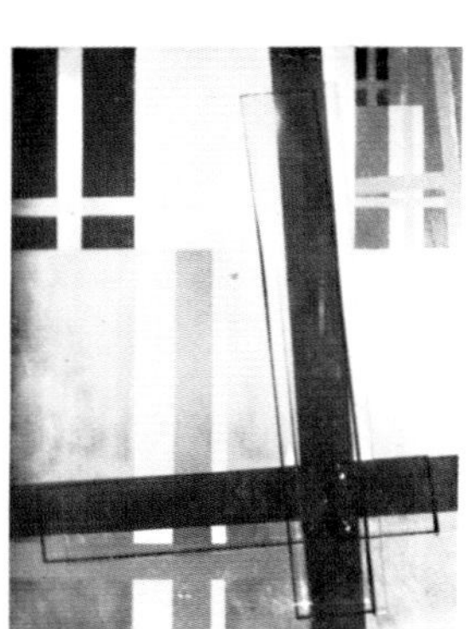

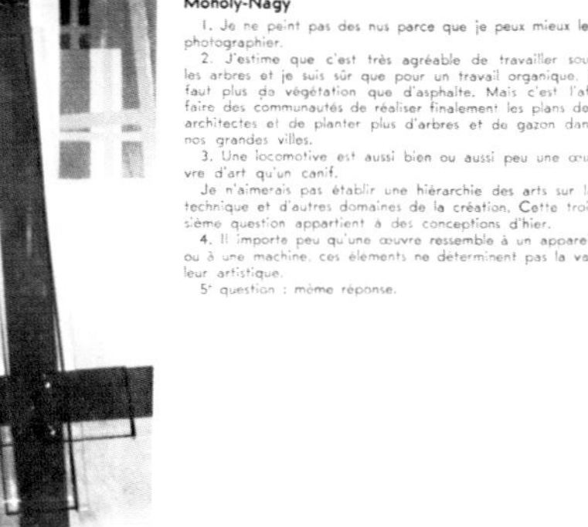

Moholy-Nagy

1. Je ne peint pas des nus parce que je peux mieux les photographier.

2. J'estime que c'est très agréable de travailler sous les arbres et je suis sûr que pour un travail organique, il faut plus de végétation que d'asphalte. Mais c'est l'affaire des communautés de réaliser finalement les plans des architectes et de planter plus d'arbres et de gazon dans nos grandes villes.

3. Une locomotive est aussi bien ou aussi peu une œuvre d'art qu'un canif.

Je n'aimerais pas établir une hiérarchie des arts sur la technique et d'autres domaines de la création. Cette troisième question appartient à des conceptions d'hier.

4. Il importe peu qu'une œuvre ressemble à un appareil ou à une machine, ces éléments ne déterminent pas la valeur artistique.

5e question : même réponse.

Moholy-Nagy 1925

Moholy-Nagy 1926

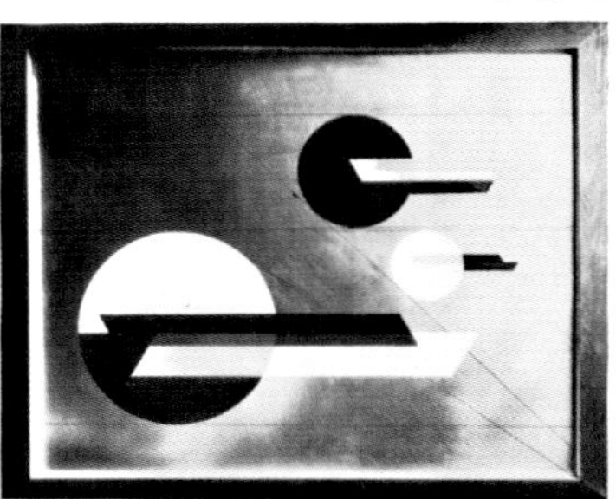

30

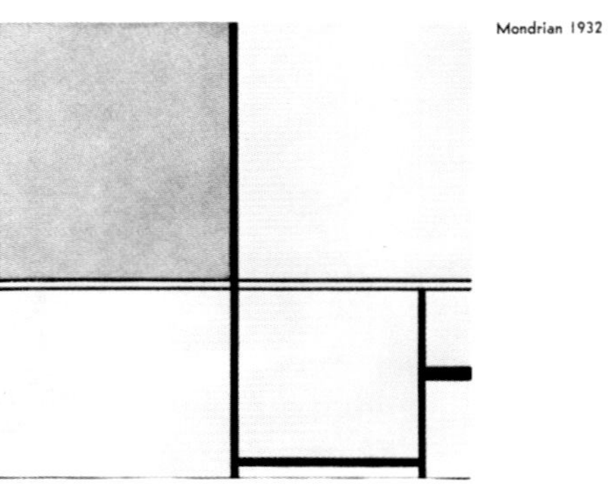

Mondrian 1932

Mondrian

L'Efficacité artistique d'une œuvre est non seulement déterminée par sa valeur artistique, mais aussi par le caractère de la représentation figurative : sujet, formes naturelles ou abstraites.

Bien que la valeur artistique soit identique dans chaque vraie œuvre d'art : éternelle, indépendante de la représentation figurative, celle-ci est d'une telle importance qu'elle détermine l'expression de cette valeur totalement. Étant changeable, la représentation figurative transforme constamment l'expression purement artistique : la capacité artistique se sert en cours du temps toujours d'autres formes ou les crée. Dans cette action réciproque, il faut donc distinguer deux valeurs : la valeur artistique et la valeur des moyens d'expression.

Il est donc clair que pour la mentalité moderne, l'œuvre à l'apparence d'une machine ou d'une création technique ajoute à son efficacité artistique par sa représentation figurative plus abstraite, c'est-à-dire par ses formes plus exactes, son manque de lyrisme classique ou romantique, etc... Cependant, c'est la valeur artistique qui détermine dans quelle mesure cette nouvelle « figuration » est annihilée et transformée en œuvre d'art.

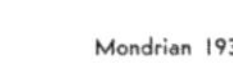

Mondrian 1932

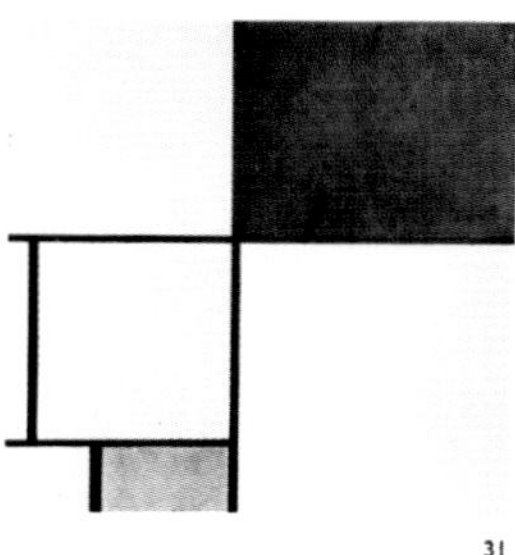

31

Abstraction-Creation cahier N° 2, 1933

seen either as a principle of universal harmony dating back to Classical Greece, or as evidence of progressive attitudes. Consequently, following the Section d'Or exhibitions of 1912, 1920 and 1925, several publications took up the question of the use of mathematics in art, of which the following examples are by no means exhaustive. Severini's *Du cubisme au classicisme*, which Ozenfant criticised in *L'Esprit Nouveau* (no. 17, 1922) for replacing 'the mysticism of the senses with that of the golden section or the triangle', while nonetheless extolling the regulating line as 'a guarantee against arbitrariness'. That same year saw the publication of the essay *Den gudomliga geometrien* (Divine geometry), 1922 by Gosta Adrian Nilsson, a Swedish friend of Fernand Léger living in Paris between 1920 and 1925. Several members of Abstraction-Création were also involved in this research, either prior to or following M.C. Ghyka's *L'Esthétique des proportions dans la nature et les arts* (1927) and *Le Nombre d'Or* (1931).

Vantongerloo's studies in *De Stijl* (no. 9, July 1918), his book *L'art et son avenir* (1924), and various articles written in Menton in 1926 and 1927 are thus significant milestones. Béothy had also applied the golden mean to an architectural project in 1919 which was later revised as a sculpture. In 1926, he undertook a study on *La série d'Or*, which was translated into French in 1932 and published in 1939. The Hungarian artist acknowledged discussing these issues with his associates during the Abstraction-Création period. In Poland, the *Compositions architecturales* (1928-29) that Strzeminski completed prior to developing Unism, as well as the sculptures of Kobro, were similarly devised through the calculation of proportions. Hélion, for his part, published an article entitled 'Art et Mathématique' in *Art Concret* (1930), in which reproductions of one of his drawings and of a variation on van Doesburg's *Composition arithmétique* demonstrate their approach. Finally, Mondrian, although not a supporter of the application

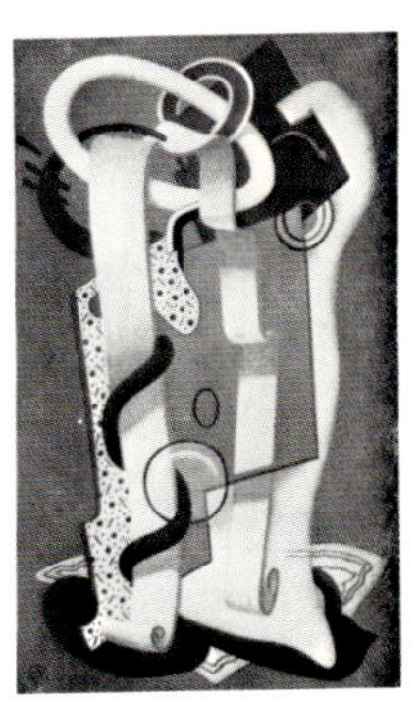

Power 1932

Prampolini

Notre temps, caractéristiquement futuriste, apparaîtra distinct dans l'histoire de l'art par la divinité nouvelle : la Machine (Manifeste de l'art mécanique — Prampolini — Mars 1923, Rome, Revue « Noi »).

La vieille esthétique se nourrissait de legendes, de mythes et d'histoire, produits médiocres de collectivités aveugles et esclaves. L'esthétique futuriste se nourrit des plus puissants et complexes produits du génie humain. La Machine est bien le symbole le plus riche de la mystérieuse force créatrice humaine. De la Machine et à travers la Machine se développe tout le drame humain.

Nous autres, futuristes, imposons à la Machine de surpasser sa fonction pratique pour s'élever dans la vie spirituelle et désintéressée de l'Art, et devenir ainsi une sublime inspiratrice.

L'artiste qui ne veut pas s'effondrer dans l'imprécis et dans le plagiat doit aimer seulement la vie qu'il vit et l'atmosphère qu'il respire.

L'unique modèle est la « machine », fille nécessaire de l'homme, nécessaire prolongement du corps humain et unique maître de simultanéité.

Il faut distinguer entre forme extérieure et esprit de la Machine.

Par esthétique de la machine, nous entendons la splendeur géométrique et numérique faite de synthèse, d'ordre

Power 1932

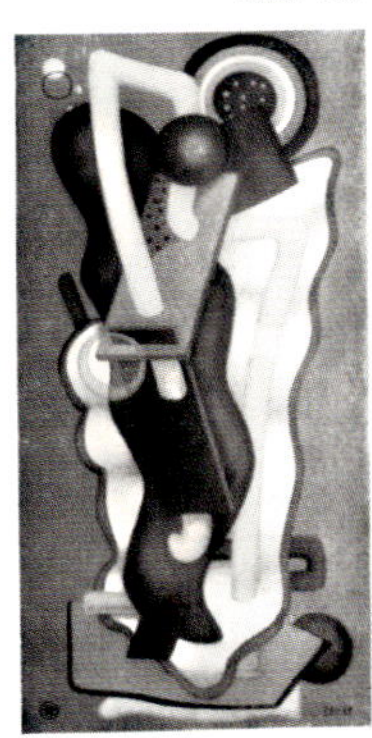

Power

Est-ce qu'une locomotive est une œuvre d'art ?

Non pas ! — une locomotive n'est pas une œuvre d'art. Une œuvre d'art, c'est une harmonie créée comme fin en soi, et un artiste est quelqu'un qui s'occupe « seulement » de l'harmonie des formes et des couleurs comme fins en soi.

Si l'harmonie des formes est le résultat d'une fonction pratique, comme, par exemple, la vitesse, la légèreté, solidité, cela n'est pas une fin en soi, c'est plutôt un moyen vers un but. Donc ce n'est pas une œuvre d'art.

C'est bien possible qu'il soit une partie d'une machine où l'auteur soit libre de choisir la courbe la plus belle, la proportion la plus fine, et cet élément seul peut avoir une valeur esthétique, mais s'il permettait qu'une valeur esthétique l'emporte sur la fonction pratique, il serait un mauvais ingénieur ; et, s'il est un mauvais ingénieur, c'est beaucoup mieux qu'il soit mort.

Un artiste, en regardant une machine parfaite, peut être inspiré et créer une œuvre d'art, mais ça c'est autre chose.

36

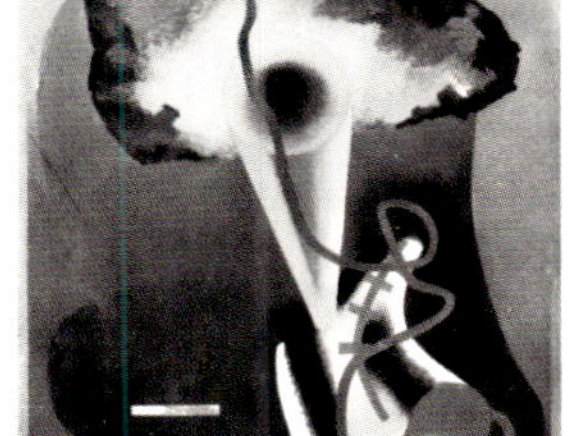

Nous n'en savons rien.
Ainsi était dieu.
L'homme —
Dieu —
Le fils de l'homme —
Le fils de dieu —
Le nom de dieu —
et cætera.

Pour créer la terre
il a copié les cieux.
Pour couronner l'œuvre
il s'est copié lui-même.
Sacré copiste de bon dieu.
L'Homme
est venu sur terre.
L'homme a chanté :
L'eau.
Voici ma sœur,
pure, simple, précieuse.
Le vent.
Voici mon frère,
sauvage, aimable.
Le feu.
Voici mon enfant,
beau, clair, gai.
La lune.
Voici ma femme,
beaux seins de montagne,
jolis trous de cratères.

Prampolini 1932

Prampolini 1932

d'essentiel, de précision d'engrenages, de mouvement, de donner-avoir, de continuité, de régularité. Cette esthétique est basée sur « l'esprit » de la machine et non sur la machine elle-même : « simultanéité de forces » qui aspirent toujours plus à leur organisation.

Séligmann

Tradition.
Au commencement
dieu
créa les cieux et la terre.
La terre
était informe, vide — rien.
Dieu
se mouvait au-dessus des eaux
(idées futures des hommes à créer.)

Verdâtre,
tacheté de rouge,
sous la ceinture
la trinité
prête à jaillir —
couronné d'un pot de tôle émaillée
et d'un bicorne d'aviateur,
tombé dans une guerre pré-biblique.

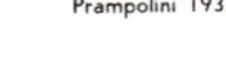

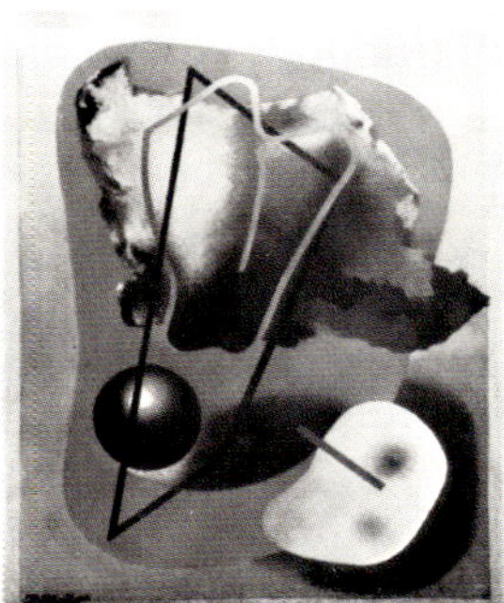

37

Abstraction-Creation cahier N° 2, 1933

of mathematics in art, introduced Schiess, a Swiss member of Abstraction-Création, to D'Arcy W. Thompson's *Growth and Form* (1917) and to the English journal *The Diagonal* (1919–20), edited by Jay Hambidge, who had studied dynamic symmetry in Greek art. From this brief overview, it can be seen that Power's book *Éléments de la construction picturale* (1932) was anchored not only to the spirit of the times, but also to the Abstraction-Création camp. Power's choice to work with the group's printer and publisher, Antoine Roche, and the inclusion in *cahier* Nº 2 of Balandier's article 'Abstraction + Création = Musique', reinforce this analysis, particularly when considering that Power, a talented pianist, was passionate about music. Balandier took up one of the ancient thesis, first advanced in the early 1910s through Canudo's written texts and Kupka's paintings, advocating music as a model for all the arts. He lauded Pythagorean harmony as an ordering principle for the universe, advocated by the eternal thought of the great 'initiates'. Faced with the chaos 'of an unbridled materialism', he concluded that 'in all the arts, let us be "musicians" of numbers and we will be become pure spirits, not only liberators, but necessarily and above all, liberated.'

In the face of this shared concern to develop an artistic autonomy, detached from all representations of the external world and symbolism, mathematics was valued in diverse ways, its impact varying according to the particular sensibility and outlook of each artist. While all saw mathematics as a precision instrument and a didactic working method, the Masonic or theosophical artists also retained the esoteric 'quality' of Numbers. Others, such as Béothy or Power, were committed to the 'truth' of numbers, that is, of a harmonic relationship to the cosmos. Finally, the materialist and formalist artists, such as Hélion in 1930, considered mathematics an indispensable tool in developing concepts of

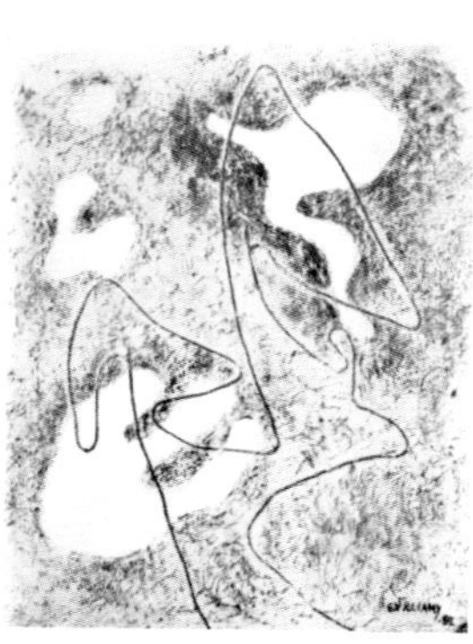

Vulliamy 1932

Vulliamy

L'être humain a peur d'engendrer contre nature. Il vit dans un état fiévreux à 40, suant à l'ombre des jeunes filles en fleurs, en les peignant maladives et chétives croyant que le Nu est beau et existe.

Quelle attitude prendre après cela ? Peindre et rester figé comme un poteau... ou se mettre en contact psychique avec le Nu. Prenez garde au courant ! Danger de mort.

... Pour me dompter et me désennuyer devant la fadaise d'un Nu je rugis dans un verre de lampe. En dernière edition sont les assassinats. Que faire entre ces deux attractions ? Crier au scandale devant l'art pour vieux messieurs devenu monotone et réduit... à dix sous pour militaires et bonnes d'enfant..

Devant la lâcheté et la stupidité de nos prédécesseurs il nous faut assassiner le Nu. Mettons alors des gants blancs de chef de rayon au contact de la laideur humaine : our contraste de formes, car j'ai peur de me perdre dans les tuyaux du radiateur... Du nu devenu article de fin de saison... Fermé pour cause de deuil.

Que penser devant pareil état de choses ? Se laisser choir et s'asseoir en prenant garde à la peinture... dans son esprit en fumant des bleues... pureté.

Devenons purs et créons. Du sens interdit, courrons à l'unique, pour aller vers l'esprit créatif et intellectuel. Le Nu n'existe plus, mais peut devenir une source de formes pures et émouvantes engendrées à travers l'émotion intellectuelle d'un état psychique. — Prenons alors de la jouvence de l'abbé Soury et rajeunissons la peinture qui ne doit plus être un art de reproduction. — Mais j'aime volontiers désaltérer mon esprit créatif à la source du Nu qui me procure par métamorphose des êtres abstraits en forme de sinusoïdes ou d'autres se mouvant dans l'espace.

Vulliamy

50

Wadsworth 1932

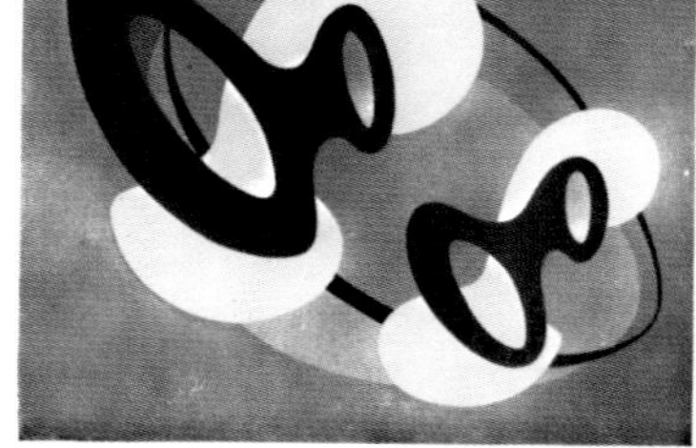

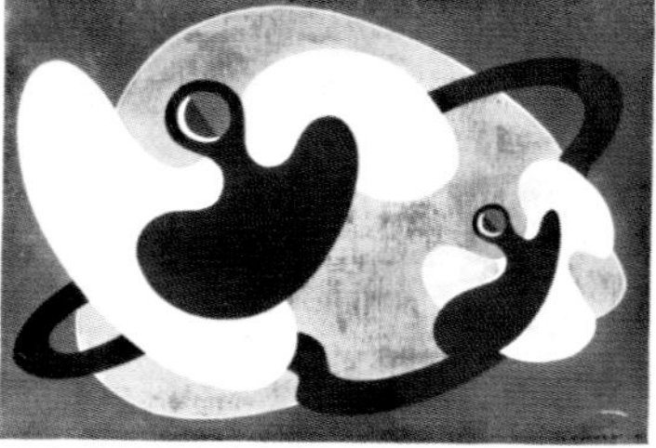

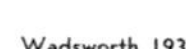

Wadsworth 1932

51

Abstraction-Creation cahier Nº 2, 1933

space-time appropriate to modernity. As he wrote in *Art Concret*, 'The Theory of Relativity specified that there is no fixed point in the universe, nor a fixed space, and that variable time itself is an essential dimension. But time exists in a painting, in that one cannot see it "in a single glance".' Many artists also fluctuated and evolved between these different points of view, often satisfying themselves with a certain theoretical vagueness, and leaving a good deal up to intuition.

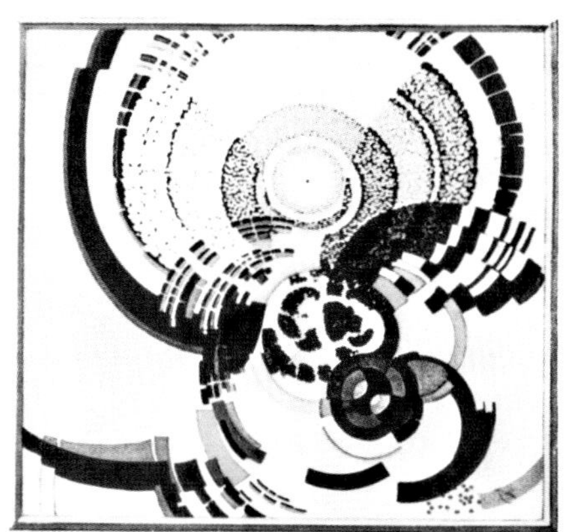

Kupka 1911-30

Kupka

l'art, habileté de saisir la Nature ?
Savants ! Cinéastes !
l'art de la transfigurer, transposer ?
Ignorants, ignorants. Fous.
Art quand même. Imaginer, créer
(Sujet dans l'objet.) Absolu, logique.

28

Kandinsky 1932

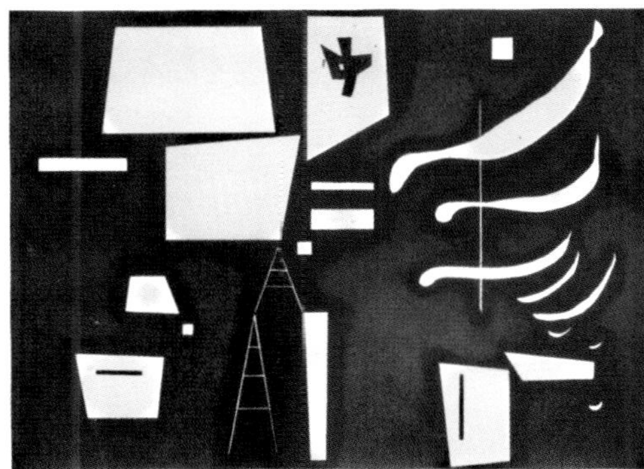

29

Abstraction-Creation cahier N° 3, 1934

A new route: an art of synthesis

CHALLENGING THEIR ELDERS, an important minority of young artists stood out in seeking a possible synthesis with Surrealism. However, Abstraction-Création, as with its predecessors Cercle et Carré and Art Concret, emerged as a rival movement. Seuphor had gathered around him all the tendencies of the avant-garde with the exception of Surrealism, which he wanted to oppose. 'I understand by Surrealism ... that little piece of shit which each of us has in his heart, to quote one of their own,' he wrote in *cahier* Nº 1. Equally vicious attacks were penned by van Doesburg in Art Concret's *revue*.

> 'Instead of dreams, the art of the future will be based on science and technique. We have the experiments by fakers of painting that show the dream is a false prophet in the field of the plastic arts. The aim of painting is not to expose one's vices or to undress in front of the viewer... Painting in the style of Jack the Ripper might be interesting to detectives, criminologists, psychologists and psychiatrists. It remains, and will remain, removed from modern life, removed from our social and artistic needs; it bears no relation to our architectural spirit and our constructive intelligence.'

In the face of these frankly hostile positions, the attitude of Abstraction-Création towards Surrealism became at once more ambiguous and more tolerant. It reflected the dilemma facing many young artists working between non-figuration and Surrealism, or even in both genres simultaneously, in a transitional period of experimentation.

Tutundjian emerged as a prime example. From 1925, his formal vocabulary simultaneously included geometric figures and dreamlike, biomorphic forms. In parallel with the precise reliefs that Tutundjian exhibited at the Galerie May in 1929, he also executed Surrealist

Power

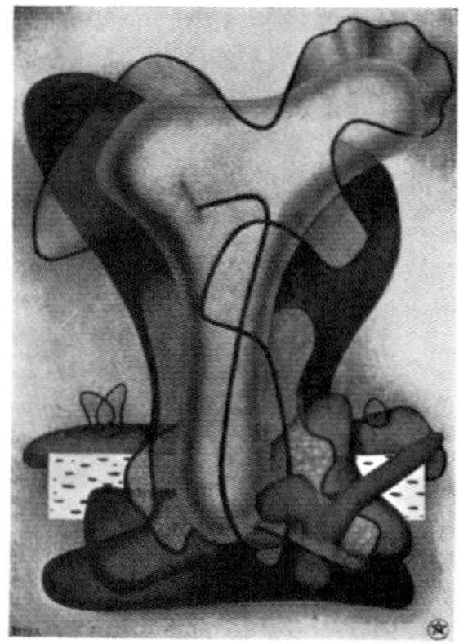

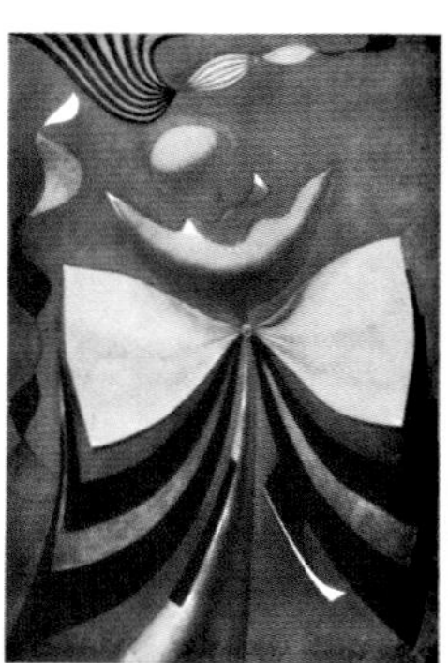

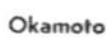
Okamoto

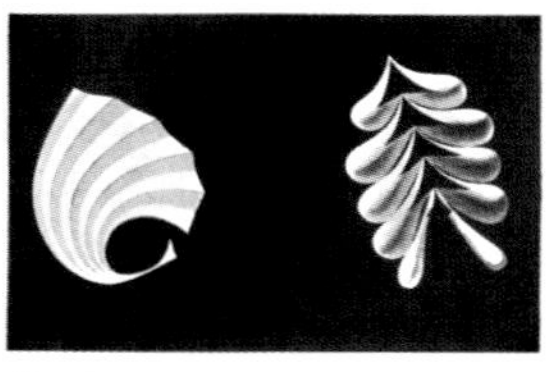
Okamoto

L'art abstrait était pour la jeunesse actuelle le moyen de s'évader de la réalité environnante ; le moyen de la remplacer par la couleur et les formes pures, les visions lyriques obsédantes.

Et si les yeux ne voyaient que la couleur de la joie, ils n'étaient plus des yeux. C'étaient des phares.

La réalité est l'expression perpétuelle du mouvement vital : la réalité picturale est la révolution permanente de la vision humaine.

Taro OKAMOTO.

Roubillotte 1936

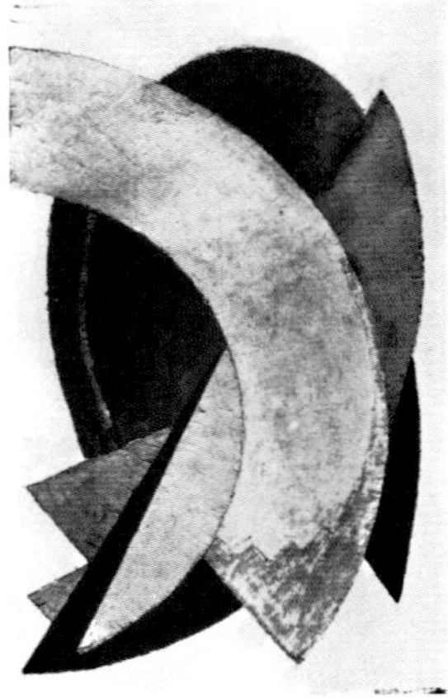

20 21

Abstraction-Creation cahier Nº 5, 1936

figurative drawings similar in style to Dali. Finally, he withdrew from Abstraction-Création in 1932, opting for Surrealism, as the painters Vulliamy, Paalen, Seligmann, Gorky and Okamoto would later do, all like Giacometti, who had never accepted the invitation to join Abstraction-Création.

Calder, too, synthesized this twofold influence of non-objective art and Surrealism throughout the 1930s. It is known that Mondrian exerted a deep influence on Calder following their first meeting in 1930, prompting Calder to relinquish the wire characters of his Circus in favour of non-objective painting. However, it was not Neoplasticism that attracted Calder, but, on the contrary, the poetic and informal universes of Tutundjian and Miro, both friends of his.[21] Several aspects of Miro's personality - his humour, his taste for simple materials salvaged from here and there and transformed according to dreams or chance - resonated with Calder. The *stabiles* he exhibited at the Galerie Percier in April 1931 project into three dimensions the poetic universe completely stripped of the inessential that one finds in the 'magnetic fields' of Miro.[22]

The majority of those members of Abstraction-Création inclined to lyrical expression, but varying in their commitment to the Surrealists, had been approached and supported by Arp. He was the only Surrealist in Cercle et Carré and was a particularly active member of Abstraction-Création. Arp refused to be bound by the categories of Surrealism and non-figurative art. He made his position known in a letter addressed to Brzekowski in 1929 and published in *l'Art Contemporain*. Surrealism only interested Arp insofar as it was devoid of any descriptive content, as an extension of Dada and a translation of emotion. He liked the technical anonymity of non-figurative art, and agreed with its premise that any work of art is a 'concretion' of creative thought without the imitation or abstraction of nature; but he disliked its lack of fantasy and intellectual coldness. 'It is an incomplete art

Power 1933

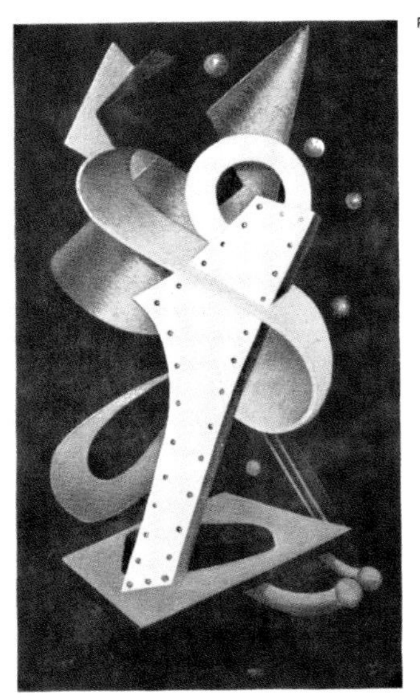

Power

.... Pour un véritable artiste, le sujet n'est qu'une excuse pour une composition toute formelle, une création pure et c'est à cause de cela, — à cause de cette recherche de la pureté absolue que l'artiste moderne fait le tableau sans sujet, le tableau-objet qui n'a rien à faire avec le monde extérieur mais qui reste une « fin-en-soi » — une création indépendante.

34

Ben Nicholson

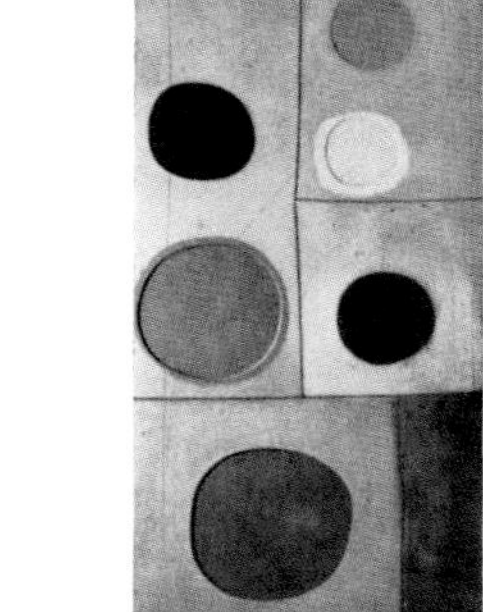

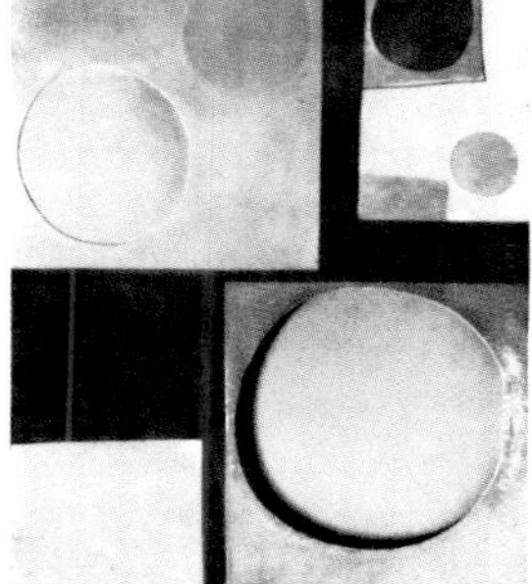

Ben-Nicholson

35

Abstraction-Creation cahier N° 3, 1934

which privileges the intellect to the detriment of the senses.' Arp adopted van Doesburg's understanding of Art Concret:

> 'Man calls abstract that which is concrete … I understand that one calls a Cubist painting abstract because the parts have been taken away from the object which served as a model for the painting. But I find that a painting or a sculpture which had no object as a model are just as concrete and sensual as a leaf or stone.'

This broad conception of Art Concret, which allowed for the inclusion of both non-figurative Surrealists and followers of geometric art, was adopted in 1936 by Max Bill in his preface to the exhibition catalogue *Zeitprobleme in der Schweizer Malerei und Plastik* (Current Problems in Swiss Painting and Sculpture) at the Kunsthaus in Zurich. Throughout the 1930s, it was used as a selection criterion for numerous exhibitions of non-objective art.

This desire for synthesis was evident in numerous works that melded apparent oppositions. Miro and his geometric reliefs, such as *Construction* (1930), and Max Bill and his lyrical wooden sculptures created in 1933 and 1934, reproduced in *cahier* Nº 4, are only some examples. Hans Erni invited artists as different as Arp, Braque, Calder, de Chirico, Derain, Ernst, Fernandez, Giacometti, Gonzales, Gris, Hélion, Kandinsky, Klee, Léger, Mondrian, Nicholson, Paalen, Picasso and Sophie Täuber-Arp to participate in the exhibition *These-Antithese-Synthese* in Lucerne in 1935, thus emphasising one of the essential aspects of the decade. In asking Hélion to write the preface for the exhibition catalogue, he also confirmed the renown of the young French painter, who represented a non-dogmatic non-figurative art, reconciling rationality and vitality. Abandoning an art based on mathematical and geometric progressions and the use of pure colour that he had prescribed in *Art Concret* (1930), Hélion defined his new approach:

> 'the superiority of nature is to present the maximum complexity of relationships. It is towards nature that I am making strides. On one hand, there are those who skirt desperately around nature without daring to enter, and on the other hand, those who, through elementary structures, try to develop a language.'[23]

His painting aroused great interest in England and in the USA where he influenced numerous artists. Myfanwy Evans, editor of the magazine *Axis*, was a fervent advocate of Hélion.

> 'His abstract painting is essentially organic, his massing and coordination of shapes is so alive that it is not even a symbol for life – it is a piece of life.'[24]

The confrontation between geometric art and Surrealism in the 1930s gave birth to an organic non-objective art, of which Arp was the undisputed father. 'The fog that is man refuses to be put in a corner,' he wrote in 1934, confirming, like many other artists such as Hepworth, Erni, Brignoni, Calder, Fischli, Freundlich and Paalen, that he preferred to follow a path in harmony with nature.

Furthermore, this tendency was shared across generations. It can be found in the evolution of Baumeister's formal vocabulary and, above all, in the biomorphism of Kandinsky's Parisian period. This organic concrete art, although very different in conception, ultimately converged in their work. This happened much sooner among the abstract artists, notably Brancusi, as well as Béothy. In this sense, it is sometimes difficult, and even absurd, to attempt to distinguish the work of an abstract painter or sculptor inspired by nature from that of a concrete artist who makes a poetic form. Art's labels often only name the inessential.

Abstraction-Création, a catalyst for non-figurative art in other countries

THE CLOSURE OF THE BAUHAUS, the rise of Nazism in Germany and finally the insecurity of Europe drove artists further and further west. They left Paris for London, and then Europe for the United States. Switzerland once again seemed to be a place of refuge and witnessed intense artistic activity: Dada in Zurich during the WW1 and Art Concret during the WW2. While Gropius (1934-37), Marcel Breuer (1935-37), Moholy-Nagy (1935-37), Naum Gabo and Mondrian (1938) spent time in London, and while Ozenfant opened a school there, the Swiss teachers (Klee, Itten, H. Meyer, 1936) and students of the Bauhaus (Bill, Fischli, Schiess, Hans Wittner, Schawinsky) returned to their country of birth. Hélène de Mandrot hosted artistic events in the Château de la Sarraz in Vaud, and a number of sculptors, architects, musicians and painters were invited to holiday there. Moholy-Nagy, Kandinsky, Schlemmer, Klee, Seuphor, Arp and Vordemberge-Gildewart found themselves in this haven of cultural exchange and peace. During the transitional period from 1931 until 1934, Abstraction-Création was the principal point for uniting artists in exile in Switzerland, England and the United States. Later, the first stirrings of local renewal occurred in numerous international groupings and in the formation of new movements: Groupe 33 (1933) and Allianz (1937) in Switzerland, Unit One (1933) in England and AAA (American Abstract Artists), (1936) in the USA. Abstraction-Création promoted the works of the principal artistic personalities who drove this renewal.

From one *cahier* to the next, one can see the progress and stylistic liberation of young artists. At the outset, the influence of Arp, for example, is evident in Barbara Hepworth, Erni and Seligmann, while Wadsworth and Power owe a great deal to Léger, and echoes of Picasso are evident in Vulliamy and Gorky.[25]

Power

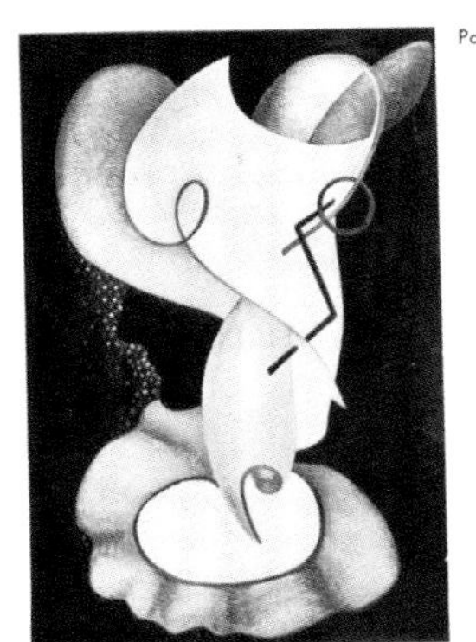

Power

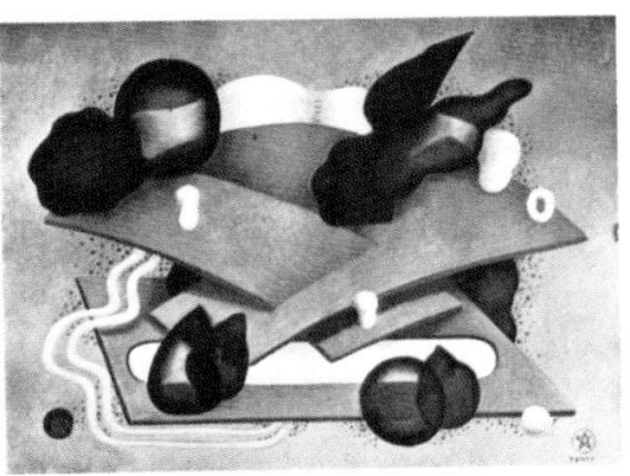

22

Melotti 1935

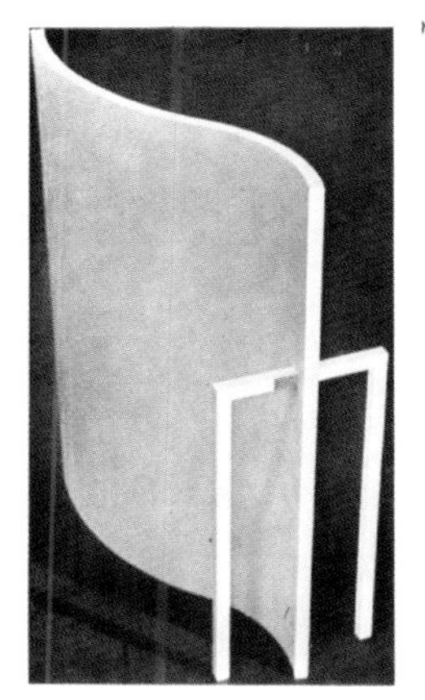

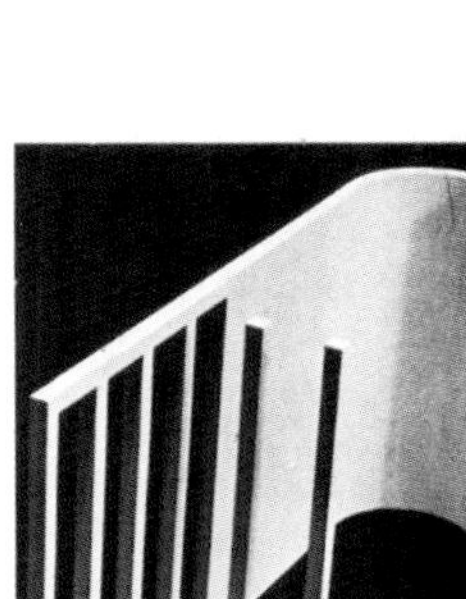

1935 Melotti

23

Abstraction-Creation cahier N° 4, 1935

The emerging renewal in Switzerland, England, and even in Scandinavia, provided new enriching experiences for this art of synthesis, of which Arp, Giacometti, Hélion and Calder were the most vocal advocates. 'Surrealism and Abstraction, the search for subjective form' was the title of an article published in *Axis* which neatly summarised one of the principal aims of English abstraction. *Axis* and *Circle* extolled the Swiss painter Erni, who, from 1935 onwards, asserted himself as one of the new protagonists of the synthetic tendency.[26] His influence on English painting is particularly marked in the work of Arthur Jackson, and raises the question of whether his balanced volumes, linked together in space through line, did not inspire, from 1937, the stringed figures of Henry Moore, even though, in principle, Moore refers uniquely to mathematical objects.

Another tendency of English and Swiss non-objective art followed stricter criteria derived from Constructivism, the Bauhaus or De Stijl. Moholy-Nagy had a particular impact in England, notably on Alastair Morton, Asley, Havinden and Paule Vézelay. Vézelay adopted for herself the multiplication of diagonal lines in order to create spatial illusions.

If, from the era of Abstraction-Création, Ben Nicholson emerged as the most original figure in English non-figurative art, Max Bill became the major driving force of this current in Switzerland. From 1934 onwards, Bill laid the foundations for an art which claimed to be purely formal, like Polish Unism, but from which it differed in its search for a systematic expression, starting from a basic material concept in order to develop seriality using geometrical and mathematical laws. *Construction en deux parties* (1934) and *Construction avec un cube suspendu* (1935-36) are the first milestones in this series of revolutions that present the same theme in different spaces (in two or three dimensions), or at another stage of material evolution. Bill's publication entitled *Quinze variations sur un même thème* (1935-38) announced this revolution: not only did it affirm purely formal aims, but it established seriality, in particular, as one of the fundamental bases of the concrete art of the future. The innovation therefore did not lie in Bill's specific example of the material application of serial progression, which others had done before him, but in his understanding of seriality, the modular element and the grid.[27] It was only towards 1939-42 that Bill's theories were considered by Swiss artists such as Lohse, Graeser and Vera Loewensberg, who sought a personal language through structural and serial systems.

The situation of art in Italy deserves special mention. Throughout the 1920s Italian art was dominated by Futurism and the Novecento, which were generally considered art of the state; one representing the avant-garde left, the other the conservative right. During this period of isolation only Pannaggi, Paladini and Prampolini were strongly influenced by European trends. The emergence of a rationalist trend in architecture (supported by the Groupe des 7 and the MIAR) and the development of a geometric tendency in the decorative arts facilitated the late burgeoning of a geometric style of painting, which recruited members from among the former painters of the Novecento and from students in the schools of applied arts. The rationalist principles of order, clarity, economy and functionality fit so poorly with Futurism that Carlo Belli, the spokesman of the new geometric art, considered his famous work *Kn* as 'the last dream of Romanticism'.[28] From 1934, geometric non-figuration competed with Futurism to be the state art of the avant-garde.

Prampolini and Sartoris worked towards expanding cultural relations between Italy and its neighbouring countries. As former members of the Union des Artistes Modernes and Cercle et Carré they effectively managed public relations. Furthermore, between 1930–32, Licini, Reggiani and Veronesi were able to visit Europe, and notably Paris. They thus had a direct knowledge of the different currents of the international avant-garde, some examples of which were shown in 1933 at Casa Bragalia in Rome. Finally, works of Vordemberge-Gildewart, Albers and Kandinsky were exhibited at the Galleria Il Milione in Milan in 1934. These contacts and events were decisive for painters at the schools in Como and Milan. Until then they had only known of contemporary art abroad through journals, particularly those of the Bauhaus. *cahier* Nº 5 of *Abstraction-Création* reproduced the very first, and initially awkward, abstract works by Veronesi, Reggiani, Bogliardi and Ghiringhelli. The influences of Moholy-Nagy on the painting of Veronesi and Manlio Rho, of Vordemberge-Gildewart on Reggiani and that of Kandinsky on Soldati, persisted until the war. Nevertheless, 1935 heralded the liberation of Italian non-figurative art, which, despite some derivative works, discovered its own direction. This date saw the opening at the Studio di Casorati e Paulucci in Turin of the *Prima mostra collettiva di arte astratta italiana* (First collective exhibition of Italian abstract art), an exhibition that already included fifteen participants. They had formulated precise aesthetic aims: 'lovers of order, we uphold the social function of the work of art. It is clear that the solution to the problem cannot reside in imitation, but ... in the field of pure creation.'[29]

In revealing to the world the existence of an Italian non-objective art, Abstraction-Création promoted genuine innovators such as Melotti and Fontana. As Maurizio Fagiolo remarked, they distinguished themselves from most non-figurative artists in Como and Milan by 'a point of subtle irrationality'. By remaining removed from the principles of the Bauhaus and geometric art in general, Melotti and Fontana were able to innovate and consequently drew closer to a *surréalisant* concrete art. According to Fontana, Melotti was one of the greatest sculptors of the interwar period. At first glance the sculptures of Melotti respond to the rationalist aesthetic. He aimed to achieve through his use of materials a harmonic presence in space. Passionate about music, he applied the art of counterpoint to sculpture. For him, 'the foundations of material harmonics and counterpoint are found in geometry'.[30] The purity of elementary geometric forms is not contrasted with any tactile value. His works are realised, like those of Kobro, in a smooth anonymous material painted white or metal. The irrational element that one encounters in many of his works, the open space that creates a strange and poetic atmosphere, are explained by the genesis of his work. Melotti began his career with metaphysical, Surrealist drawings of monumental arcades, rocks with windows, and mysterious boxes. At first, the style of these sketches approaches that of a Surrealist Picasso, de Chirico, Miro, or indeed Giacometti. A timeless, weighty and enigmatic atmosphere bathes these bizarre architectural structures. Throughout the years 1932–36, these themes were revised, pared back and rendered geometric, and the style became more precise and dry, without cast shadows. His sculptures could then emerge like the three-dimensional working drawing of a rationalised dream universe, like a harmonic presence in a timeless space.

Fontana, like Melotti, searched for the elementary but adopted an *anti-plastique* style marked by a deliberate awkwardness and by being open to chance and experimentation. His shaky drawing style bears a relation to graffiti, to those spontaneous marks that man has throughout history projected onto the wall to appropriate space. It is the instant of the automatic gesture that leaves its imprint on the material. This almost raw substance was nevertheless structured by geometric forms. From 1931 Fontana declared himself, 'for free abstraction, against absolute abstraction,' for 'space, against volume'. His abstract output of the 1930s foreshadowed his postwar art. It already corresponded to aims later defined in his *Manifiesto blanco* (White Manifesto) of 1946 which rejects a strictly rationalist art. For him, only 'an art based on forms created by the subconscious, balanced with reason, constitutes a true expression of being and a synthesis of the historical moment.'

Finally, Abstraction-Création had repercussions as far away as the USA, contributing to the evolution of American non-objective art. In this respect, the particularly active role of Hélion must be mentioned. He acted on the one hand as friend and advisor to the painter Gallatin, founder of the Museum of Living Art (1927), and for whom he wrote the preface 'Evolution of Abstract Art', and on the other hand as a model of this art of synthesis.[31] Indeed, numerous American galleries and museums began to exhibit Helion's painting during his second trip to the United States (1933-34). Further, Abstraction-Création included up to 33 American 'friends' and members, among whom were Calder, Holty, F. Kann, Gorky and W. Einstein. When in 1936 Abstraction-Création came to an end, Holty, along with Harry Hotzman, Paul Kelpe, Balcomb Greene, Ibram Lassaw, Charles G. Shaw and Warren Wheelock, founded the group American Abstract Artists (AAA) which had clear ties to Abstraction-Création. Although reserved for American art, AAA welcomed recently naturalised European painters, such as Albers and Glarner, both former members of Abstraction-Création. During this period, Calder participated in the *Concretionist* exhibition organised by Gallatin, the show that confirmed the advent of an American non-objective art. Most of the artists involved had studied in Paris. Aware that New York was gradually becoming the new international centre for art, Sophie Täuber-Arp dedicated an edition of her journal *Plastique* (1937–39) to the rising stars of American non-figuration. Two exhibitions held in 1939, *Plastique* and the *Salon des Réalités Nouvelles* organised by Yvanhoé Rambosson and Frédo Sidès, proved to be the final incarnation of Abstraction-Création's spirit before the WW2.

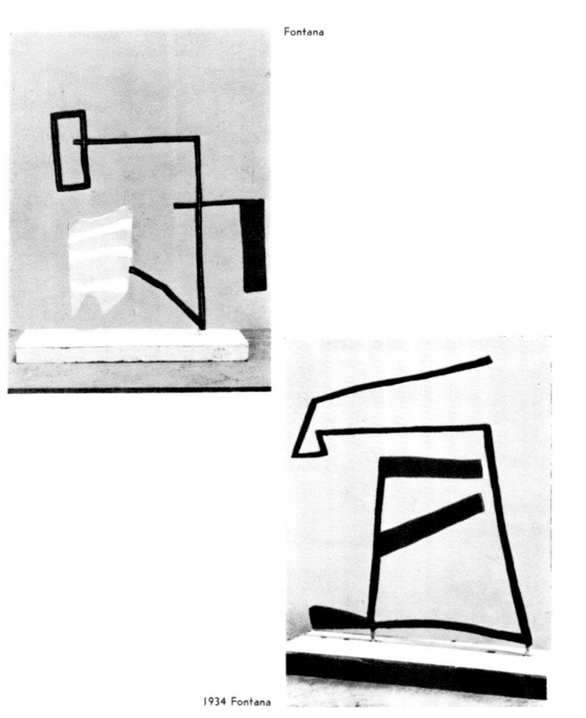

Garcin

La matière n'est jamais une contrainte pour le créateur de formes.

Tout au contraire, c'est dans ses luttes avec elle qu'il augmente singulièrement sa puissance, et, chose étrange, c'est seulement lorsqu'il se laisse guider par ses exigences qu'il en devient le maître, qu'il la dépasse en quelque sorte, et à travers elle aboutit à l'idée, mais cela sans préméditation et simplement parce que celle-ci lui est suggérée par son moi profond et que, de ce fait, elle s'impose à lui comme une nécessité : double mouvement simultané et qui avance toujours sur le même rythme sans que jamais l'un ne précède l'autre.

Grâce à cette stricte observance, il obtient un moyen d'expression dont l'efficacité est au delà de l'iconographie. Ce langage plastique n'obtient sa plénitude que lorsqu'il est avant tout fidèle à ses propres lois. Il peut « être ou ne pas être » figuratif, là n'est pas la véritable question.

La force est en elle-même un contenu formel dont la valeur est exactement égale à l'esprit de celui qui l'a créée. Epreuve redoutable et difficile victoire qui engage l'homme tout entier, mais qui justifie la valeur humaine de l'art.

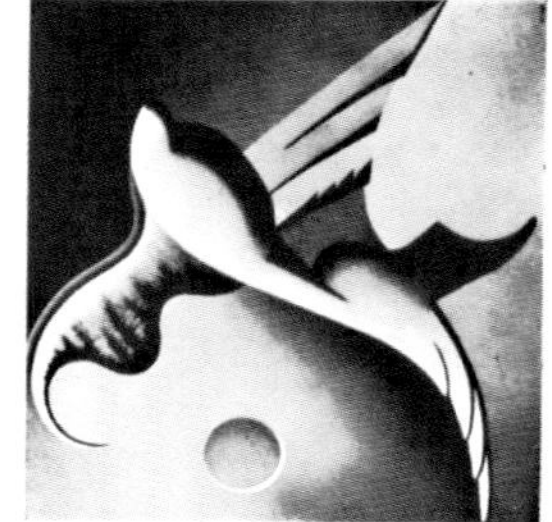

Garcin

Ghiringhelli 1934

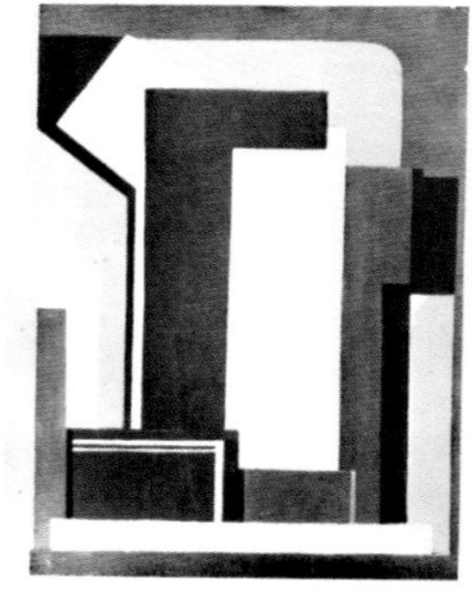

1934 Ghiringhelli

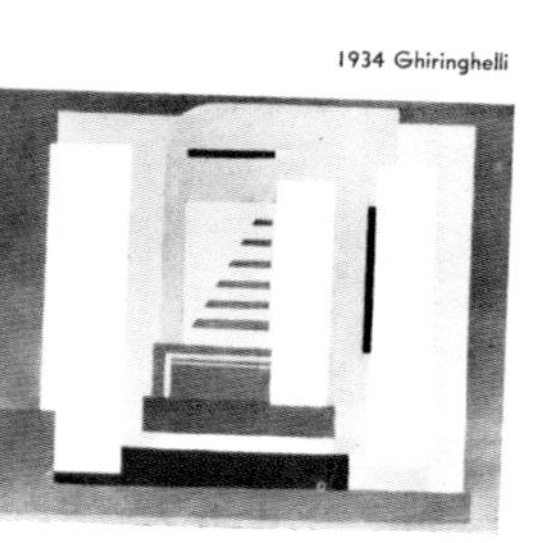

9

Abstraction-Creation cahier N° 4, 1935

Notes

1. Michel Seuphor (F. Berckelears), *Les évasions de Olivier Trickmanshholm* (Ed. du Pavois, Paris 1946), p. 101. In his autobiographical novel, Seuphor points out that for foreign artists, German inflation was a godsend. In Berlin, the poor foreigner became almost rich. The changing parity of the mark with the dollar during the year 1923:

June 1923	100 000 marks
July 1923	350 000 marks
August 1923	4 600 000 marks
September 1923	100 000 000 marks
October 1923	25 000 000 000 marks
November 1923	4 200 000 000 000 marks

Cf. 'Theater in Der Weimarer Republik' Kunstamt Kreuzberg und Institut für Theaterwissenschaft der Universität Köln, Berlin 1977, p. 171. In 1924, a phase of stabilisation began that would last until 1929. It also marks the start of the departure of foreign artists for Paris.

2. First Salon, June 1931, at the Galerie de la Renaissance. Second Salon, January 1932, Parc des Expositions, Porte de Versailles.
3. *Exposition Sélect d'Art Contemporain* (Selective exhibition of contemporary art). With the participation of Arp, Marcelle Cahn, Campigli, Charchoune, Cupera, Daura, Despujol, Théo van Doesburg, Engel Rozier, Ferat, Fernandez, Freundlich, Torrès Garcia, Crotti, Kosnick-Kloss, Kupka, Miro, Mondrian, Monteiro, Planas, Picasso, Poznanski, Shwab, Survage, Tutundjian, Villon.
4. These artistic groups had their dances, meeting places and patrons. The Café Voltaire was the preferred haunt for Seuphor and Mondrian's circle of acquaintances. In 1930, the followers of 'Cercle et Carré' could also be found there, including Vantongerloo, Servranckx, Arp and Sophie Täuber, Russolo, Francisca Clausen, and Marcelle Cahn. Abstraction-Création took up the baton. The Delaunays preferred the Closerie des Lilas, where the regulars included Ivan and Claire Goll, Chana Orloff and Prampolini.
5. Willy Rotzler in his work *Constructive Concepts* A.B.C. Edition Zurich 1977, p.118, clarifies that the "conception of an Art Concret, in the sense of concretisation of a pictorial thought independent of visible reality, is not the invention of van Doesburg. The German Constructivist Max Burchartz used it before him, no doubt after the publication of the 1922 edition of *Aesthetics* by the German philosopher Georg Wilhelm Friedrich Hegel. In accordance with his dialectical method, Hegel explains the process of art as the concretisation of an abstract thought, thus considering the term 'concrete' as the opposite of 'abstract'.
6. Michel Seuphor, *Cercle et Carré* Pierre Belfond ed. 1971, preface to the re-edition p. 19. Further, see the editorial of issue no. 2 of *Cercle et Carré*, 15 April 1930, in which Michel Seuphor wrote, 'My friend Théo van Doesburg, officially invited on 7 January 1930 to participate in the formation of our group, thought it necessary to refuse. And apparently for reasons of simple pride, clearly seeing that he could never act as dictator (which he believes himself to be) or as "destructivist"... And today he sends us a very long letter, attacking our group and our journal, giving free rein to his angry blunders, but in a way that leaves no doubt as to the true nature of this man, who claims to dislike negiligence, advocating concrete and "arithmetical art"'.
7. Letter published in *Holland Dada* by K. Schippers, ed. Querido's Uitgeverij, Amsterdam, 1974, p. 186
8. Wantz practised in van Doesburg's studio throughout 1929–30, completing Neoplastic works, but the following year, he abandoned painting definitively to devote himself to Communist propaganda.
9. Shwab did not sign the manifesto, since commitment of any kind did not suit his anarcho-nihilistic character. He nevertheless attended some meetings and agreed for one of his paintings to be reproduced in the pamphlet.
10. cf; Aldo Pelligrini: *New tendencies in art* Jacobo Muchnik Ed. 1966. Chapter 1.
11. Document 2, Gladys Fabre, *Abstraction-Création*, 1978, p. 52.
12. Document 7 and Document 8, Gladys Fabre, *Abstraction-Création* , 1978, pp. 54-56.
13. Alexander Calder, *An autobiography with pictures*, New York, Pantheon Books, 1966, p. 130.
14. In a letter to Kupka, van Doesburg writes, 'Since it is absolutely impossible to organise interesting exhibitions or publications by placing overly strict limitations on the participants, we are obliged to come together on a wider basis. The best artists in Paris and abroad should participate, even if we do not share their leanings.' Daniel Abadie, 'Art abstrait/Art Concret', *Paris-New York*, Centre Georges Pompidou, catalogue. Musée d'Art Moderne, 1 June – 19 September 1977, p.407.
15. Op cit note 11, p.406.
16. Michel Seuphor, *l'Art abstrait* 1918–38, Maeght 1972, p. 104 and Dora Vallier, *l'Art abstrait* Livre de poche. Librairie générale française 1967, p. 223 and 225.
17. AAER was founded by Vailland Couturier, Aragon and Léon Moussinac in 1932. The main idea was to create a unionism of letters, arts and sciences, aligned with trade unionism (see also note 17).
18. Vantongerloo, 'Evolution', *Abstraction-Création, cahier* N° 4, 1935.
19. Herbin, *Abstraction-Création, cahier* N° 4, 1935, p. 13.
20. Rosenberg in *cahier* N° 1, p. 47.
21. In a letter to Tutundjian dated 13 May 1958, Helion asserts that 'you impressed and influenced more than one artist who is now well-known, like Calder, for example, who admired you enormously, and who saw in you the acute relationships between solid spheres and fine lines, from which you made beautiful objects, bristling with life, and powerful pictures.'
22. On this subject, see *Joan Miró: Magnetic Fields*, exhibition catalogue, Guggenheim Museum, New York. Essay by Margit Rowell.
23. *Hélion*, exhibition catalogue. *Archives de l'art contemporain* no. 15, Centre national d'art contemporain, Dec. 1970 – Feb. 1971, p. 88
24. Myfanwy Evans, 'Hélion To-day: a Personal Comment', published in *Axis* no. 4, 1935, London, pp. 4-9, quoted in Micha, René, *Hélion*, Crown Publishers, 1979 p.8.
25. Barbara Hepworth writes, after a visit to Arp's studio in 1932: 'I thought about the poetic in Arp's sculptures. I had never had any first-hand knowledge of the Dadaist movement, so that seeing his work for the first time freed me ... to see the figure in landscape with new eyes ... Arp had fused landscape with the human form in so extraordinary a manner. Perhaps in freeing himself from material demands his idea transcended all possible limitations. I began to imagine the earth rising and becoming human. I speculated as to how I was to find my own identification, as a human being and a sculptor, with the landscape around me.' Barbara Hepworth, *A pictorial autobiography*, Adams & Dart, Bath, Somerset, 1970, p.22.
26. *Circle: International Survey of Constructive Art* by Ben Nicholson and Naum Gabo, edited by J.L. Martin, London 1937, re-edition Faber and Faber Limited 1971.
27. See Gladys Fabre, 'De l'enseignement des arts décoratifs à l'avènement de la forme pure' [From teaching decorative arts to the advent of pure form], *Aspects historiques du Constructivisme et de l'art concret*, exhibition catalogue. Musée d'Art Moderne de la Ville de Paris, 3 June – 28 August 1977.
28. Carlo Belli, *Kn*, 1935, re-edition, Milan: Vanni Scheiwiller, 1972.
29. Paolo Fossati, 'Veronesi le ragioni astratte', *Nadar* 8, Martano, Turin 1970, p.66. The participants were Bogliardi, De Amicis, D'Errico, Fontana, Ghiringhelli, Licini, Melotti, Reggiani, Soldati, Veronesi, among others.
30. Fausto Melotti, *Il Milione*, no. 40, 10 May – 24 May, 1935.
31. Hélion, 'Evolution of abstract art', preface to the catalogue for the Gallery of Living Art, New York, 1933.

*Gladys Fabre's essay was written to accompany the exhibition *Abstraction-Création 1931-1936* held at Musée d'Art Moderne de la Ville de Paris and the Westfälisches Landesmuseum fur Kunst und Kulturgeschichte Münster in 1978. We are most grateful to Fabre for generously making her text available for this first English translation, and for editing and making additions to her text. Some documents reproduced in the original text are referred to in footnotes. As the original essay accompanied an exhibition, certain references to artworks have been deleted.

Index

Page numbers in italic indicate illustrations.

Acknowledgements

The curators would like to express their gratitude to the following individuals and institutions that have made this exhibition possible:

Sydney: Mitchell and Robyn Martin-Webber, Michael Whitworth and Candice Bruce, Kenneth R. Reed, Russell Robertson, Penelope Seidler and Terence Maloon.

The University of Sydney: Power Institute: Professor Mark Ledbury, Emma White and Amelia Kelly; Schaeffer Library: Anthony White; University Archives: Julia Mant; Rare Books & Special Collections: Sara Hilder; Chancellors Committee; Julia Horne and Margaret Harris.

University Art Gallery: David Ellis, Luke Parker, Maree Clutterbuck, Julie Taylor, Alayne Allvis, Nicole Kluk, Christopher Jones and Li-Fu Lu.

Museum of Contemporary Art: Elizabeth Ann Macgregor, Judith Blackall, Megan Williams and Claire Campey.

National Art School: Anita Taylor, Stephen Little, David Serisier and Susan Andrews.

Art Gallery of New South Wales: Steven Miller.

Mitchell Library: Richard Neville

Melbourne: Heide Museum of Modern Art; Jason Smith, Linda Michael and Lesley Harding; State Library of Victoria.

Canberra: The National Library: Pictures and Manuscript Collection.

London: Bertram family, David Jaffe and Sarah Wilson; Tate Archives; Courtauld Institute Library.

Brussels: Gladys Fabre.

Paris: Bibliothèque de l'Institut national d'histoire de l'art; Bibliothèque Kandinsky, Centre de Documention et de Recherche du Musée national d'art moderne, Centre Georges Pompidou, Paris; Bibliothèque Forney.

Pontoise: Musées de Pontoise: Christophe Duvivier.

Caen: Institut Mémoires de l'édition contemporaine.

Princeton: Marquand Library of Art and Archaeology, Princeton University: Jessica Hoppe Dagci and John Blazejewskii.

Our research draws upon the accumulated research of a number of art historians, notably: Anthony Bradley, Clive Evatt, Adam Geczy, Lesley Harding, Donna Lee Brien, Linda Michael, Bernice Murphy Emeritus Professor Virginia Spate, and the Bathurst Historical Society.

We would also like to particularly thank Luke Parker, Susan Best, Peter Thorn, Ross Peck, Michael Myers, Anna McMahon, Matthys Gerber, Rex Butler, Andrew McNamara, Antonia Fredman and Chris Andrews.

Finally our families, Margaret Balding and Lotte Donaldson, and Alan and Margaret Donaldson; and Marian Dzurik, Miloš Stephen and Valery and Ninian Stephen.

All works by J.W. Power are from the Edith Power Bequest, 1961, University of Sydney, managed by the Museum of Contemporary Art, unless otherwise indicated.

All plate photography by Jenni Carter.

Contributors

A.D.S. Donaldson is an artist, curator, art historian and lecturer at the National Art School, Sydney. He studied at the University of Sydney, the Kunstakademie Düsseldorf and the Royal Danish Academy of Fine Arts. His 2002 survey exhibition was held at the University Art Gallery, The University of Queensland.

Gladys Fabre is an art historian and curator. Her exhibitions include *Léger et L'Esprit Moderne: une alternative d'avantgarde à l'art non-objectif 1918-1931* (1982), *Abstraction Création 1931-1936* (1978), and *Van Doesburg & the International Avant-Garde: Constructing a New World* (2009).

Virginia Spate is emeritus professor of art history at Sydney University. Her books include *The Colour of Time: Claude Monet*, winner of the Mitchell Prize for Art History in 1993 and *Orphism: The evolution of non-figurative painting in Paris 1910-1914*.

Ann Stephen is an art historian and senior curator of the University Art Gallery at the University of Sydney. Her books include *On looking at looking: The art and politics of Ian Burn* (2006) and *Modern Times: The untold story of modernism in Australia* (2008), co-edited with Andrew McNamara and Philip Goad.

Published in conjunction with the exhibition
J.W. Power: Abstraction-Création, Paris 1934
University Art Gallery, The University of Sydney
24 September 2012 – 25 January 2013, and
Heide Museum of Modern Art, Melbourne, 2014

Exhibition curators and editors: A.D.S Donaldson and Ann Stephen
Managing editor: Luke Parker

Graphic design and print production: Peter Thorn
Printed in Australia using Forestry Stewardship Council approved paper
Published by Power Publications in conjunction with the University Art Gallery, The University of Sydney

National Library of Australia Cataloguing-in-Publication entry
Author: Donaldson, A. D. S
Title: J. W. Power: Abstraction-Création, Paris 1934 / by A.D.S. Donaldson and Ann Stephen, with contributions by Virginia Spate and Gladys Fabre.
ISBN: 9780909952402 (hbk.)
Subjects: Power, J. J. W. (John Joseph Wardell), 1881-1943--Exhibitions
Art, Abstract--20th century--Exhibitions.
Painting, Abstract--20th century--Exhibitions.
Art, Australian--20th century--Exhibitions.
Art, Abstract--France.
Other Authors/Contributors:
Stephen, Ann.
Spate, Virginia, 1937-
Fabre, Gladys.
Dewey Number:
709.994

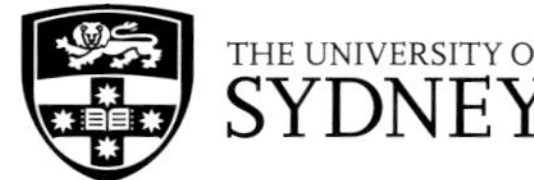

POWER PUBLICATIONS

Endpapers based on the cover of J.W. Power's *Éléments de la Construction Picturale* 1932.

Frontispiece photograph of J.W. Power in Paris, c. 1935 by Frank Wardell, University of Sydney Archives, G3/224/1420.

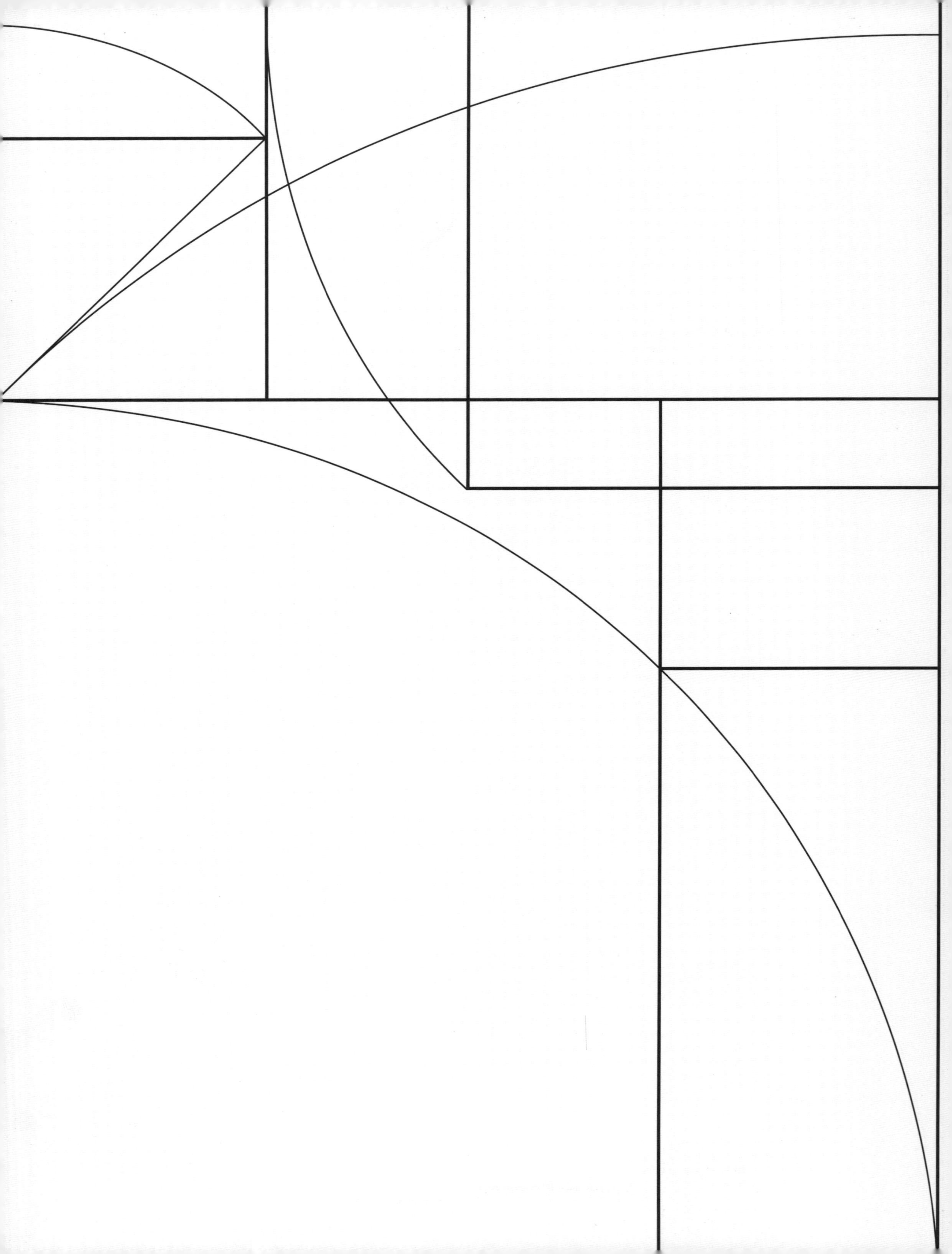